A Freethinker's
A-Z of the New World
of Business

The **Capstone Business** Catalog

A Freethinker's
A-Z of the New World
of Business

Words: **Stuart Crainer**

Advisors: **Bruce Tulgan** and **Watts Wacker**

CAPSTONE

Copyright © Stuart Crainer 2000

The right of Stuart Crainer to be identified as the author of this work has been asserted in accordance with the Copyright, Designs and Patents Act 1988

First published 2000 by
Capstone US
Business Books Network
163 Central Avenue
Suite 2
Hopkins Professional Building
Dover
NH 03820
USA

Capstone Publishing Limited
Oxford Centre for Innovation
Mill Street
Oxford OX2 0JX
United Kingdom
http://www.capstone.co.uk

CIP catalogue records for this book are available from the British Library and the US Library of Congress

ISBN 1-84112-014-6

Typeset by
Sparks Computer Solutions Ltd, Oxford
http://www.sparks.co.uk
Printed and bound by
T.J. International Ltd, Padstow, Cornwall

This book is printed on acid-free paper

Substantial discounts on bulk quantities of Capstone books are available to corporations, professional associations and other organizations. If you are in the USA or Canada, phone the LPC Group for details on (1-800-626-4330) or fax (1-800-243-0138). Everywhere else, phone Capstone Publishing on (+44-1865-798623) or fax (+44-1865-240941).

Introduction

Companies, commentators, consultants and the usual array of charlatans have talked about the pace of change for a decade or so. Speed freaks have talked up downsizing and rationalized it as rightsizing. They have debated their way through the mire of re-engineering and emerged the other side clutching straws. Now, they want a break, breathing space, peace and quiet. Let's take it easy. Time out.

Then the reality kicks in. Things are scary. Change doesn't stop while we all go for a latte. It keeps on rolling and no one is immune. Not even tenured professors. Not even Wall St stars. And certainly not CEOs. 'Taking risks, breaking the rules, and being a maverick have always been important, but today they are more crucial than ever,' says strategy luminary Gary Hamel. 'We live in a discontinuous world – one where digitalization, deregulation and globalization are profoundly reshaping the industrial landscape.'[1] Change on.

Whether you are a CEO, a lathe operator or a bonds trader, fear is a reasonable response. When the going gets discontinuous, the exec

zeitbite#1
Marshall
McLuhan

"Electric light is pure information."

gets as scared as any other human being. And there is plenty to make you fearful – even more to make you think. The combined brain power of the world's computers has now outstripped the brain power of human beings. Change on. Computers are smarter than all of us. Who'd have thought Microsoft's capitalization would exceed IBM's and Seattle would be fashionable?

Only the ill-advised – or the ill – are not scared. But, look around and there is still smug complacency on show. Senior execs in companies named Blahblah.com or Blah! are pretty sure of themselves. Pity their delusions.

Take a look at the books in an airport book store. Smug squared.

At a time when uncertainty is a universal business experience whether you are in Tokyo, Munich or Dallas, the certainty of their prescriptions has the hollow ring of a placebo. Bullet points are meaningless wish lists. Sucked eggs. Tidiness and order (if they ever existed) are elusive. Without their backbone of certainty most business books collapse in a heap.

Certainty RIP. Change on. Uncertainty is uncharted territory. For the first time traveler, it is bedeviled by ambiguity, abstract thoughts, unusual metaphors and a distinct unwillingness to launch into a short sharp diagnosis followed by an equally pithy prescription. The journey is harder, and as likely to leave the curious with even more questions as provide any answers.

Viva questions. The circle has not been squared. In Silicon Valley $3.5 billion is frittered away annually because of clogged highways and gridlocks.[2] We could change the world if we could get to our desks.

We are in wild times. But times which are less novel than we are sometimes led to believe. Remember Joseph Schumpeter's definition of capitalism as 'Gales of creative destruction.' The gales have been howling since time immemorial.

What lies ahead? There are plenty who reckon that they know. The future has never been a bigger industry. According to the futurist think tank First Matter: "Many of the commercial opportunities to emerge in the next millennium will be based on changes that will occur in the social agenda. These changes will center around four new individual freedoms: To Go, To Be, To Do, To Know."[3]

The individual is king. The ultimate global capitalism. The free agent world where we move from one interesting assignment to another. It happens. But, for most people, it does not.

The individual is king. Understanding yourself and humankind is the challenge. Spirituality. Getting in touch. Again, it happens. But, for many people, spiritual awakening is neither yearned for nor desired.

The reality is that the individual has never been king. Cash is not king. If it is we are hurtling nowhere. Once more into the void. Capitalism is a black hole unless it creates communities, teams, units, networks, links. Capitalism is a series of complex relationships conducted within a variety of different environments and cultures between an even greater array of people and organizations. The driving force of capitalism is not money. The relationships are driven by trust, faith, fear, respect, need, hunger, desire, demand, greed, hate and many other elements.

The end result is a commercial tornado, a recklessly random array of connections and contradictions. *The Freethinker's A–Z* is your guide to this smorgasbord. It is not a book of cast iron answers. There are none. *The Freethinker's A–Z* is the business book of our times, defining the zeitgeist. Change on.

The freethinker's route map
The Freethinker's A–Z is ordered alphabetically and, on page xi, the entries are divided according to their subject matter. The subject areas covered are:

People
- Commentators
- Corporate suits
- Tech chiefs
- Gurus and thinkers

- Self-help, spirituality and motivation
- Entrepreneurs
- Neteratti
- Money makers
- Ads, fashion and design
- Information and education
- Media and publishing

Organizations
- Think tanks, policy and pressure
- Retailers
- Consulting firms
- Brands
- Information and entertainment
- Up-tech
- Beans, bean counters and bean shifters
- Education
- Makers
- Servers
- Communicators

Ideas
- Tools and concepts
- Tools for competing
- Tools for money making
- Tools for living
- Tools for working
- Events
- Places
- Phenomena

What is clear from the entries in *The Freethinker's A–Z* is that the business world has gone through – and is going through – incredible change. The movers and shakers are different people working in different organizations in different ways than those we might have picked out a decade ago. (No surprise when you consider that in 1900 73 percent of US employees worked in production; this fell to 57 percent by 1940; and just over one-third by 1980. It is still falling.)

The Freethinker's A–Z is not the final word. The only Z in the contemporary alphabet can be found on *Sesame Street*. The selection is eclectic, international and occasionally irrational. Many people were canvassed for their views on who and what should be included. The only general criterion for inclusion was that entries had to be people, things or organizations that were changing things.

The end result is a selection with hardly a smokestack in sight. High-tech companies abound. Service *uber alles*.

But this does not mean that Palo Alto, CA is the center of the universe. It is an important place, but it would be a mistake to think that the world has become globalized and wired up only to impose geographical limitations on itself. The future is global. We are centers of our universes.

This is reflected in the make-up of the entries in *The Freethinker's A–Z*. Today's thinkers are as likely to be shaven-headed professors from the Stockholm School of Economics as tenure-seekers from Harvard. Today's benchmark CEO is as likely to be a Korean with a steady supply of old world aphorisms as a WASP educated to the hilt in the latest business jargon. Today's leading edge organization is more likely to be a fledgling start-up with a bright idea and a weird way of doing things than a multinational corporation. (Come to think of it, all of these things were probably always true – it was just that living in the shadows of corporate might we never thought they were true.)

Feedback

The Freethinker's A–Z is not all-embracing. People, companies, organizations, ideas, products and many other things have been overlooked. No book could honestly claim to be able to contain the corporate ferment we see all around. We are under no illusions. Also, you will find opinions, as well as intemperate and ill-conceived remarks, scattered throughout the text. They are there for your pleasure. Adjust your blood pressure accordingly.

We operate an intellectual returns policy. If there is anything in *The Freethinker's A–Z* with which you disagree or which intrigues you or which is plainly incorrect you can contact the editor, Stuart Crainer at capstone_publishing@msn.com

Thanks

The Freethinker's A–Z was the idea of *Mark Allin* and *Richard Burton* of Capstone Publishing. They generated the first list of headings. Debate followed. Various people helped with ideas and suggestions. Entries were added, discussed and discarded right up to the last possible minute. Ideas for headlines came from *Watts Wacker*. Wit, wisdom and opinion also came in from *Gerry* ('There's no i in team') *Griffin*; *Tom Brown* of Management General; *Peter Cohan*; *Richard Castle*; and *Eddie Obeng* of Pentacle – The Virtual Business School. Thanks are also due to Bruce Tulgan of Rainmaker Thinking Inc.

Words in *The Freethinker's A–Z* are the work of *Stuart Crainer* unless otherwise stated. The other contributors are *Des Dearlove* and *Georgina Peters* of Suntop Media; *Trevor Merriden, Gerry Griffin* and *Stephen Coomber* who also contributed greatly to the research.

The logistics of turning the manuscript into this book were down to *John Duggan* and *Tom Fryer* of Sparks.

Stuart Crainer
Summer 1999

x

⊗people⊗cat#1
Commentators
Scott Adams
John Byrne
Don Imus
Art Kleiner
Peter Schwartz
Ken Shelton

⊗people⊗cat#2
Corporate suits
Percy Barnevik
Gordon Bethune
Sabheer Bhatia
Sir Peter Bonfield
John Browne
Michael Eisner
Aaron Feuerstein
Niall Fitzgerald
Terry Leahy
Göran Lindahl
Lyndsay Owen-Jones
Dennis Stevenson
Jack Welch

⊗people⊗cat#3
Tech chiefs
Sabheer Bahtia
George Bell
Michael Dell
David Duffield
Larry Ellison
Bill Gates
Andy Grove
Steve Jobs
Stan Shih

⊗people⊗cat#4
Gurus and thinkers
W. Brian Arthur
Peter Drucker
Robert Fritz
Sumantra Ghoshal
Gary Hamel
Charles Handy
W. Chan Kim
Kam-hon Lee
Regis McKenna
Chris Meyer
Ikujiro Nonaka
Kjell Nordström
Richard Scase
Amartya Sen
Don Sull
Fons Trompenaars

⊗people⊗cat#5
Self-help, spirituality and motivation
Stephen Covey
David Firth
Daniel Goleman
Anthony Robbins
Benjamin Zander

⊗people⊗cat#6
Entrepreneurs
Paul Allen
Jeff Bezos
Richard Branson
James Dyson
Elwin Giel
James Lavelle
Jonathan Ledecky
Mark Levin

Ian Schrager
Howard Schultz
Leigh Steinberg
Perween Warsi

⊗people⊗cat#7
Neteratti
Tim Berners-Lee
Vinton Cerf
Esther Dyson
David Gee
Jon Postel
Don Tapscott

⊗people⊗cat#8
Money makers
Warren Buffett
Abby Cohen
George Soros
Ann Winblad

⊗people⊗cat#9
Ads, fashion and design
Serena Kelsey
Alex McQueen

⊗people⊗cat#10
Information and education
Michael Bloomberg
Michael Milken

⊗people⊗cat#11
Media and publishing
Waheed Alli
Matt Drudge

Michael Lynton
Elisabeth Murdoch
James Murdoch
Lachlan Murdoch
Rupert Murdoch
Tony O'Reilly
John Cowper Powys
Gail Rebuck
Harriet Rubin
Marjorie Scardino
Ted Turner
Oprah Winfrey
Anna Wintour
David Yelland

⊗organizations⊗cat#1
*Think tanks, policy and
pressure*
Demos
Global Business Network
MIT Media Lab
Santa Fe Institute

⊗organizations⊗cat#2
Retailers
Amazon.com
Benetton
GAP
Gateway 2000
IKEA
Online Originals
Republic Industries
Rubbermaid
Wal-Mart

⊗organizations⊗cat#3
Consulting firms
Cap Gemini
Covey Institute
Ernst & Young
Helios Consulting
PA Consulting
Renaissance Solutions
Strategos

⊗organizations⊗cat#4
Brands
Absolut
Daewoo
Disney
National Basketball Association
Lexus
Manchester United
Nike
Saturn
Virgin
Wyeth

⊗organizations⊗cat#5
Information and entertainment
Brill's Content
Fast Company
Dreamworks SKG
Management General

⊗organizations⊗cat#6
Up-tech
Adobe Systems
Cisco Systems
International Business Machines
LG
SAS Institute

Starwave
Xybernaut

⊗organizations⊗cat#7
Beans, bean counters and bean shifters
Berkshire Hathaway
E*Trade

⊗organizations⊗cat#8
Education
Apollo Group
Disney University
British Aerospace Virtual University
Motorola University
Pensare
Knowledge Universe
Wharton Business School

⊗organizations⊗cat#9
Makers
Anglian Water
Asea Brown Boveri
General Electric
Home Depot
Mercedes-Benz
New Pig Corporation
Oticon
Sumitomo Rubber

⊗organizations⊗cat#10
Servers
easyJet
Healtheon Corp.
Iridium

xiii

SOL
Starbucks
St Luke's
?What *If!*

⊗**organizations**⊗**cat#11**
Communicators
Bertelsmann
Wordworks

⊗**tools and ideas**⊗**cat#1**
Concepts
adhocracy
bit head
career management
leadership RIP
loyalty
motivation
perception management
power
reputation management
storytelling

⊗**tools and ideas**⊗**cat#2**
Tools for competing
balanced scorecard
brands
business bites
business schools
competency tracking
co-opetition
core competents
corporate legacy
corporate memory
corporate universities
data warehousing
diversity advantage

division of mental labor
ecommerce
employee value proposition
empty marketshare
feminizing the boardroom
game theory
grassroots leadership
human capital
increasing returns
intellectual capital
marketspace
Neuro-Linguistic Programming
NPR costs
On-line analytical processing
organizational agility
thought leadership
value migration
values

⊗**tools and ideas**⊗**cat#3**
Tools for money making
derivatives
rock star securitized loans
shareholder value
spread betting

⊗**tools and ideas**⊗**cat#4**
Phenomena
book buying
branding consulting firms
CEO agency
clusters
connectivity
Cool Britannia
corporate divorces
discontinuity
dumbing down
executive churn

executive search
executive shortages
faculty free agents
Generation X
ghostwriting
golden hellos
motivational speakers
spin doctors

⊗**tools and ideas**⊗**cat#5**
Tools for living
Barbie
Coca-Cola Wear
continuous learning
free agents
smart cards

⊗**tools and ideas**⊗**cat#6**
Tools for working
Big Mac Index
business books
e-mail
groups
iMac
ineffective habits
job titles
mobile information

⊗**tools and ideas**⊗**cat#7**
Events
World Economic Forum

⊗**tools and ideas**⊗**cat#8**
Places
The Internet
Sophia Antipolis

Notes
1 Hamel, Gary, "Killer strategies that make shareholders rich," *Fortune*, June 23, 1997.
2 "A nip in the valley," *The Economist*, September 5, 1998.
3 Wacker, Watts, *The 500 Year Delta*, Capstone, Oxford, 1997.

Absolut

Forget Stolichnya, Absolut has emerged as the vodka brand of our times. It is the number one imported vodka in the United States with 60 percent of the market. Absolut's success has been built on a clever ad campaign. Developed by TBWA Chiat/Day, the ads, with their variations on the Absolut bottle, have become classics – so much so that a book of the ads sold a staggering 150,000 copies. (If you want an insight into the modern ad industry it is a decorative and impressive starting point.)

The most surprising thing about Absolut is that it is produced by a state-owned industry. Owned by the Swedish state, Absolut is probably the best possible advertisement for state control. Indeed, in these privatized times Absolut is increasingly the only ad for successful state control.

SEE: BRANDS
MORE INFO: www.absolutvodka.com
SOURCES: *USA Today*; Richard W. Lewis, *Absolut Book: The Absolut Vodka Advertising Story*, 1996

Adams, Scott

Cartoonist and sometime corporate staffer, Scott Adams (born 1957) is the creator of the eponymous Dilbert cartoon strip. Dilbert, with its wry take on the abject tedium of much of corporate life, is now syndicated to 1700 newspapers in over 50 countries and has spawned a series of bestsellers.

Adams is a failed inventor with an MBA from the University of California at Berkeley ("I'm far more of the businessman who draws cartoons," he says) who found much of his inspiration working as an engineer for Pacific Bell. (He also worked at Crocker National Bank and is a certified hypnotist.) It is amazing to think that he actually hung onto this job until 1995 – "I really didn't know until about 1994 that the cartooning was going to work. For the first several years it just limped along at fewer than 100 newspapers."

Adams, now based in Danville, CA, receives around 350 e-mails a day from readers – this gives him much of his materal. With Dilberts everywhere, Adams has signed a reputed $20 million contract for five more Dilbert books.

Not everyone is a fan. "Dilbert is the bestselling business book of all time. It is cynical about management. Never has there been so much cynicism," laments Gary Hamel, not himself automatically associated with a positive slant on business life. Such comments overlook the fact that managers tend to be among the most cynical people on the planet.

SEE: GARY HAMEL; BUSINESS BOOKS
MORE INFO: ScottAdams@aol.com
SOURCES: *Financial Times*, November 22/23, 1997

adhocracy
The antidote to the burdensome bureaucracy envisaged by Max Weber is the adhocracy, a word coined by the American thinker Warren Bennis (born 1925). An adhocracy is characterized by blurred divides between roles, functions and departments. It is an organization founded on ambiguity rather than clarity utilizing small groups to achieve clearly specified goals. Such freewheeling has usually proved beyond organizations.

Robert Waterman – co-author of *In Search of Excellence*, later defined adhocracy as "any form of organization that cuts across normal bureaucratic lines to capture opportunities, solve problems, and get results."

The concept was taken up by the futurist Alvin Toffler (born 1928) in his 1970 book *Future Shock*, which predicted (way ahead of its time) that "businesses were going to re-structure themselves repeatedly. That they would have to reduce hierarchy and [adopt] what we termed adhocracy." Toffler later noted that "This sounded sensational to many readers." Thirty years on, it still does. After decades assembling carefully constructed hierarchies and ornate bureaucracies, companies saw no reason to dismantle them. Many still do not.

SEE: GRASSROOTS LEADERSHIP; POWER
MORE INFO: Warren Bennis, *The Temporary Society*, 1968; Alvin Toffler,
            Future Shock, 1970
SOURCES: Rowan Gibson (editor), *Rethinking the Future*, 1997

Adobe Systems

Adobe Systems was founded by John Warnock (now CEO and chairman) and Charles Geschke (president and chairman). Both worked at Xerox's famous Palo Alto Research Center. Geschke arrived there via Carnegie Mellon and Xavier University. Warnock took a more circuitous route by way of the Evans & Sutherland Computer Corp, Computer Sciences Corp, IBM and the University of Utah.

Adobe helped ignite the revolution in desktop publishing in the early 1980s. Its software includes Adobe Acrobat and Adobe Photoshop. Headquartered at San José, CA, it now employs 2700 people. Adobe's interests include Adobe Ventures and Adobe Ventures II, venture capital partnerships with Hambrecht and Quist which have earned over $100 million since 1994.

SEE: ECOMMERCE
MORE INFO: www.adobe.com
SOURCES: www.adobe.com

Allen, Paul

With a perpetually amiable look, Paul Allen (born 1953) looks as though he is just about to pop into the kitchen to get a beer before finishing another great story. This may well be true, but Paul Allen is also one of the richest men on the planet – actually the third richest according to *Forbes*. He is currently founder and chairman of The Paul Allen Group; and was previously one half of the founding duo of Microsoft, a computing firm. Allen resigned from Microsoft in 1983 after illness. At the time it had 476 employees and revenues of $50 million. His stock in the company is now estimated to be worth some $22 billion.

Paul Allen could have elected to take it easy and count his money. He has given over $100 million to worthy causes and has dabbled – in a fairly serious financial sort of way it must be said – in a number of companies through the Paul Allen Group. He clearly believes that money is there to be used.

Upside magazine has labeled him "High-tech's fairy godmother." This title has been earned through a stream of high-profile and huge investments in high-tech companies since Allen collected his Microsoft golden egg. During 1998, he spent $2.8 billion on Marcus Cable and $4.5 billion on Charter Communications. The future is cable, until the next great investment opportunity comes along.

SEE: BILL GATES
MORE INFO: Des Dearlove, *Business the Bill Gates Way*, Capstone, 1998.
SOURCES: www.upside.com

Alli, Waheed

Waheed Alli (British, born 1964) is an increasingly influential and successful figure in the British media industry. He is joint managing director of Planet 24 (of which he owns one-third). As an openly gay Asian businessman he is something of a role model. Though he does not give interviews, he sits on the British government's Panel 2000. His current wealth is estimated at £10 million.

SEE: COOL BRITANNIA

Amazon.com

With 2.5 million books, Amazon.com is Earth's biggest bookstore. It is the exemplar of electronic commerce and its founder Jeff Bezos recipient of plaudit after plaudit – though not, as yet, profit upon profit.

Back in the electronic mists, the first books ordered through Amazon were dispatched in the fall of 1994 (personally packed by Bezos and his wife); in 1997 Amazon sold its one millionth book. In 1997, sales approached $148 million, an eight-fold increase year on year. In 1998 sales grew 838 percent.

The original model for Amazon.com was to provide the world's largest bookshop, but it quickly found that it was actually selling information as much as books. Today, for example, Amazon ("the toast of cyberspace" according to the *Financial Times*) will send customers an e-mail every time a new book comes out on a subject in which they have registered an interest. That information also helps the company better understand its customers and target its marketing.

The world's largest on-line book stores

Bookstore	Country	Deliverable titles (million)
Amazon.com	US	2.5
Alt.bookstore	US	2.0
Abiszet Bucherservice	Germany	1.3
Foyles	UK	1.0
Barnes & Noble	US	1.0
The Co-op Bookshop	Australia	1.0
Libro Web	Spain	1.0
Internet Bookshop IBS	UK	0.92
JF Lehmanns	Germany	0.75
Book Stacks Unlimited	US	0.5

Company: Amazon.com, Inc.

Address:
1516 Second Ave. Seattle, WA 98101
Phone: 206-622-2335
Fax: 206-622-2405
http://www.amazon.com

Business
Specialist retailers – books, music, videos on-line.

Statistics, fiscal year end December

Employees	1997 614
Annual sales (million)	1998 $610.0
Annual results (million)	1998 ($124.5)
Other facts	Amazon.com sells 1.5 million in-print titles and 1 million out of print titles via the Internet.
Hoover's 500	—
Fortune 500	—

The site also encourages "chat" among its users as part of its service. To encourage discussion, it not only posts book reviews from leading newspapers, it also encourages customers to send in their own reviews which are published on the Amazon site. This, say McKinsey consultants John Hagel and Arthur Armstrong in their book *Net Gain*, is a powerful form of "community building" – a new trick for electronic channels – something that adds value to web transactions.

Despite its popularity with consumers, business journalists and academics, Amazon.com has yet to make a profit. Suggestions are that it is struggling with its new music format and a host of imitators and competitors lurk. It may already be looking elsewhere – in 1998 Amazon bought Junglee Corp and PlanetAll, two Internet companies.

Georgina Peters

SEE: JEFF BEZOS; ECOMMERCE
MORE INFO: www.amazon.com
SOURCES: Jonathan Bowen/Oxford University Computing Laboratory

Anglian Water

In 1989, the UK Government privatized the nation's water industry. Overnight, regional water companies were transformed into commercial organizations. Some have turned out more commercial than others. It is a trick that Anglian Water has managed. Headquartered in Huntingdon, Cambridgeshire, 60 miles to the north-east of London, Anglian has emerged as one of the largest water companies in the world, serving more than five million people with operations in the Americas, Europe, Asia, Australia and New Zealand and over 5000 employees worldwide. In the US, its activities include the joint venture American–Anglian which has sales of $40 million and serves one million people – including a $50 million contract to supply water to Buffalo, NY. Anglian's stated intention is to be the number one water company in the UK and one of the best globally by 2007.

Anglian's is a textbook transformation – from being a public organization burdened with bureaucracy and comfort zones into a global player. Central to this has been its management of innovation. Anglian was one of the first UK companies to appoint a director of innovation. It argues that innovation is multi-functional and includes all 5000 employees; innovation is managed with the same rigor as other processes; and innovation is closely aligned to learning and knowledge development (producing Anglian's use of the phrase "kennovation," condensing knowledge – "ken" – and innovation into one). Anglian's entire approach to learning is embodied in Aqua Universitas – known to all as the University of Water – a virtual corporate university.

SEE: CORPORATE UNIVERSITIES
MORE INFO: www.anglianwater.co.uk
SOURCES: Company reports; interviews

Apollo Group

B-schools take note. Based in Phoenix, Arizona, the education provider Apollo has recorded average growth over the last five years of 29 percent. Its 1997 sales were $266 million from which its net income was $30.2 million. It has a market value of $2,194 million.

Apollo was the brainchild of John G. Sperling, still its CEO and owner of just under 20 percent of the company (stock valued at $415 million). Working at San Jose State University, Sperling was refused support for an adult degree program. Undaunted, he started his own business in adult, degree programs. Long before the idea was fashionable, Sperling believed that lifelong employment with a single employer would be replaced by lifelong learning and employment with a variety of employers.

Sperling's first contract came from the University of San Francisco. Now, his educational business is highly profitable and expanding rapidly. Apollo more than doubled its total enrollments and revenues between 1993 and 1997. Its businesses include the University of Phoenix (40,000 students at 51 campuses in 13 states plus 2600 students through virtual classrooms), the Institute for Professional Development, the College for Financial Planning and Western International University. All in all it has 100 campuses in 32 states and activities in Puerto Rico and London, UK. It has also formed a company with Hughes Network Systems to provide satellite-based learning.

SEE: BUSINESS SCHOOLS; CORPORATE UNIVERSITIES; MOTOROLA
                UNIVERSITY; DISNEY UNIVERSITY; KNOWLEDGE UNIVERSE
MORE INFO: www.apollogrp.com
SOURCES: Stuart Crainer & Des Dearlove, *Gravy Training*, 1998

Arthur, W. Brian

The economist W. Brian Arthur is based at the Santa Fe Institute where he is Citibank Professor. He has an MA in math from the University of Michigan (1969) and a PhD in operations research from the University of California Berkeley (1973). He was later Dean and Virginia Morrison Professor of Population Studies and Economics at Stanford and Professor of Biology at Stanford (1983–96).

Given his multi-skilled résumé, it is perhaps just as well that Arthur now refers to himself as an "applied mathematician." Arthur's central gripe about economics as a discipline is that it has become distanced from reality. "I would like to see economics become more of a science, and more of a science means that it concerns itself more with reality," he says. "We're facing a danger that economics is rigorous deduction based upon faulty assumptions."

This is of concern, says Arthur, because we are moving to a "technically based economy" in which the rules of economics are being challenged and changed. Understanding of the new commercial realities requires radical new insights from radical new economists.

Underpinning Arthur's arguments is a move away from solutions and foolproof models to questions and frameworks. "Economics has always taken a shortcut and said, assume there is a problem and assume that we can arrive at a solution. Now, I would say, assume there's a situation, how do players cognitively deal with it? In other words, what frameworks do they wheel up to understand the situation?" Making sense of the situation is the critical first step. Assuming there is an economic model that will spit out a solution is a sure route to diminishing returns.

SEE: SANTA FE INSTITUTE; DECREASING RETURNS
MORE INFO: Brian Arthur, Steven Durlauf & David Lane (editors), *The
                Economy as an Evolving Complex System II*, 1997
SOURCES: *Strategy & Business*, 2nd Quarter 1998

Asea Brown Boveri

Asea Brown Boveri (ABB) is one of the most lauded and reported on companies of our time. Case studies abound. ABB is routinely decorated with corporate baubles as Europe's most admired company. Commentators praise; analysts purr.

Headquartered in Zurich, Switzerland, ABB is the world's leading power engineering company employing over 213,000 people in 50 countries. A $31 billion company it is broken down into 35 business areas with 5000 profit centers ("5000 perceived companies," says chief executive officer Göran Lindahl).

ABB came about from the merger of the Swedish company Asea, then led by the redoubtable Swede Percy Barnevik, and the Swiss company, Brown Boveri. It was the biggest cross-border merger since Royal Dutch Shell's oily coupling. Barnevik became the CEO of the resulting ABB and revolutionized its organization and performance until being succeeded by Lindahl in 1997.

When the Asea Brown Boveri merger was announced on August 10, 1987, the corporate world was stunned by its suddenness. The *Wall Street Journal* said that it was a merger "born of necessity, not of love." This overlooked the uncanny fit between the two companies. It was truly a marriage made in corporate heaven. Brown Boveri was international, Asea was not. Asea excelled at management, Brown Boveri did not. Technology, markets and cultures fitted together. Of course, whether this was luck or strategic insight is a matter of continuing discussion.

Then, quite simply, Barnevik made it work. "The challenge set by Barnevik was to create – out of a group of 1,300 companies employing 210,000 people in 150 countries – a streamlined, entrepreneurial organization with as few management layers as possible," write Kevin Barham and Claudia Heimer in their book on the company. To enable this to happen, Barnevik introduced a complex matrix structure – what Lindahl has called "decentralization under central conditions." The company is run by an Executive Committee with the organization below divided by business areas; company and profit centers; and country organizations. The aim is to reap the advantages of being a large organization while also having the advantages of smallness.

ABB's matrix structure has been the source of much debate. It has been hailed as a new organizational model and Barnevik as GM's Alfred P. Sloan reincarnated. Barnevik argues that the matrix system is simply a formal means of recording and understanding what happens informally in any large organization. The spider's web of the matrix is a fact of life.

While it may prove unwise to copy ABB slavishly, the company is inspirational in other ways. You could summarize ABB's management style and philosophy as management for and by grown-ups. None of this happened overnight or easily. But, it all happened deliberately. Throughout its activities there is a keen sense of commonsensical managerial decisions leading to a greater corporate destiny. Clarity and communication abound.

SEE: GORAN LINDAHL; PERCY BARNEVIK
MORE INFO: Kevin Barham & Claudia Heimer, *ABB: The Dancing Giant*, 1998;
            www.abb.com
SOURCES: Kevin Barham & Claudia Heimer, *ABB: The Dancing Giant*, 1998

II

Bahtia, Sabheer

If you want a model for the new career, Sabheer Bahtia provides it. Bahtia is co-founder and general manager of the Hotmail Group. Formerly with Apple, Bahtia's bright idea was to offer a free email service supported by advertising. Bahtia worked on the idea in his garage *à la* Hewlett and Packard circa 1937. He then sat in his car and recruited staff. Before long, Hotmail had 1 million subscribers and was sucked into the Microsoft empire in 1997 for around $400 million. With ad revenue increasing by a massive 15 to 20 percent per month, Hotmail is an e-business that makes money. A novel idea, but unlikely to catch on.

SEE: ECOMMERCE
MORE INFO: www.hotmail.com

balanced scorecard

Developed by David Norton and Robert Kaplan, the balanced scorecard is "a strategic management and measurement system that links strategic objectives to comprehensive indicators."

Norton is co-founder of the consulting company, Renaissance Solutions, and Kaplan is Marvin Bower Professor of Leadership Development at Harvard Business School. The duo developed the concept at the beginning of the 1990s in research sponsored by KPMG.

They had a simple message for managers: what you measure is what you get. Kaplan and Norton compared running a company to flying a plane. The pilot who relies on a single dial is unlikely to be safe. Pilots must utilize all the information contained in their cockpit.

Identifying the essential measures for an organization is not straight-forward – around 20 measures are par for the course. According to Kaplan and Norton, a "good" balanced scorecard contains three elements. First, it establishes "cause and effect relationships." Rather than being isolated figures, measures are related to each other and the network of relationships makes up the strategy. Second, a balanced scorecard should have a combination of lead and lag indicators. Lag indicators are measures, such as market share, which are common across an industry and, though important, offer no distinctive advantage. Lead indicators are measures which are company (and strategy) specific. Finally, an effective balanced scorecard is linked to financial measures. By this, Kaplan and Norton mean that initiatives such as reengineering or lean production need to be tied to financial measures rather than pursued indiscriminately.

The balanced scorecard is now widely championed. Indeed, it has somewhat ironically become a management fad. Its argument – that blind faith in a single measurement or a small range of measures is dangerous – is powerful, but effective measures of elements, such as management competencies or intellectual capital, remain elusive.

SEE: RENAISSANCE SOLUTIONS
MORE INFO: www.rens.com; Robert S. Kaplan & Robin Cooper, *Cost and
            effect: Using integrated cost systems to drive profitability
            and performance*, 1998; Robert S. Kaplan & David P. Norton,
            The Balanced Scorecard: Translating strategy into action, 1996

Barbie

Often said to be the most successful toy in history, Barbie celebrated her 40th birthday in 1999. The world celebrated. "Forty years of dreams" proclaimed Barbie's makers, Mattel. Forty or not, Barbie defies the ageing process in a defiantly old-fashioned sort of way. No cellulite in sight, Barbie has long legs and a figure as shapely as shapely could be. Translated from doll size into reality, Barbie would stand seven feet tall with five feet long legs. Her stats would be 40–22–36. One might have thought that the sexist freak show Barbie-style would now be outdated. After all, children now have PCs and Game Boys. Not so. A Barbie is bought every two seconds. Barbie, who first saw the light of day at the annual Toy Fair in New York in 1959, is now a $1.9 billion industry.

Barbie was the idea of Ruth Handler, wife of Elliott Handler, one of the founders of the toy company Mattel. Mrs Handler saw her daughter playing with paper dolls and was inspired to make something a little more permanent and realistic. "If a little girl was going to do role-playing of what she would be like at 16 or 17, it was a little stupid to play with a doll that had a flat chest. So I gave her beautiful breasts," said Mrs Handler. (The Handlers eventually sold most of their interests in Mattel in 1989.) The breasts haven't

Stretching Barbie

Barbie should have stretch marks, given the number of times the Barbie brand has been extended. Extensions include:

- 1961: The advent of Ken, the man in Barbie's packed life.
- 1963: Midge, Barbie's friend, invented to provide a shoulder to cry on. (Reborn in 1988.)
- 1964: Skipper, Barbie's little known younger sister.
- 1968: Barbie pushes back the cultural frontiers with her black friend, Christie.
- 1988: The Hispanic friend, Teresa, becomes Barbie's confidante.
- 1990: Kira, Barbie's Asian friend.
- 1992: Barbie's much younger sister, Stacie.
- 1995: Unfeasibly young sister, Kelly.
- 1997: Becky, confined to a wheelchair.

always worked in Barbie's favor. In Japan sales were initially sluggish. Market research found that girls and their parents thought that Barbie's breasts were too large. Mattel eventually changed the doll for the Japanese market. The licensee in Japan quickly sold two million of the smaller breasted Barbie.

Though Barbie is a universal and (usually) standardized product, part of its success has been the number of costume variations on offer. Over 100 new costumes are added each year. This is necessary because Barbie is a Renaissance woman. You can have it all. Just look at Barbie – "She's a successful businesswoman, a member of a rock band, and a Women's World Cup Soccer Player," Barbie's Web site informs us. And she also has a man in her life, Ken. He is suitably coincidental. Introduced in 1961, Ken has lurked in the background, content presumably to see Barbie make such a success of her multi-faceted life. Barbie also has her friend, Midge, who first saw the light of day in 1963 before slipping into obscurity prior to a stunning 1988 comeback.

Barbie has moved with the times. Indeed, she has embraced virtually every sad and temporary fashion with something approaching abandon. Barbie was inspired by the Beatles, then became, of all things, a Mod. She has also, along the way, reflected the "prairie look," whatever that may be, and been into disco music. In the 1980s, she got into power dressing. She still found time to be an aerobics instructor. This sporting theme has continued. The late twentieth-century Barbie is a basketball and soccer player.

Barbie's makers are proud of Barbie's multi-career approach. "Barbie has the unique ability to inspire self-esteem, glamour, and a sense of adventure in all who love her," Mattel gushes. "She has been a role model to women as an Astronaut in 1994, 1986 and in 1965 – nearly 20 years before Sally Ride! As a college graduate in 1963, surgeon in 1973, business executive in 1986, 'Summit Diplomat' and airline pilot in 1990, a presidential candidate in 1992, and a dentist in 1997, the Barbie doll has opened new dreams for girls that were not as accessible in the early 1960s. As a matter of fact, the world's most popular fashion doll has actually had 75 careers since her inception." Unfortunately, Mattel does not record the success of the Career Diplomat version.

Barbie

Now Mattel, the Californian maker of the doll on perpetual heat, has entered the fashionable world of mass customization. Barbie now comes complete with 15,000 combinations. Change the outfit, the eyes, the color – but don't even think about the legs. All for $40 (double the usual price). The management gurus were right. Mass customization is child's play.

zeitbite#4
Ray Bradbury

"Put me in a room with a pad and a pencil and set me up against a hundred people with a hundred computers – I'll outcreate every goddamn sonofabitch in the room."

SEE: MASS CUSTOMIZATION
MORE INFO: www.barbie.com
SOURCES: *The Times*, 11 November 1998; www.barbie.com

Barnevik, Percy

Percy Barnevik is the former CEO of Asea Brown Boveri. He is now a non-executive director of General Motors and ABB chairman.

Barnevik (born 1941) is one of the most celebrated CEOs of our time. He has been portrayed as a kind of European Jack Welch. There are similarities. Both men have a long-held and passionate disdain for bureaucracy. Barnevik developed an aversion to bureaucracy and hierarchy when he worked at the family print firm as a child. As an adult, Barnevik developed his 30 percent rule – on taking over a company 30 percent of headquarters staff are fired; 30 percent moved to other companies in the group; 30 percent spun off into separate profit centers; leaving 10 percent to get on with the work. Both Barnevik and Welch are inveterate and powerful communicators who have managed to maintain a heady tempo of change. They have changed then changed again.

Undoubtedly the biggest coup of Barnevik's career was the merger of Asea and Brown Boveri in 1987. Negotiations were conducted in secret. When the boards were shown the draft agreement for the first time, some directors had no idea a merger was afoot. They had an hour to read the papers. The entire process was extraordinarily quick. Due diligence was notable for its absence as Barnevik pushed to clinch the deal. When a draft agreement was generated, Barnevik read it out line by line in front of both negotiating teams. Objections were ironed out on the spot. If voices weren't raised, it was taken as agreed. "We had to be fast; there could be no leakage; we could not have lawyers around; we had to trust each other," Barnevik reflected.

Barnevik's management style is forthright, entrepreneurial and upfront. The level of trust was perhaps the most striking thing about the merger. Both sets of management recognized that it was a good idea. There was no political manouvering. Secret discussions remained secret. Decisions were made and kept to. This atmosphere of mutual respect and trust was probably helped by the fact that it was a merger rather than a takeover – "A takeover would have destroyed a lot, psychologically, politically and commercially," says Barnevik.

A restless, high-octane workaholic, Barnevik created a sophisticated matrix system for ABB; reduced hierarchy and bureaucracy with great zeal; and created one of the first effective, truly global organizations. He also managed his succession with characteristic ease.

SEE: ASEA BROWN BOVERI; GÖRAN LINDAHL
MORE INFO: Kevin Barham & Claudia Heimer, *ABB: The Dancing Giant*, 1998;
              www.abb.com
SOURCES: Kevin Barham & Claudia Heimer, *ABB: The Dancing Giant*, 1998

Bell, George

George Bell is the CEO of Excite, the search engine that now attracts some 20 million visitors per month. Bell is not some whiz-kid who has spent his life fiddling with the hard drive. He is a sometime writer and producer of documentaries. This saw him climb Everest. He was also senior VP of Times Mirror Magazines and launched the cable network, Outdoor Life. Bell's message is that when the going gets tough, the tough guys move in – "We've finished the cocktail-party conversation of the Web's growth." Bell is, according to *Wired*, "legendary for his dealmaking hustle." He professes to have a simple business philosophy: "I try to come in, switch the lights on, do as much as I can each day, then switch the lights off. And come back the next day." Simple.

SEE: ECOMMERCE
MORE INFO: www.excite.com
SOURCES: *Wired*, September 98

19

zeitbite#5
Walter
Wriston

"Information about money has become more valuable than money itself."

Benetton

In 1965 Giuliana Benetton decided to knit a brightly colored sweater. If only she'd known where it would lead. Over 30 years on, Giuliana and her three brothers, Luciano, Gilberto and Carlo, have a global retail chain of 7000 stores in 120 countries selling brightly colored sweaters. Giuliana controls the work of over 200 designers at Benetton's Design Center.

Benetton's Castrette industrial complex in Northern Italy is among the world's most advanced. The factory produces almost 100 million garments every year. It includes an automatic distribution system, which handles over 30,000 packages every day. This process is managed by a mere 19 people – a traditional system would require at least 400.

While Benetton has been one of retailing's most eye-catching performers of recent decades – latest worldwide annual sales were worth 2871 billion lire – it now stands on a knife edge. The next few years will determine if the brand has longevity as Benetton expands into new markets and new regions.

Its brands now include Zerotondo, Sisley and 012. In 1997 it moved into sportswear and sporting equipment through such brands as Prince, Nordica and Rollerblade.

zeitbite#6
Esther Dyson

"I'm convinced that in the long term, the Internet will come to be regarded as the medium of truth."

Benetton is now taking its brand to bigger and bigger stores. It has opened megastores in major European cities and its US flagship is the 1200-square-meter store in New York's Scribner Building on 5th Avenue.

Growth is backed by Benetton's surprising, or offensive, advertising. One features Luciano Benetton naked except for the line "I want my clothes back." Then there are the shocking images of people dying. Gratuitous? Perhaps it is, but it has largely succeeded in cementing Benetton's niche as a colorful outsider.

SEE: ABSOLUT; BRANDS
MORE INFO: www.benetton.com

Benetton

Berkshire Hathaway

Headquartered in Omaha, Nebraska, Berkshire Hathaway is Warren Buffett. The two are inextricably linked – in corporate fact and stock market mythology. The reality is that Berkshire Hathaway is a corporate entity, a shell inhabited by 38,000 employees and made real by the passage of dollars to and fro – but a shell with a market capitalization of around $60 billion.

Berkshire Hathaway's subsidiaries include Helzberg's Diamond Shops, Flight Safety International, GEICO and HH Brown & Dexter. A more peculiar assortment of companies it would be difficult to imagine. From candy (See's) to insurance (National Indemnity), the company remains a law unto itself.

Buffett – and his cohort Charlie Munger – is the company's life force. Whether Berkshire Hathaway will continue without Buffett remains a point of perennial, if useless, debate, GEICO's Lou Simpson is usually touted as Buffett's successor. Sorry Lou. He is a hard, if not impossible, act to follow.

SEE: WARREN BUFFETT
MORE INFO: www.berkshirehathaway.com
SOURCES: Berkshire Hathaway Annual Report

Berners-Lee, Tim,

Tim Berners-Lee is based at MIT's computer science lab. He is head of the World Wide Web Consortium (W3C) which is attempting to create some sort of order on the Web. As one of the inventors of the Internet – perhaps the inventor – Berners-Lee is qualified for the job. (To help things along, he has recently been given a $270,000 "genius grant" courtesy of a helpful foundation.)

Berners-Lee is British and built his first computer when he was studying physics at Oxford University. After graduating in 1976, he worked for Plessey and then a firm writing typesetting software. In 1980 he spent six months consulting at CERN, the European Particle Physics Lab in Geneva, Switzerland. "I needed to be able to keep track of things, and none of the computer programs that you could get would let you make this random association between absolutely anything and absolutely anything," he later recalled.

Berners-Lee developed a program called ENQUIRE ("Enquire within for everything"). He returned to CERN in 1984 and developed the idea of running hypertext across the Internet. He went on to develop browsers and protocols. In 1992 the Internet exploded. Berners-Lee probably deserves to be a multi-billionaire. Instead, he is talking up the next stage in the Internet's development – the transformation from the bewildering mass now in operation to a smooth running, accessible, reliable tool.

SEE: THE INTERNET
MORE INFO: Tim Berners-Lee, *Weaving the Web*, 1999
SOURCES: *The Observer*, 19 April 1998

Bertelsmann

Long-established, low profile and traditional, the German company Bertelsmann is perhaps the most surprising participant in the contemporary media bonanza. Based in Gütersloh in northern Germany, Berteslmann is 163 years old and remains a private company (90 percent controlled by Reinhard Mohn, a descendant of Carl Bertelsmann). Yet, it has quietly snuck onto the top table alongside the likes of Rupert Murdoch, Pearson and the American media titans. (If you are into rankings, it is the media number three behind Time Warner and Disney.) In 1998, Bertelsmann truly marked its arrival with the purchase of Random House for an estimated $1.5 billion. This helped it to become the second biggest English language publisher in the world.

The Bertelsmann empire was built after the company was wiped out during World War II. First the company was closed down by the Nazis because its head was a devout Christian, then the British compounded things by bombing its factory. With book-club and magazine interests (including the German magazine, *Stern*), Bertelsmann revived, slowly putting feelers into the American market and ventures such as TV and music. It now owns 50 percent of Barnes & Noble's Web site business (bought for $200 million); 49 percent of European broadcasting company, CLT-UFA; and has a stake in AOL and a German sports information provider. Internet-related businesses now bring in DM1.4 billion of its revenues.

Bertelsmann

The great challenge for Bertelsmann and its chief executive, Thomas Middelhoff (born 1953) is how to change its traditional way of working – decentralized to a fault and German-dominated – and how to fend off Internet competition at the same time as joining the Internet bandwagon.

SEE: **RUPERT MURDOCH**
MORE INFO: www.berteslmann.de
SOURCES: www.hoovers.com; www.bertelsmann.de

Bethune, Gordon

Talk turnaround these days and you're talking Gordon Bethune. Bethune is chairman and CEO of Continental Airlines. He took on the job in 1994. It didn't appear to be the greatest career move. In fact, it appeared to be the career equivalent of suicide. Continental was in disastrously bad shape. The previous CEO, Frank Lorenzo, had followed a cheap fare strategy, which had got the airline nowhere. It had been in Chapter 11 and seemed stuck in the red. Its market capitalization of $230 million was actually less than the trade-in value of its planes. (This must rank as one of the most inglorious achievements in recent managerial history.) Continental lost $204 million in 1994. Blue skies were far away.

Things were bad. "We even had pilots turning down the air conditioning and slowing down planes to save the cost of fuel. They made passengers hot, mad, and late," says Bethune.

On arrival Bethune took the double locks off the executive offices on the 20th floor. He ordered that the planes be repainted so that they were all the same color. He instructed staff to ensure that the planes were cleaned three times more often. He announced that every month that Continental was in the top five airlines on on-time performance everyone got $65 – the company lost $6 million per month by being late. In the first month Continental was seventh; in the second it was fourth and in the third, first.

In 1996 Continental made profits of $556 million and its market capitalization is now $3 billion. *Fortune* selected it as the Most Improved Company of the 1990s. "We don't spend a lot of time on strategy; we spend more time on implementation, making sure we

zeitbite#7
Larry Bossidy

"Productivity is a mind-set."

23

Bethune, Gordon

get it done," says Bethune who has proved single-handedly that management is not aeronautic science: great management is simple.

SEE: EASYJET
MORE INFO: www.flycontinetal.com
SOURCES: *The Art of Taking Charge*, January 98

Bezos, Jeff

Jeff Bezos (born 1963) has a 41 percent share in Amazon.com. This is now reputed to be worth some $910 million. His career has been quite successful. A Princeton graduate, he ended up as the youngest vice president at Banker's Trust in New York. Then he made his break – "I tried to imagine being 80 years old, looking back on my life. I knew that I would hardly regret having missed my 1994 Wall Street bonus. But having missed being part of the Internet-boom – that would have really hurt." Trouble is that most people didn't even know the Internet boom was going to happen. Bezos did. How long his particular boom continues is open to debate. For the moment, he remains an entrepreneurial model.

SEE: AMAZON.COM; ECOMMERCE
MORE INFO: www.amazon.com
SOURCES: *New World* 2/98

Big Mac Index

Not so long ago, the opening of a McDonald's outside the US was an event. A McDonalds in Moscow? The press flocked to see the roubles flow. Now, McDonalds has conquered the world. The mystery has gone; now comes the measurement. The ultimate tool is the Big Mac Index.

The Index was developed by the sardonically excellent *Economist* magazine as a measure of the strength of worldwide currencies. It takes the price of Big Mac – available in over 100 countries – as the currency benchmark for the world. So if a Beijing Big Mac costs $1.16, an American Big Mac $2.42 and a Swiss Big Mac $4.02, the Chinese yuan is undervalued and the Swiss Franc over-valued.

Simple and robust, the Big Mac Index has been around for over a decade. During this time it has endured the usual vicissitudes of market forces. When McDonalds cut the price of a Big Mac by 65 percent, the markets shook with shock. The Whopper Index may only be a bite away.

SEE: BALANCED SCORECARD
SOURCES: *Economist* 12 April 97

bit-head

Someone who is overly dedicated to the internal workings of anything with a hard drive. To some it may be a term of endearment. A geek with added scientific credibility. To most inhabitants of the world (beyond Palo Alto, CA) it is understood pejoratively.

zeitbite#8
Al Neuharth

"Never hesitate to steal a good idea."

Bloomberg, Michael

After running the company's equity trading and technology systems, Michael Bloomberg (born 1942) left Salomon Brothers in 1981. With a group of fellow ex-Salomon employees, Bloomberg founded Innovative Market Systems. The company was later renamed Bloomberg. It now has annual revenues in excess of $1 billion and Bloomberg is CEO. The company includes Bloomberg Financial Markets, Bloomberg News Radio, Bloomberg Business News and Bloomberg Information TV.

Bloomberg was educated at John Hopkins University and Harvard Business School. His public pronouncements suggest arrogance – "I could literally walk up to any crowd anytime, and speak for as long as you like, and they would love it," he told the *Financial Times* for no apparent reason. His autobiography is accurately entitled *Bloomberg on Bloomberg*. This is tempered by fears of individual and corporate mortality. "If you don't keep improving, someone else will; clean your clock," he says. "No company in history has gone on forever. It's scary. Of the Fortune 500 when we started the business in 1981, only 160 are left." Bloomberg has prepared for the company's demise, or at least purchase, after his death: his will lays down that the business will be sold to the highest bidder within two years of his death.

25

Bloomberg retains 80 percent of the business (the remaining share is owned by Merrill Lynch). He remains resolutely blunt in his managerial philosophy: "Management, accountants, and other outsiders can say anything they want. Clients and employees never lie."

The lobby of the company's New York office is dominated by a giant perimeter-circumscribing fish tank. Care for a swim?

SEE: MICHAEL MILKEN
MORE INFO: www.bloomberg.com
SOURCES: *Bloomberg on Bloomberg*, 1997; John Gapper, "Is it a mayor? Is it a god? No, it's Michael Bloomberg," *Financial Times*, 11 May 1998

Bonfield, Sir Peter

Sir Peter Bonfield (born 1944) is chief executive of British Telecommunications (BT). His role as leader is best known – to date at least – for his unsuccessful courting of MCI. BT put $4.3 billion into the company and there were protracted talks concerning a possible merger. Eventually BT lost out to Worldcom who paid $37 billion for MCI.

Bonfield, educated at the sporty Loughborough University and formerly with ICL, bounced back. BT joined up with AT&T in a $10 billion network alliance. With 129,000 employees and sales (1998) of $26,145 million, BT is a big telecoms player ready to punch its weight through a variety of global alliances.

MORE INFO: www.bt.com

book buying

Writers are not usually renowned for their willingness to buy their own works. They expect them gratis from their grateful publishers. Trouble is, all writers are not created equal. In the wacky world of business books, authors are more than willing to buy their own books. (They are often keener to buy them than to write them.) Sometimes they buy them in huge numbers. As a result (and completely unbeknown to the innocent authors, I might add) the books sometimes find themselves on the bestsellers list.

When this happens, investigative journalists tend to suggest that this is cheating. The authors protest that it is simply marketing. Most famously the authors of *The Discipline of Market Leaders* arranged the purchase of over 10,000 copies of their book. James Champy bought 7500 copies of his *Reengineering Management*. The trick is to buy the book from the right bookstore – only certain stores contribute to the bestseller rankings. For highly intelligent consultants with egos the size of continents and ambitions on a global scale, this is not a difficult task. The business book may well be the most expensive calling card ever invented.

SEE: GHOSTWRITING; WORDWORKS
SOURCES: *Across the Board*, November/December 1998

branding consulting firms

Consulting firms have discovered branding. The consulting arms of the Big Five auditing firms, in particular, have embraced it with uncharacteristic zeal. The leading consulting firms now spend $50 million or more – sometimes much more – every year on brand-boosting advertising.

And it is not just mass media advertising that consulting firms deploy. More subtle means of brand enhancement are utilized. Traditional firms now invest heavily in bolstering their brands through "thought leadership" products, events, publications and associations – everything from lavish magazines to book awards. It may lack the impact of a direct appeal through a glamorous full color ad, but the aim of thought leadership endeavors is identical: brand development – and rapid brand development at that.

Over the past couple of decades, the big consultancy firms have been growing at a frenetic rate, spreading their empires across the globe. The problem facing them now is how to sustain that level of growth as the market becomes ever more saturated. The trouble is that after a while one consultant can look very much like another, so how do you differentiate yourself?

In addition, many have expanded so rapidly, growing arms and legs at such a rate, that even their own clients – and employees – don't understand their total capability.

The answer, the big firms have decided, lies with branding. The brand's the thing. The allure of branding for consulting firms can be attributed to a number of factors. First, there remains some confusion and vagueness about what it is that consultants actually do. Effective branding helps consultants to explain their role in the corporate firmament to potential customers and, it must be said, to themselves: branding has an external and internal audience.

Second, just as traditional branding has convinced consumers that one washing powder is different from another, so it helps differentiate one consulting firm from another. The more commoditized the market, the more branding matters.

Third, branding enables consulting firms to communicate with the entire population of buyers of consultancy in organizations. Previously, consulting firms were brought in by CEOs or board directors. Now, less senior managers also regularly employ consultants. While the entire potential market for a firm may once have rested with 200 or 300 CEOs, now there are often 20, 30, even 40, people in an organization buying consulting services. Communicating with this much bigger and broader audience requires branding as well as the nurturing of one-to-one relationships.

The fourth element is that branding can actually help consulting firms communicate with their own people, binding together what might otherwise be a rag bag of different brand personalities in different markets.

Finally, branding helps firms attract and retain the best people. In a knowledge-centered business, this final factor is of rapidly increasing importance. There is a 15–20 percent attrition rate among many top firms. Little wonder then that much of the advertising by consulting firms is directly targeted at potential recruits.

Some take a different approach, by seeking to appeal to the idealism of potential recruits. "Not everyone can wait ten years for a new drug to come to market," reads a three-page spread from the now laboriously named PricewaterhouseCoopers featuring a portrait of a man from an underdeveloped country who has just been inoculated. Do you want to help? Of course. Do you think the ad is for a drug company? Probably. Then you read the tag line: "We're helping make sure they don't have to. Join us. Together we can change the world."

The overall challenge for consulting firms is to implement branding strategies that appeal to a variety of audiences. If firms get their branding right, they create a virtuous circle.

Of course, there is nothing new in this. Consulting firms have long been aware of the power of branding, but have generally done little to systematically develop their brands. Prior to the 1990s, consulting firm brands developed in an ad hoc way. Generally, they were backed by little advertising – deemed too crass and inappropriate for a business relying on word-of-mouth recommendation – and haphazard promotion.

In the modern era, the starting point for the branding frenzy, was the operational split of Andersen Consulting from Arthur Andersen in 1989. Overnight a new giant emerged. Its birth was backed by a brand building bonanza. The new consulting firm's early ads asked if we remembered the geek in the class who was good at calculus. They went on to say that the geek now worked for Andersen. This was aimed primarily at the company's internal audience. The message was that Andersen people were bright, numerate, problem solvers. Its aim was to build confidence inside the fledgling giant. Yesterday's geeks suddenly became today's corporate saviors. The geeks started billing.

Andersen Consulting remains the most notable and lavish exponent of one of two brand building strategies pursued by consulting firms. Andersen invests heavily in mass media image advertising. Such advertising is a relatively new adventure for consulting firms. "Most consulting is sold through referral. Image advertising is the very antithesis of the traditional relationship marketing in consulting," says Tom Rodenhauser, long-time commentator on the consulting industry and editor of the *Rodenhauser Report*.

Image advertising by consulting firms is now a mainstay of business magazines and newspapers. One issue of a business magazine included 14 color ads from Andersen. In the name of brand building, golf veteran Jay Sigel is sponsored by the company, and the van Gogh exhibition at London's National Gallery was an Andersen Consulting event. (No suggestion that Sigel or van Gogh are geeks.)

branding consulting firms

And where a giant treads, another is sure to follow. "Andersen raised the bar for the mega firms," says Tom Rodenhauser. "Now, they feel obligated to follow." Experts suggest that Ernst & Young will spend about $100 million globally this year and KPMG invests $60 million annually on brand building. The battle is on.

The competitive battle is a war of words and images. KPMG proclaims that it's time for clarity – this did not prevent one of its recent ads being headed by the lines: "Giving your business the means to get where it needs to go doesn't amount to much if you're heading in the wrong direction in the first place." No-one ever suggested that clarity is easily achieved. Elsewhere, in the quest for what it calls "unified global branding," KPMG proclaims that its consultants have an average of 13 years of experience. Its television and print advertising features a crowd of children leaving a school bus. "They skip into the building each morning, so young, so innocent, so helpless. Are we referring to your children or your consultants?" Neat but, of course, it all depends on how you calculate experience.

More combative is Deloitte-Touche's comparative advertising, which targeted McKinsey. The only thing that hasn't yet happened is a more personal slant to the advertising. This, for the moment at least, is regarded as unprofessional. But it is probably not long before we see the CEO of a big firm presenting himself as the friendly face of management consulting.

In the mean time, messages are fired off from all sides and opinions differ on the merit of the individual campaigns. "Pricewaterhouse-Coopers, Ernst & Young and KPMG need to rethink. Their advertising doesn't stand out, it doesn't make a case," says Sam Hill. "Deloitte's advertising looks different. It is simple and has a condensing message. It is very powerful."

Some also have reservations about the general tone. In appealing to widely different audiences there is the danger of firms presenting themselves as all things to all men. "Firms say they can do anything for anyone anywhere. There is a tendency to over simplify and to over sell. They tend to create an image of what they want to be versus what they are right now," warns Tom Rodenhauser.

The trouble is that in the quest to differentiate themselves, the big consulting firms give the appearance of slavishly following each other. "They are all doing much the same thing – full page ads in the *Wall Street Journal* and *Financial Times* – so you have to question the effectiveness of much of the activity," says Tom Rodenhauser, going on to predict that more skirmishes lie ahead: "The gloves are likely to come off in terms of advertising."

Perhaps more significantly, there are suspicions that the big bucks spent are not necessarily leading to big rewards. "If you press them on the effectiveness of advertising, they become wishy-washy about whether it translates into business. The question must be whether it is necessary in that sort of business. If these were public companies rather than partnerships, shareholders would say 'My God' when they saw how much was being spent," says Rodenhauser.

For clients and potential recruits, the question must be whether the carefully created brand is real or a meaningless mirage. Messaging that communicates the authentic brand is most likely to succeed.

"Companies should ask themselves how they are going to target different audiences," says Tom Rodenhauser. "Promoting knowledge to the target audience is the key. Instead of broad stroke advertising, they should be promoting a single practice group to a specific audience."

But whatever the pros and cons of the latest spate of consultancy brand building, the signs are that the battle of the brands is only just beginning. One thing is sure: the ad agencies aren't complaining.

SEE: BRANDS; HELIOS CONSULTING
MORE INFO: www.kpmg.com; www.ac.com; www.mckinsey.com;
            www.ey.com; www.pwcglobal.com
SOURCES: Interviews; *Management Review*, October 1999

brands
Brands are an ever-present part of our lives – from the clothes we wear, to the food we eat; from the toys our children play with, to the

drinks we consume; from our mobile phones to our cigarettes. We read about brands in our carefully branded newspapers. We are loyal to brands and almost everything appears to be capable of being branded – from eggs to countries. The potential for branding appears limitless. And, the effort is sometimes worth it – "It's just like Pepsi Cola!" noted Eduard Shevardnadze at the opening of the new Coke bottling plant in Tblisi, Georgia.

There is no escape. "Your T-shirt with the distinctive Champion 'C' on the sleeve, the blue jeans with the prominent Levi's rivets, the watch with the hey-this-certifies-I-made-it icon on the face, your fountain pen with the maker's symbol crafted into the end ... You're branded, branded, branded," says Tom Peters.

Not only has the world of brands expanded to take in virtually everything that can be made, provided or breathed, it has re-invented its traditional relationships. Small, locally available products have been converted into nationally and internationally renowned money-earners.

Once the world of brands was dominated by fast moving consumer goods. Now it is filled with retailers – from Benetton to Wal-Mart – and financial services companies. For all this, the function of brands is fundamentally straightforward. Brands are little more than prompts, symbols and representations – activities which have been used since we started buying and selling things. Brands are marketing shorthand which companies hope will lead us to purchase their particular products.

Brands have become associated with the hard-selling entrepreneurial superficiality of the 1980s when deals were everything and brands changed hands as readily as stolen watches. Brands have been brought back to earth. Companies now appreciate that brands are neither frivolous nor a necessary evil, but important, expensive and potentially lucrative investments. That they are now all-embracing is a fact of life – caused in part by the human need for re-assurance, labeling and ease of identity.

Brands are exciting. For business people and consumers, the world of brands appears invigorating and sometimes glamorous. It is the world of Bacardi advertisements and multi-million pound campaigns.

But, there is much more to brands than this alluring image. There is also, for example, a comfort factor. Brands may pander to our dreams and aspirations – beaches, sunshine, not a worry in the world and a glass of spirits too – but they also re-assure. We like the idea of a life of excitement and unlimited finance, but settle for having a drink in the comfort of our home. The brand becomes a surrogate for our ambitions and dreams. The successful brands are the ones that we are comfortable with, but which are not complacent. They sell us Caribbean dreams at an affordable price. We know what the brand does, what it looks like and how much it costs. And the best brands continually meet and exceed our expectations.

At its simplest, branding is a statement of ownership. Cows are branded and, in the commercial world, branding can be traced back to trademarks placed on Greek pots in the seventh century BC and, later, to medieval tradesmen who put trademarks on their products to protect themselves and buyers against inferior imitations. (Of course, in the modern world people are adept at copying trademarks – whether they are Lacoste, Sony, Rolex or Le Coq Sportif – and producing imitations, which are often highly accurate.)

Today, brands are a ready source of information as well as identification. They are also an experience. Customers used to buy things; now, they experience them. We are in a new era, where brands are positioned as having emotional and life-style benefits which are transferable across several products, rather than being narrowly identified with a particular product.

In this new era, brands are driven by consumers. They are psychological, as well as physical. Brands are about hearts and minds. "A brand is a promise, and, in the end, you have to keep your promises. A product is the artifact of the truth of a promise. Coke promises refreshment; Gateway Computer promises to be your wagon master across the Silicon prairie. There is no difference between what you sell and what you believe," says futurist Watts Wacker. Selling is believing.

SEE: ABSOLUT; BRANDING CONSULTING FIRMS; VIRGIN
SOURCES: *Fast Company*, August–September 1997; *Entrepreneur*, April
            1997

brands

Branson, Richard

Richard Branson (born 1950) wears colorful jumpers and dropped out of school aged 16. He sports a beard and is good fun. He likes high-jinks and japery: flying around the world in a balloon (failed), posing naked with a book covering his genitalia (unnecessary) and PR stunts of any type (collecting litter for Margaret Thatcher and many other similar offences – including Mike Oldfield's execrable *Tubular Bells*). His column inches are only matched by his wealth.

Branson's gifts are many. He is an entrepreneur whose timing is often impeccable. He has a talent for publicity. His business secret is simply to go into stuffy markets where customer service, strong brands and competition are notable by their absence. He then shakes things up.

Richard Branson is the ultimate brand-builder. Through his company, the Virgin Group, he has created a unique business phenomenon. Never before has a single brand been so successfully deployed across such a diverse range of goods and services. The distinctive red and white Virgin logo, it seems, is as elastic as Mates condoms that are just one of the many products it promotes.

Branson started his first business at the age of 16, and was a millionaire at 24. Now, his personal wealth has been estimated at $2.7 billion, but it's hard to get an accurate tally, since his companies are private, constantly dividing and multiplying, and are controlled via a series of tax-efficient offshore trusts.

His derring-do outside of business life is matched by the boldness of his escapades in it. He has repeatedly used the Virgin brand to take on aggressive market leaders and shake up complacent markets – first the big record companies, then the airlines and more recently soft drinks and financial services. These commercial adventures have almost bankrupted the company on several occasions.

Today, Branson is the driving force at the center of a web of somewhere between 150 and 200 companies, employing more than 8,000 people in 26 countries. His commercial interests span travel, hotels, consumer goods, computer games, music and airlines. You can even buy a Virgin pension or investment plan.

Branson deliberately targets markets where the customer has been consistently ripped-off or under-served, and the competition is complacent. He delights in casting Virgin as the cheeky underdog, faster on its feet and nipping at the heels of big business. No one plays David to the Goliath of big business better than Richard Branson. It is a marketing strategy that appeals to millions.

Remarkably, he has also managed to keep a veil around the inner workings of his financial empire. In 1986 he floated his Virgin business on the London Stock Exchange, only to buy it back because he didn't like the constraints a market listing brought with it.

According to Tim Jackson, author of *Virgin King*, the unofficial Branson biography, Branson's motto should be "ARS EST CELARE ARTEM" – the art lies in concealing the art. This is the essence of the Branson management style, and the cornerstone of the Virgin empire.

Des Dearlove

SEE: VIRGIN; BRANDS
MORE INFO: www.virgin.com
SOURCES: Des Dearlove, *Business the Richard Branson Way*, 1998

Brill's Content

A new voice in the media, calling for accurate and fair reporting, has emerged. Entitled *Brill's Content*, after its driving force Stephen Brill, it is a US-based magazine that reports on how everybody else is reporting.

On one hand, the magazine calls for a return to the founding principles of journalism – checking your sources, providing a fair and proper context for the story. On the other hand, it seems to have an iconoclastic streak – arguing that Microsoft is better at (or at least as good at) media spin-doctoring than it is at technology. *Brill's Content* also has a sneaking admiration for the giant-toppling antics of Internet hack Matt Drudge.

The magazine's basic approach is to take US (and some international) organs of the media to task for blurring the line between informing the public and merely entertaining it or selling to it. In a world of increasingly lurid and headline-driven media, it argues for and is an example of thorough-going and balanced journalism: the Microsoft article weighed in at an impressive 8,780 words. The magazine also believes in giving ample space and prime position to its detractors – the letters page commanding a prominent position and generous amount of space within the magazine.

The media world is undergoing speedy transformation. *Brill's Content* is a self-conscious anachronism that shows us how far we have traveled when it comes to the mass-market consumption of news and information.

Gerry Griffin

SEE: MATT DRUDGE
MORE INFO: www.brillscontent.com
SOURCES: www.brillscontent.com

British Aerospace Virtual University

In April 1998, British Aerospace, one of Europe's biggest defence and aerospace companies, unveiled plans to create a virtual university in partnership with outside academic institutions. Called the British Aerospace Virtual University, the initiative involves a massive financial commitment by the company. In the next decade, it is pledged to investing more than £1.5 billion on building up the company's all-important "knowledge base" for the future. The virtual university marks one of the biggest investments in Europe in workplace development and one of the most significant developments in corporate universities.

SEE: CORPORATE UNIVERSITIES
MORE INFO: www.bae.co.uk
SOURCES: www.bae.co.uk

Browne, John

John Browne (born 1948) now finds himself as one of the most influential executives in the world. The Cambridge-educated Browne led the oil giant BP into its August 1998 takeover of AMOCO. The £30.3 billion deal was one of the most stunning of the 1990s in scale and surprise. Browne managed to emerge still relatively unknown. This is a substantial achievement given that he is also a non-executive director of Intel and of Smith Kline Beecham.

MORE INFO: www.bpamoco.com
SOURCES: www.bpamoco.com

Buffett, Warren

Warren Buffett (born 1930) is the greatest investor of our age. And, if not, the Sage of Omaha is certainly the best known. If in 1965 $10,000 had been invested in Warren Buffett's company, Berkshire Hathaway Inc., it would now be worth some $22 million. By 1997, a single Berkshire Hathaway share was worth nearly $20,000. These impressive figures have been much quoted as Buffet's success has been examined from every angle. Yet, if emulation is a measure of understanding, it appears little understood.

Above the maelstrom of analysts, commentators and private investors, stands Warren Buffett, a man of resolutely simple tastes, someone who oozes old-fashioned decency from every pore. As he has become more famous and Berkshire Hathaway ever more successful, Buffett's public utterances and writings have become more gnomic.

Buffett's career is simply summarized. He worked in his father's brokerage firm and then a portfolio-management company in New York. He founded the Buffett Partnership and then took over Berkshire Hathaway, a small textile company in Bedford, Mass.

Buffett advocates "focused investing." When gauging the wisdom of an investment, investors should look at five features: "The certainty with which the long-term economic characteristics of the business can be evaluated; the certainty with which management can be evaluated, both as to its ability to realize the full potential of the business and to wisely employ its cash flows; the certainty with which management can be counted on to channel the reward from the business to the shareholders rather than to itself; the purchase price of the business; the levels of taxation and inflation that will be experienced and that will determine the degree by which an investor's purchasing-power return is reduced from his gross return."

Time and time again, Buffett returns to the issue of sound management. The trouble is that there are a great many poor managers. "The supreme irony of business management is that it is far easier for an inadequate CEO to keep his job than it is for an inadequate subordinate," lamented Buffett in 1988, going on to criticize the comfortable conspiracies of too many boardrooms. "At board meetings, criticism of the CEO's performance is often viewed as the social equivalent of belching."

Buffett believes that executives should think and behave as owners of their businesses. Buffett's own management style is characteristically down to earth. "Charlie [Munger] and I are the managing partners of Berkshire," he explained in 1996. "But we subcontract all of the heavy lifting in this business to the managers of our subsidiaries. In fact, we delegate almost to the point of abdication: Though Berkshire has about 33,000 employees, only 12 of these are at headquarters." In fashionable books this would be called empowerment; to Buffet it is brazen commonsense.

Buffett is a ponderous minimalist in an age of hyperactive behemoths. "Charlie and I decided long ago that in an investment lifetime it's too hard to make hundreds of smart decisions ... Indeed, we'll now settle for one good idea a year. (Charlie says it's my turn.)" he wrote in 1993.

In the Berkshire Hathaway boardroom, belches are welcomed. Buffett admits to mistakes and errors of judgement in a most un-executive way. Perhaps the single most important aspect of Buffett's management style is that 99 percent of his and his wife's net worth is in the company's shares. The investment secret of Warren Buffett is revealed: Put all your eggs in one basket.

Georgina Peters

SEE: **BERKSHIRE HATHAWAY**
MORE INFO: www.berkshirehathaway.com

Buffett, Warren

SOURCES: Lawrence A. Cunningham, *The Essays of Warren Buffett:*
Lessons for Corporate America, 1997

business-bites

The corporate catch phrase – the business-bite – is a relatively recent development. Business-bites distill complex issues into punchy one-liners. Forget the detailed academic argument. The idea is to capture the very essence of your business philosophy or message into a simple but highly memorable sentence. "IBM was yesterday; Microsoft is today; Oracle is the future," says Larry Ellison with customary elan. In so doing, the owner and originator hopes to achieve two not entirely unrelated objectives. First, to become instantly recognizable to managers around the globe; and second to sell business books and consultancy services.

The intellectual sound-bites are phrases such as, *Only the Paranoid Survive*, a bestseller for Andrew Grove, head of Intel. We can only guess at how the book might have fared had his original altogether less snappy title *Navigating Strategic Inflection Points* not been rejected by the publisher. "Managers do things right; leaders do the right things" is a hardy perennial from leadership guru Warren Bennis. "Don't automate, obliterate" was the re-engineering call to arms. James Champy and Michael Hammer also produced "Good products don't make winners; winners make good products."

Meanwhile back in nerd-land, "A PC in every home" could only be Bill Gates. While there is "Trade not Aid" from Anita Roddick of the Body Shop, and the slightly less sassy but no less true, "Corporations are not things, they are the people who run them," from Charles Handy.

Business-bites differ sharply from mission statements – which are typically bland corporate statements. They belong to the individual rather than the company. So, for example, "Any color you like as long as it's black," goes with Henry Ford and not with the eponymous car company he founded.

Some have been quicker on the uptake than others. The man who coined the phrase "nanosecond nineties," Tom Peters, has had more bites than just about anyone. More recently, his bite has been: "Crazy times call for crazy organizations."

Business bites are important business weapons. No business leader ever achieved anything if no one understood him or her. At their best, they communicate complex ideas simply, quickly and understandably. At worst, they are meaningless bastardizations.

Such is the premium placed on business-bites that it is not unheard of for them to be followed by a copyright symbol or even the letter "TM" denoting trademarks of the author. This is more likely where there are consultancy products and services to be sold on the back of the intellectual property they represent.

Des Dearlove

SEE: CHARLES HANDY; BUSINESS BOOKS

business books
You once knew where you stood with business books. They were dull and unreadable. And, to make matters worse, they looked dull and unreadable. The decision to pass the business books and head to the section marked fiction was made easily.

No more. Over the last 15 years, the business book market has been revolutionized. A small segment of the publishing world has been turned into a global market with publishers hurrying to find the latest purveyor of managerial jargon. Business books even look like novels with their garish covers, punchy titles and hard sales lines.

Thanks to the eponymous *Dilbert Principle* by Scott Adams, business books have gone mainstream with a vengeance. Their titles are hip – or at least would like to be. Harvard's John Kao wrote *Jamming,* a eulogy to jazz creativity and how it could be the future of business. Then there are the bright and zany titles. This trend was established with the success of *When Giants Learn to Dance,* by another Harvard star, Rosabeth Moss Kanter. Professor Moss Kanter is a serious academic who prides herself – justifiably – on the quality of her research. She is, however, responsible for a steady stream of books with silly names. Charles Handy picked up on Kanter's example early on – he wrote *The Age of Unreason* and, more biblically, *Waiting for the Mountain to Move.* A title like Handy's *The Empty*

40

Raincoat is – in this market at least – pure genius. It defies analysis and begs a number of important questions – why is the raincoat empty? What can and should be inside? The fact that the answer is doughnuts and shamrocks only adds to the confusion.

Things have got a little out of hand. Now, no business book is complete without a surreal title and a detailed sub-title that attempts to tell you its contents in less than 12 words. Alternatively, for those who don't thrive on subtlety and ambiguity, another alternative is the shocking title which has blockbuster and bestseller written all over it. Tom Peters has cornered this particular market with titles such as *Thriving on Chaos* and *Liberation Management*. These give managers the impression that the contents are all about action and action is their fatal attraction.

All of this is good news for publishers. In 1991, McGraw Hill published 25 business titles; in 1996 it published 110. Marketing budgets at the esteemed (and un-Dilbert) Harvard Business School Press are estimated to have almost doubled in the last four years. In the UK alone 2,931 business titles were published in 1996 – compared with a paltry 771 in 1975. Happy days are here.

SEE: BOOK BUYING; WORDWORKS; GHOSTWRITING

business schools

First the good news. Business schools are a huge international business. From Helsinki to Auckland, their coffers are brimming. The global executive education market has been calculated at some $12 billion. A place on the nine-week Advanced Management Program at Harvard will set you back $40,500. Over the last 50 years, business schools have created a formidable industry.

And now the bad news. Business schools are at a crossroads. After 20 years of booming business, they face intensifying competition and fundamental questions about their role. Increasingly the message must be: change or face extinction.

Competition comes from a number of fronts. There are a growing number of corporate universities, centers funded by companies to train their staff. Then there are consulting firms. Once the big business ideas came out of business schools. Now, they tend to emerge from consulting firms like McKinsey & Co., which increasingly consider themselves to be in the ideas market. There are upstarts and start-ups in abundance. Many specialize in distance learning delivered by the latest technology.

The final source of competition to business schools comes, somewhat surprisingly, from their own faculty. Business-school faculty can increasingly be found running their own lucrative consulting businesses. Then there is the seminar and conference merry-go-round.

The end result of growing competition is likely to be a shakedown in business-school numbers. At the moment there are now some 800 business schools in the US and Europe producing well over 100,000 MBA graduates a year. The future may well see a three-tier system with a small elite of global schools at the top, nationally competing schools below and a final tier of local competitors.

Chris Lederer of Chicago-based Helios Consulting argues that the only the best business school brands will survive. "American schools such as Harvard, Wharton, Amos Tuck, Northwestern, the University of Virginia's Darden and MIT's Sloan School have successfully created brands which are separate from their universities," says Lederer. "With the proliferation of schools and the MBA now almost generic, business schools have to develop brands which differentiate them from the competition."

With branding pre-eminent, Lederer presents an intriguing scenario: "A quarter of Harvard Business School graduates receive job offers from consulting firm, McKinsey. So, think of the potential of the Harvard Business School/McKinsey MBA. With the blurring of divides between consulting firms, corporations and business schools it could make sense. Students could spend a year learning through the case-study method at Harvard and the following year working on McKinsey assignments. It would be a powerful coupling of brands." Other brands which are already reputed to be sniffing out opportunities are Microsoft and News Corporation. In the age of info-tainment, a link between a media or high-tech giant and a business school could be a match made in heaven.

Of course, the entire issue of business schools behaving like brands arouses academic indignation. Phrases such as academic integrity are used. The trouble is that business schools have never quite established whether they wish to be considered as academic institutions or businesses. The result is that they tend to perform badly on both counts.

As academic institutions, business schools increasingly have to acknowledge an indifferent record in generating new thinking. Then there are matters of academic impartiality. The business-school habit of seeking corporate funding for everything from chairs (Professorial and others) to wallpaper means that anomalies can arise. The holder of a professorship sponsored by a particular company is hardly likely to publish a damning case study of the company's management techniques. Little wonder that much business literature is banal and self-congratulatory.

And, if business schools are to be treated as businesses, their record is equally questionable. Business schools appear adept at shooting themselves in the foot and remain perpetual hostages to charges of not running themselves according to the precepts they champion in the lecture theater. Business schools may protest about the unfairness of being judged by their practical application of the theories they so eloquently espouse. But, how many business schools re-engineered themselves at the beginning of the 1990s? How many have identified their core competencies and, as a result, changed their organizational structure? How many really know what business they are in?

Until such issues are clarified, a steady stream of stories of managerial incompetence will continue to surface. Clearly, there is an inherent unfairness attached to such stories. No organization is perfect. Management is an imprecise art. The trouble is that business schools have led managers to believe that running a business can be a precise, measurable and, therefore, manageable science. Being measured by their own yardsticks is inevitable. The challenge for them is to re-evaluate the yardsticks. Those that fail to do so will bite the corporate dust.

SEE: CORPORATE UNIVERSITIES; APOLLO GROUP
MORE INFO: www.mba.org.uk; www.mbaplanet.com
SOURCES: Stuart Crainer & Des Dearlove, *Gravy Training*, Capstone, 1998

Byrne, John

John Byrne is the *BusinessWeek* columnist who ran the magazine's bi-annual survey of business schools. "Some deans refer to John Byrne, the *BusinessWeek* journalist responsible for compiling the rankings, not altogether jokingly as 'the most important man in North American management education'," wrote George Bickerstaffe in *Which MBA?*. Byrne no longer has this onerous responsibility, but remains at the magazine.

SEE: BUSINESS SCHOOLS

44

Cap Gemini

The European information systems consulting and integration company. Big in Europe, it now has a US subsidiary in New York. With more than 31,000 employees, Cap's 1997 net income was $127 million. A French holding company, CGIP, owns 26 percent of the firm.

SEE: **BRANDING CONSULTING FIRMS**
MORE INFO: **www.capgemini.com**
SOURCES: **www.capgemini.com**

zeitbite#9
Charles
Handy

"Corporations are not things, they are the people who run them."

career management

Career management is a new phenomenon. In the distant past, life unrolled before you. It was largely not yours to control. Then, during the twentieth century, the corporation emerged as the determiner of careers. Now, careers increasingly have to be managed by individuals. It is us, as individuals, who make the choices and call the shots.

The objective, Peter Drucker has observed, is simple enough. Happiness comes from working at what we are good at and in ways that suit our abilities. The trouble is that this rarely happens. The reason, says Drucker, is because we often have little idea of what we are good at. We should ask what are our strengths? How do I perform? What are my values? Where do I belong? What should my contribution be?

The route to outstanding performance is to identify and improve your unique skills, and then to find jobs, or assignments, which match your skills, values etc. Ask questions, find the answers, and then you are equipped to make the right decisions for your career – and life – development.

SEE: EXECUTIVE CHURN; EXECUTIVE SHORTAGES; PETER DRUCKER
SOURCES: Peter F. Drucker, "Managing oneself," *Harvard Business Review* March–April 1999

CEO Agency

In the near future, superstar CEOs will call the shots. They will demand and receive high salaries. They will also take on the jobs that interest them most. When that interest fades, they will leave.

Already, we see interim executives – Apple's iCEO Steve Jobs being the best-known example.

Renaissance men and women are rare. This explains why there are talent shortages: "Leadership in a modern organization is highly complex and it is increasingly difficult – sometimes impossible – to find all the necessary traits in a single person," says Jonas Ridderstråle of the Stockholm School of Economics. "In the future we will see leadership groups rather than individual leaders."

All of this means that "Show me the money," the phrase from *Jerry Maguire*, could have new resonance for top executives in the next few years. The movie starred Tom Cruise in the role of a wheeler-dealer sports agent. How long before top executives start hiring their own agents?

Not long at all if Leigh Steinberg has anything to do with it. Today, his law firm, Steinberg & Moorad, represents more than 100 athletes and negotiates multi-million dollar deals for some of America's best-known sports stars. Steinberg is now exploring ways of expanding his business to include negotiating on behalf of top business talent. The CEO Agency is surely only a matter of time.

It's enough to strike terror into the hearts of recruiters everywhere – which may be just the shock they need to start taking the issue seriously. According to Generation X expert and trend follower, Bruce Tulgan, the process is already underway: "More and more of the best talent are acting like free agents," he says. "Many have consultancies of one – they sell some unique skill or knowledge on the open market. Many are happy to represent themselves. As agents emerge to represent these free-agent knowledge workers, such agents will be successful to the extent that they are able to demonstrate that they add significant value to the equation. Already plenty of executive recruiters play a similar role as do some of the consulting firms that pull in outside independent consultants to work on key projects."

SEE: EXECUTIVE SEARCH; EXECUTIVE CHURN; LEIGH STEINBERG
MORE INFO: www.leighsteinberg.com
SOURCES: *Management Review*, August 1999

Cerf, Vinton

Vinton Cerf is one of the founding fathers of the Internet and senior vice president of Advanced Internet Architecture for MCI WorldCom. He unravels the technological future. And the future is "seamless interaction."

Cerf studied at Stanford and UCLA. Between 1976 and 1982 he worked at the US Department of Defense's Advanced Research Projects Agency and from 1982–1986 he was vice president of MCI Digital Information Services. He has also been vice president of the Corporation for National Research Initiatives. More intriguing, Cerf was a technical advisor to Gene Roddenberry's "Earth: Final Conflict" TV show. (Suitably, in 1994 *People* included him as one of its "25 most intriguing people.")

Cerf co-designed the TCP/IP protocol, the computer language that effectively gave birth to the Internet. He was founding president of the Internet Society (1992–95).

As Cerf points out, there is plenty of room for growth in Internet usage. Sixty percent of US homes do not have Internet access. Explosive growth disguises the fact that the Internet has grown since the 1960s. Behind the revolution is a story of diligent evolution. He is also quick to refute notions that the Internet is a limited commercial tool laden with security problems. Dell, says Cerf, records daily sales of $6 million through the Internet and Cisco Systems totals annual sales of $2 billion through its site.

He envisages a future where access to the Internet is constant – "The idea of having to dial a phone to make a temporary Internet connection – which is the way many people use the Net today – will seem pretty odd. We're going to evolve to the point where network access is provided like electricity – in other words, always on."

SEE: TIM BERNERS-LEE; ECOMMERCE
MORE INFO: www.mci.com
SOURCES: Brody, Herb, "Net cerfing," *Technology Review*, May/June 1998

Cisco Systems

John Chambers, a 50-year-old former salesman, became CEO of Cisco Systems in January 1995. Since then Chambers – ex-IBM and Wang – has put his very firm imprint on Cisco. Under his leadership the share price has gone up by almost 800 percent and Cisco's market value is now in excess of $100 billion – putting it ahead of GM. It was the fastest company to reach this mark in history. Revenues have leapt from $1.3 billion to $8.5 billion.

Cisco, now the third-largest company quoted on the NASDAQ, is the basic plumber of the Internet and corporate networks. It does the grunt work of data-networking equipment. (It is the number one networking gear supplier.) It was founded by Stanford staffers Leonard Bosack and Sandra Lerner in 1984.

Now, Chambers is moving it into telecoms equipment. Typically, he visited the heads of 90 out of the 100 top phone companies in the world. Chambers wears his ambitions on his sleeve: "I want Cisco to be a dynasty. I think it can be a company that changes the world."

SEE: ECOMMERCE
MORE INFO: www.cisco.com
SOURCES: *Fortune*, September 7, 1998

clusters

Harvard Business School's Michael Porter is one of the titans of business thinking. His five forces framework, developed in the 1980 bestseller *Competitive Strategy*, is one of the most popular – and plagiarized – business models in history.

While the merits, or otherwise, of the five forces continues to be debated and taught, Porter studiously has moved on. His work is notable for its academic rigor and weighty tone. He is no populist and takes on some of the received orthodoxies of globalization.

Theory suggests that the globalization of markets, rapid transportation and high-speed communications capability should allow companies to source anything from anywhere, anytime. But, argues Porter, the reality is very different.

The global theory fails to explain the remarkably high success rate of firms specializing in the same disciplines operating in close geographical proximity.

Porter points to clusters, critical masses of linked industries and institutions in a particular place that enjoy unusual competitive success in a particular field. The most famous examples, he says, are computer firms in Silicon Valley and the Hollywood film industry, but other such clusters are dotted around the globe.

The proximity of organizations within these clusters – including suppliers, academic institutions and government agencies – appears to affect competition in three broad ways. First, they increase the productivity of companies in the region. Second, they drive the direction and pace of innovation. Third, they stimulate and trigger the genesis of new businesses within the cluster.

According to Porter, this phenomenon is probably best explained by the notion of a closer-knit community; one where geographical, cultural, and institutional closeness confer insiders with special access to each others skills and ideas.

Porter's hot house theory is hard to refute, although it does not explain the success of a company such as Microsoft which deliberately chooses to position itself out of Silicon Valley.

SEE: SOPHIA ANTIPOLIS

SOURCES: "Clusters and the new economics of competition," *Harvard Business Review*, November/December 1998

Coca-Cola Wear

With a market capitalization of $142,164 million and an annual turnover of $18,868 million, Coca-Cola remains hugely robust. Interestingly, however, it is moving towards more adventurous brand stretching than it has previously succeeded in pulling off. In the 1980s it made an attempt to launch a clothing range with no less than Tommy Hilfiger (then unknown). It came to nothing. Now, Coca-Cola Wear is a reality. This is based on the belief that "consumers feel a special relationship with Coke that encompasses more than

50

just the drinking experience." Perhaps, but even the strongest brand can soon become over-stretched if pulled in the wrong direction.

SEE: BRANDS
MORE INFO: www.cocacola.com

Cohen, Abby

Abby Cohen (born 1952) glories under the title of "the world's most influential market forecaster." She is a partner at the investment bank Goldman, Sachs – one of a mere 14 women among The Brotherhood's 245 partners.

Cohen was born in Queens, New York, the daughter of an accountant. She went to Cornell University and worked at the Federal Bank and then T Rowe Price Associates. More interesting, she joined Drexel Burnham Lambert, which later went bankrupt. A brief spell at Barclays de Zoete Weld preceded her joining Goldman Sachs in October 1990.

Cohen's reputation has been built on a formidable dedication to the bull market. "Many investors price in the expectation of recession. We do not think that's right," she says. So far, so good.

SEE: WARREN BUFFETT
MORE INFO: www.gs.com
SOURCES: *Guardian*, October 24, 1998; *Observer*, October 25, 1998

competency tracking

In the beginning came competencies. Companies labored long and hard to identify the competencies required in specific jobs. The downside was that this produced a mountain of paper, and a lengthy list of training and development requirements. The plus side was that training could be targeted more appropriately. Clearly defined competencies could result in timely and targeted training.

While the competency-training link makes clear, logical and powerful managerial and competitive sense, it has not always worked in practice. Indeed, as in so many cases, practice lags behind the neatly phrased and entirely logical theory.

While lots of companies engage in skills gap analysis, often they do not move forward to the next stage. The gaps inevitably remain as organizations ponder the wisdom of investing in training to fill them.

And then there are the sheer number of actual and potential competencies. While some companies have managed to distill the core competencies they require to a meager 12, most finish with far more. Many have a profusion. This may be entirely accurate, but means that actually managing them is usually impossible. Monitoring the developmental achievements and needs of someone in a job with 47 identified competencies requires more than one man and a flip chart.

For many, the reality is that linking competencies to appraisal and assessment systems, as well as to training, simply produces an array of paperwork. Even companies with carefully mapped out and understood competency frameworks have struggled with monitoring what has happened, what needs to happen and what is happening regarding training.

Now, technology is bringing new rigor and efficiency to the divide between theories and practices. Use of competency tracking software is increasing as organizations seek solutions to long running problems. Competency tracking is enabling companies to overcome some of the logistical challenges in ensuring that training and development is constantly related back to competencies, as well as being planned ahead with competencies in mind.

Among those who are taking advantage of the potential of managing competencies more positively is Prudential Assurance. It has introduced new competency software which aims to halve the administrative workload for those whose job it is to track and record employee development and standards. It breaks down employees' roles into four areas – technical knowledge, processing knowledge, behavioral skills and systems awareness. In time the software will track competency across them all. In the first instance, however, the company is focusing on those areas which are critical for compliance.

As well as taking much of the labor out of the competency process competency tracking takes the subjectivity out of management assessment. And may help companies with their succession planning.

competency tracking

More generally, demand for competency tracking is liable to expand as the quantity of administration and the complexity of compliance issues increases workloads in HR and training administration. Closer ties between competencies and reward and remuneration packages may further stimulate growth. Competency-based pay is a reality in mainland Europe, competency tracking may convince companies elsewhere to follow this route.

SEE: CORE COMPETENTS
SOURCES: *IT Training*, September 1999

connectivity

Understanding connectivity is like coming to terms with the childhood revelation that we are all, somewhere along the line, related. A whole new family suddenly emerges before you go on to ponder the awful impossibility of it all. In the information economy, small things are connected in a myriad of ways to create complex adaptive systems. Instantaneous, myriad connections are speeding the economy up and, more critically, changing the way it works.

The difference in the information economy is that the small things are connected in a myriad of ways to create a "complex adaptive system." "We have multiplied the instant connections among individuals, organizations and information itself. Attention has been focused on the resulting acceleration of business. But connections are doing more than accelerating the economy; they are changing the way it works," says Chris Meyer, co-author of *Blur*. "As the number of connections among the elements of a system grows, the system no longer behaves predictably – the system as a whole begins to exhibit unforeseen, *emergent* properties."

The trouble is that the connections are so many and so complex, that they can bring things to a grinding, inexplicable halt. "The stock market crash of October 1987 was caused by computerized trades, none of which were linked explicitly. The damage was done by the interaction of independent investor instructions – a kind of connected network of trading programs," write Stan Davis and Chris Meyer in, *Blur*. So, the stock market crash was not a frenzy of capitalism, but a connectivity short circuit. Such short circuits – akin to butterflies fluttering their wings in Mongolia and changing the climate of the world while also causing a run on the Deutsche Mark – are likely to occur with greater regularity.

SEE: CHRIS MEYER
MORE INFO: www.ey.com
SOURCES: Stan Davis & Christopher Meyer, *Blur*, Capstone, 1998

continuous learning

A 1995 study by the National Center of the Educational Quality of the Workforce looked at 3,100 US workplaces. The research found that than an average 10 percent increase in the workforce's educational level led to a 8.6 percent increase in productivity. In contrast, a 10 percent increase in plant and equipment increased productivity by 3.4 percent. Conclusion? Training and developing people is the greatest and most effective investment in a company's future. While this is a truth almost universally acknowledged, it remains a truth generally overlooked when executives consider their investment priorities.

SEE: BUSINESS SCHOOLS

Cool Britannia

zeitbite#11
Steven J Ross

"If you're not a risk taker, you should get the hell out of business."

Many in Britain awoke on May 2nd 1997 with a slight hangover and a mysterious spring in their step. The newspapers carried unconfirmed reports of people actually smiling at each other and engaging in conversation on the London underground. In the next few weeks, the weather seemed unusually bright and, perhaps most surprisingly of all, British sporting performances revived. The English cricket team beat the Australians. Greg Rusedski and Tim Henman cut a swathe through the Wimbledon seeds. The English and Scottish soccer teams qualified for the World Cup. Then a Briton shattered the land speed record. It seemed only a matter of time before there was a British winner of the Tour de France, a British Pope and the first Briton on Mars.

After the Labour Party landslide, Britain suddenly appeared a nation at ease with itself. It was confident, young and European. Cool Britannia was born. Tony Blair was to be seen hurtling along Amsterdam streets in a bicycle race with other European leaders. With youth on his side, he won – while, the newspapers quickly pointed out, Helmut Köhl walked. The cabinet even began using each

Rebranding Britain

Old brand	*New brand*
Stiff upper lip	Opinionated
Skeptical	Optimistic
Euroskeptic	European
Formal	Informal
Warm beer	Chilled lager
Class obsessed	Classless
Head	Heart
Surnames and titles	Christian names
Inward	Outward
Nationalistic	International
Andrew Lloyd-Webber	Spice Girls
Suspicion	Tolerance
Frank Bruno	Prince Naseem

other's christian names at meetings. Informality was in; pointless traditions were out. Stiff upper lips were cast aside, as ministers began speaking their minds.

People laughed at the candor of it all. Change – even political change which has little immediate effect on people's lives – appeared to herald something of a new beginning. Green shoots of recovery turned, almost overnight, into an overheating jungle – galling for the previous administration which had spent five years eyeing the ground expectantly. The wave of optimism was catching and about more than mere politics.

The change of mood was exemplified by the public outpouring of grief following the death of Diana, Princess of Wales. Nothing similar had ever been experienced. The once reserved British were suddenly gathering en masse to openly display their emotions. They queued in long, orderly lines as the British have always done but, after being kept under wraps for decades, hearts were worn on sleeves. The people were calling the tune and even the monarchy was shuffling into line.

With a new government, a surge of optimism and changes to the fabric of British life, Britain was re-branded, revamped and ready for the new millennium. In a few short months, the British brand was reinvented and no-one was more surprised than the British.

SEE: DEMOS

co-opetition

American academics, Adam Brandenburger (of Harvard Business School) and Barry Nalebuff (of Yale School of Management), suggest the new onus should be on "coopetition," an unwieldy combination of competition and co-operation. They argue that looking for win-win strategies has several advantages. First, because the approach is relatively unexplored, there is greater potential for finding new opportunities. Second, because others are not being forced to give up ground, they may offer less resistance to win-win moves, making them easier to implement. Third, because win-win moves don't force other players to retaliate, the new game is more sustainable. And, finally, imitation of a win-win move is beneficial not harmful.

co-opetition

SEE: GAME THEORY

MORE INFO: www.mayet.som.yale.edu/coopetition

core competents

A relatively small number of executive high achievers increasingly hold corporate power. Shortages of executive talent mean that the truly talented will have their choice of the plum roles. This, in turn, will mean that the old style administrator will become in less demand and will have to settle for positions below mahogany row. It will also spark a redefinition of what it means to be an executive.

For the select few, the world will be their oyster. Have talent; will travel. "Geography will be much less important in future. A new pattern of graduates and post-graduates is emerging," says Richard Wall of headhunters Heidrick & Struggles. "But more to the point, there is much less of a country-focus to jobs. Executives are more willing to look across borders. I think we are going to see a workforce which is much more transient, moving between companies and even continents."

Talented executives will be in demand and will be able to attract substantial salary and remuneration packages. In effect, corporate power will be concentrated in the hands of the few. "What is critical in the firm of the future is not so much the core competencies as the core competents," predicts Jonas Ridderstråle of the Stockholm School of Economics. "These walking monopolies will stay as long as the company can offer them something they want. When that is no longer the case they will leave."

Ridderstråle points to a growing array of supporting evidence. Bill Gates has reflected that if 20 people were to leave Microsoft, the company would risk bankruptcy. In a study by the Corporate Leadership Council, a computer firm recognized 100 "core competents" out of 16,000 employees; a software company had 10 out of 11,000; and a transportation group deemed 20 of its 33,000 employees as really critical.

So few, yet so powerful. According to Randall E. Stross, professor of business at San Jose State University and a research fellow at Stanford University: "In the software industry, a single programmer's intellectual resources, through commercial alchemy, can create

zeitbite#12
Warren
Buffett

"The business schools re-ward difficult complex be-havior more than simple behavior, but simple behav-ior is more effective."

57

entire markets where none existed before. Compare the cumulative worldwide gross revenues of the studio that captures the next Steven Spielberg compared to the rival who has to settle for the second-round draft pick. Differences separating the rewards generated by the top tier versus the second tier are geometric, not arithmetic." At the top of the organization, that difference is likely to be exponential.

SEE: KJELL NORDSTRÖM
MORE INFO: www.funkybusiness.com
SOURCES: www.funkybusiness.com

corporate divorces

Inevitably the huge movie star salaries now paid to top executives lead to huge movie star style divorces and suitably excessive movie star silliness. (Silliness: Jocelyn Wildenstein, wife of art dealer Alec, was not allowed to spend her divorce settlement on plastic surgery.)

The amazing thing is that it took so long. Two hefty divorces stand out. First, was the split between GE Capital chief Gary Wendt and his wife of years. Lorna Wendt claimed she was entitled to a 50 percent share of the couple's wealth because she had spent years as a "corporate wife." She failed. Instead, this loyal corporate wife was awarded a settlement of $20 million by the Connecticut courts. Lorna Wendt has since formed the Foundation for Equality in Marriage, and Wendt has unexpectedly left GE.

The second (on-going) divorce is that of Anna and Rupert Murdoch – first announced in Liz Smith's *New York Post* gossip column (much better to give your own newspaper the scoop). In July 1998 Anna Murdoch filed for divorce in California, citing irreconcilable differences, after 31 years of marriage to the media tycoon. The Murdoch case was complicated by the fact that Anna Murdoch is not a passive corporate wife but a director of News Corporation.

Only nine US states currently split assets equally between husband and wife. California is one of them. More metaphorical dirty corporate linen is sure to find its way into court rooms.

SEE: RUPERT MURDOCH

corporate legacy

Do you ever stop to wonder what you will leave behind when you step down from your job? Do any of us really think about the legacy we bequeath for those who follow? The answer, if you are a chief executive, should be a resounding yes. It's what marks out a great CEO from the rest.

"You can walk around any country graveyard to remind yourself that you will be under grass eventually," Peter Job, CEO of Reuters, observed when interviewed. "It's sensible, therefore, to say how long do I want my company to go on after me? This company has been going since 1851."

The concept of "corporate legacy" came out from research examining the impact of values on business. The values handed down from one generation to the next are an important dimension of the legacy.

Clearly defined corporate values can play an important role in the success of a business by engaging the energy, enthusiasm, and loyalty of employees.

The notion of corporate legacy, however, extends beyond the here and now. It raises the issue of what one generation of management should pass on to the next. In any long lived company, generations of CEOs will preside over the culture of the organization, inheriting them from their predecessor, passing them on to their successor.

Under Jack Welch, for example, General Electric has explicitly linked the performance of its managers to the company's values. Welch carries a laminated card in his pocket bearing the GE values. Failure to live those values is grounds for dismissal. At one meeting Welch surprised his audience saying: "Look around you: there are five fewer officers here than there were last year. One was fired for the numbers, four were fired for (lack of) values."

Some organizations go to remarkable lengths to preserve their distinctive cultures and safeguard their corporate legacy. Merrill Lynch, for example, has its five "Principles" engraved on plaques lining the corridors of its world headquarters. Johnson & Johnson has its values written down in a book – the "Credo" – which dates back to the founding fathers of the company. Hewlett-Packard has the H-P Way, which employees write out by hand and pin up next to the picture of their family.

In their book *Built to Last*, James C. Collins and Jerry Porras studied the factors that characterized companies that were successful over many years. A set of core values, they found, provided continuity and a sense of identity.

These companies place their values above profit maximization. Yet research suggests that they out perform companies that put profits first, providing a better return to shareholders over time. The companies identified by Collins and Porras, for example, had outperformed the general stock market by a factor of 12 since 1925.

More recently, Arie de Geus looked at corporate longevity in his book *The Living Company*. De Geus, writes about the managers of long-lived companies: "They succeeded through the generational flow of members, and considered themselves stewards of the longstanding enterprise. Each management generation was only a link in a long chain."

Stewardship is an idea that is increasingly relevant to business. How successive leaders deal with this corporate legacy, however, is rarely discussed. It goes beyond traditional ideas of succession planning – deciding who the baton will be passed to and developing the next generation of managers – or even the work on corporate memory carried out by the American management writer Art Kleiner.

The idea of corporate legacy asserts that senior management is the custodian of the values that underpin the culture, conserving them on behalf and for the benefit of the company in the future. It goes right to the heart and soul of the business: what it exists for and the values it holds most dear.

This is particularly critical when the founder or founders of a company hand over control. What marks out the great CEOs from the rest is their ability to ensure that the company goes on after

corporate legacy

them. Bill Gates and Richard Branson are both great leaders in their own right, but what legacy will they leave behind?

But there is another critical dimension to the legacy issue. As economic conditions change with the passage of time there is often pressure within companies to deviate from the values, drop them altogether, or take on new ones. The question that then has to be answered is can values change or be replaced, or are they sacrosanct?

Opinion varies on this point. "Our basic principles have endured intact since our founders conceived them," said John Young, former CEO of Hewlett-Packard in 1992. "We distinguish between core values and practices; core values don't change, but the practices might."

Writing in *Fortune* magazine, Thomas A Stewart, draws a different conclusion: "Over time self-interest distorts corporate values ... to bring them back, top management must constantly reiterate, refresh, reinterpret and rename."

If the original sense of the values has been lost – if the values have evolved in the wrong direction – it is the top team's role to redefine and reinterpret the values so that they are relevant.

Cadbury-Schweppes is one company that has tackled this issue. Today, the soft drinks and food giant distributes its branded products in more than 200 countries, but it can trace its history back to the 1800s when John Cadbury first started selling tea and coffee in Birmingham.

During the 1970s, the company faced a period of transition following its merger with Schweppes. In 1976 Sir Adrian Cadbury, then chairman, took steps to ensure that the Cadbury values would be permanently enshrined in the new company's culture.

The Cadbury values were printed in a document, "The Character of the Company." They include a commitment to:

- competitive ability;
- quality;
- clear objectives;

- simplicity;
- openness; and
- responsibility to stakeholders.

These values have helped Cadbury-Schweppes maintain its position in a changing world. It is a legacy that has been handed down.

In these days of short-term thinking, more senior managers should think about their legacy. The future is unwritten.

Des Dearlove

SEE: ART KLEINER

corporate memory

Some managers have worked in companies for 20 years only to accumulate one year's experience twenty times. Companies can do much the same. They amass a track record but no understanding of what worked and what didn't work. Mistakes are repeated. Learning happens by default. But, what if the experience of the company and the people who make up the company could be organized and utilized? What if companies remembered?

To do so, the American researchers and writers Art Kleiner and George Roth suggest companies use a tool called the *learning history*, "a narrative of a company's recent set of critical episodes, a corporate change event, a new initiative, a widespread innovation, a successful product launch or even a traumatic event like a downsizing." Other techniques to organize and gather together corporate experiences are being explored – for example, technology enables databases of personal experience to be assembled.

The aim is the creation of corporate memory, a readily accessible fund of useful knowledge about how and why the company has done things. Corporate memory aims to allow an organization to transfer experience from one generation to the next and, more mundanely, from one office to the next. It is based on the understanding that intellectual capital is not simply a contemporary phenomenon. Knowledge is – or should be – cumulative. All our insights come from retrospect, we just have to make the past available and then be able to put the past into perspective. The corollary is that if you want to stall a decision, you can always say: "Let's examine the corporate memory on that" or ponder aloud: "What would they have done in 1957?" Corporate memories can play tricks on you.

SEE: ART KLEINER

corporate universities

There are now over 1,000 corporate colleges operating in the US. They come in all shapes and sizes, and cover virtually every industry. The Ohio automotive-parts manufacturer, Dana Corporation, has Dana University; Ford has a Heavy Truck University in Detroit; Intel runs a university in Santa Clara; Sun Microsystems has Sun U; and Apple has its own university in Cupertino, California.

When they were first established, corporate universities raised a few academic eyebrows. There were sniggers at the thought of McDonald's Hamburger University or Disney University in Florida. The mirth has subsided and suspicion has taken over. If corporations can train their own executives, their reliance on business schools is reduced.

The scale of the corporate universities is, in many cases, impressive. Hamburger University, located in Oak Brook, Illinois, may not, in the eyes of some, have a great deal of academic credibility, but it is celebrating its 35th anniversary and boasts over 50,000 graduates. It has 30 resident professors, suggesting that its programs go a little beyond the art of frying. Indeed, the McDonald's educational empire has spread in parallel with the growth of its business – there are now ten international training centers in the UK, Japan, Germany and Australia – and technology enables programs to be delivered simultaneously in 22 languages.

Corporate universities are not for the faint hearted. They are highly expensive. Research in the US by Jeanne Meister calculated that the average operating budget for a corporate university was $12.4 million (though 60 percent reported budgets of $5 million or less).

The chief downside of corporate universities has been that they often do not offer anything other than an internal qualification. In an effort

63

to broaden their appeal, corporate universities are establishing partnerships with a wide range of organizations. Courses are increasingly affiliated to those of a more traditional academic institution.

Herein lies a major threat to business schools. Some corporate universities are attempting to develop degree awarding powers themselves. The consulting firm, Arthur D Little, has already pursued the degree route at its Boston-based school. But a survey of 100 corporate university deans carried out for the AACSB, by Corporate University XChange, suggested a change of heart – 40 percent of corporate universities now plan to offer degrees in partnership with higher education institutions, mostly in business administration, computer science, engineering and finance. It is down to business schools whether they believe this constitutes an opportunity or a risk.

It is also doubtful whether corporate universities can produce meaningful or useful research. Their close allegiances tarnish thoughts of objectivity and independence. Whether the growth in corporate universities will continue is a matter of some debate – most obviously within business schools.

Georgina Peters

SEE: MOTOROLA UNIVERSITY; DISNEY UNIVERSITY; CORPORATE
            UNIVERSITY XCHANGE
SOURCES: 1998 Survey of Corporate University Future Directions,
            Corporate University Xchange

Covey, Stephen

Stephen Covey (born 1932) is founder, chairman and president of the Covey Leadership Center at Provo, Utah. He has an MBA from Harvard Business School and spent the bulk of his career at Brigham Young University where he was first an administrator and then professor of Organizational Behavior. His doctoral research looked at "success literature." In 1984 he founded his Leadership Center aiming to "serve the worldwide community by empowering people and organizations to significantly increase their performance capability in order to achieve worthwhile purposes through understanding and living principle-centered leadership."

Covey reached a huge global audience with the success of *The Seven Habits of Highly Effective People* (1989) which has sold over six million copies. Along the way, the devout Mormon transformed himself into an end of the century Dale Carnegie. "He has sold himself with a brashness that makes the overexcited Tom Peters look like a shrinking violet," noted *The Economist*. Another commentator observed that "Mr Covey has a knack of dressing up spiritual principles in pinstripes." In fact, Covey's "principles" are a mixture of the commonsensical and the hackneyed – "be proactive; begin with the end in mind; put first things first; think win/win; seek first to understand, then to be understood; synergize; sharpen the saw." Yet, it is their very simplicity and accessibility which partly explains Covey's astonishing success. The Covey Leadership Center, now reincarnated as Franklin-Covey, employs over 700 people and has an annual turnover of $70 million.

SEE: **ANTHONY ROBBINS; INEFFECTIVE HABITS**
MORE INFO: www.franklin-covey.com

zeitbite#13
Vaclav Havel

"It is clearly necessary to invent organizational structures appropriate to the multicultural age."

65

Covey, Stephen

Daewoo

Back in 1967, when many were thinking only of free love, one man was thinking only of cheap textiles. Kim Woo-Choong decided to set up a company called Daewoo Industrial with five employees and $10,000 in capital. Within five years the firm had increased its exports from nothing to $40 million. Then just when textiles were peaking the astute Kim diversified his business successfully; first into heavy and industrial chemicals in the 1980s and then later into telecoms, shipbuilding, automobiles, consumer electronics and home appliances. In other words, he had his fingers in just about every pie possible.

In the 1990s, the conglomerate embraced overseas acquisitions in order to become a genuine global player, building up a presence in markets, such as Eastern Europe, where many others fear to tread. *Fortune* ranked Daewoo as the world's 24th largest business in its 1997 survey after the company increased its revenues in one year by nearly 30 percent. In spite of the economic crisis in Asia it seems likely that the Korean giant is set to hold onto many of its gains. Certainly, its founder (and still chairman) seems to have lost little of his appetite. Last year, Kim Woo-Choong spent two-thirds of his year outside South Korea on business in 42 different countries.

Daewoo's ingenuity was brilliantly demonstrated when it moved into the UK car market. It created a radical channel approach to meet fundamental customer needs not satisfied effectively by the existing channel. It started the process with an extensive market research campaign about what customers wanted from a new car company. The campaign was conducted with a toll-free telephone number and a promotion for 200 free one-year test drives. The result was a database of 200,000 target customers.

The actual Daewoo product was not mentioned at this stage. Instead, the company tapped into the residue of ill feeling among consumers. Daewoo found that, consistent with research in the US, customers were not happy with the current system. In particular, they disliked how they were treated when buying a car. They also didn't like the after-sales service they received. In effect, Daewoo positioned itself as the customer's ally.

Daewoo

Company:
Daewoo Group

Subsidiaries include: Daewoo Motor/Daewoo Securities Co Ltd;
Daewoo Electronics

Address:
541 Namdaemunno 5-ga, Chung-gu, Seoul, Korea.
Phone: +82-2-759-2114
Fax: +82-2-753-9489
http://www.daewoo.com

Business:
Motor Vehicles and Parts

Statistics, fiscal year end December

Employees	1997	265,044
Annual sales (million)	1997	$71,526.0
Annual results net inc (million)	1997	$527.0
Other facts	Daewoo Group has more than 30 domestic companies and about 400 foreign subsidiaries.	
Hoover's 500	—	
Fortune 500	# 18 – Global 500	

Daewoo recognized the inherent dealer/manufacturer conflicts of interest and decided that a conventional franchise dealer network would not achieve the desired results. In response it began selling its cars through three channels: 30 flagship, wholly-owned car sales outlets, which do not provide service or sell used cars; 100 secondary, wholly owned sites, which sell new cars, perform service and also sell used cars; and, finally, 136 tertiary service sites, which are located at an independent chain of parts and service facilities, Halfords, but which are staffed by Daewoo personnel.

Independent and different, Daewoo's approach resulted in unprecedented success for a new entrant.

Trevor Merriden

SEE: REPUBLIC INDUSTRIES
MORE INFO: www.daewoo.com

data warehousing

One million people live in the German city of Cologne. Every day as they go about their daily lives they generate piles of statistics which are dealt with by computer systems in 70 different council departments. And then, rising above departmental computer systems, is a data warehouse which collects crucial data for the city's planners. Cologne's data warehouse is one of a growing number. Banks, supermarket chains, researchers and companies in virtually every business are keenly leaping aboard the new technological bandwagon. Suddenly, instead of having scraps of data on customers, companies have reams. Mainframes have largely been consigned to the corporate equivalent of Jurassic Park; dusty files have become data warehouses.

Data warehousing has gathered apparently unstoppable momentum. It has emerged as a world market worth around $4 billion. Predictably, though nightmarishly for linguistic purists, it has spawned a fresh deluge of acronyms – DSS (Decision Support Systems); EIS (Executive Information Systems); OLCP (On Line Complex Processing) and OLAP (On Line Analytical Processing) are a small selection. If the acronyms weren't daunting enough there is also a Data Warehousing Institute, which boasts 3500 members in over 45 countries. It is easy to feel you have missed the boat – or the technological equivalent. No fear. You are not alone. Indeed, one survey found that 60 percent of IT specialists admitted to having a limited knowledge of data warehousing.

So, what are data warehouses? Pithy definitions are thin on the ground – there is "a subject-oriented, integrated, time variant, non-volatile collection of data in support of management's decision making process" or, more understandably, a data warehouse offers "a single image of business reality." Cut away the jargon and data warehouses are simply databases.

Data warehouses have become popular because the explosion of new technology has run parallel to hyper competition in markets throughout the world. Companies need the best and most accurate information about customers; and they need it now.

Retail companies have led the way. In the US, Wal-Mart and Procter & Gamble were among those who set up data warehouses before anyone invented the term. They spent huge amounts with the aim of generating more information about customers to secure their loyalty. Since their pioneering work, costs have plummeted. The average cost of installing a data warehouse is now estimated at less than $3 million and one estimate puts the price at a tenth of the cost of a few years ago.

Seán Kelly, founder and director of the Data Warehouse Network, as well as author of *Data Warehousing: The Route to Mass Customization,* argues that there are only three ways by which a company can grow its revenue – by acquiring new customers, selling additional goods and services to existing customers, and by extending the duration of customer loyalty. The second and third methods benefit from the kind of customer behavior analysis which data warehousing enables companies to carry out. "Once companies began to study the behavior patterns of customers, it became evident that ensuring customer loyalty over long periods would dramatically enhance profitability and offered enormous potential," says Kelly.

So, data warehousing is driven by the simple need to use information to gain a competitive advantage. As the quality of the data is vital, it is no surprise that the bulk of the investment for many companies is

data warehousing

not the software and hardware, but "cleansing," sorting and loading data from a variety of mainframe systems and into the warehouse.

The end result is – or should be – a dynamic and huge database. Companies can use the database to pinpoint more accurately than ever before who their best customers are and what they require from them. Data warehousing enables companies to carry out intricate analyses of various aspects of their business. This leads to mass customization; a company knows so much about the customer that it can deliver exactly what an individual customer wants. Henry Ford RIP.

SEE: WAL-MART
MORE INFO: Seán Kelly, *Data Warehousing*, 1997
SOURCES: www.dw-institute.com

Dell, Michael

The company which Michael Dell built is not the biggest in the world. Nor are its products the most innovative. Dell Corporation is that rarity: a corporate model, the benchmark for how companies can be organized and managed to reap the full potential of technology. Michael Dell is the Alfred P Sloan of the high-tech age. But, while it took Sloan decades to meld General Motors into his organizational image, Michael Dell is still a young man – born in 1965.

Dell started young. Famously, while at the University of Texas, he rebuilt PCs and sold them. His business was kick-started with a $1000 investment. Dell's 16 percent share of the company is now worth some $5 billion.

Dell's inspiration was to realize that PCs could be built to order and sold directly to customers. This had two clear advantages. First, it meant that Dell was not hostage to retailers intent on increasing their mark-ups at its expense. Dell cut out the middlemen. By doing so, he reduced the company's selling costs from a typical 12 percent of revenue to a mere 4–6 percent of revenue.

Second, the company did not need to carry large stocks. It actually carries around 11 days of inventory. "The best indirect company has 38 days on inventory. The average channel has about 45 days of inventory.

So if you put it together, you've got 80 days or so of inventory – a little less than eight times our inventory level," says Michael Dell.

In any language, high profit margins and low costs make business sense. In the fast growing computer business they are nirvana. In its first eight years Dell grew at a steady rate of 80 percent. It then slowed down to a positively snail-like 55 percent. Its 1998 revenues were $12.3 billion.

Little wonder, perhaps, that Dell's competitors look pedestrian in comparison. While Dell has been growing explosively, Compaq has been growing at less than 20 percent. In terms of market share Dell is now closing in on Compaq in the US (14.1 percent versus 15.8 percent in the third quarter of 1998) and is number two in worldwide share behind Compaq. Dell may well end up having the best performing stock of the 1990s. Dell's market capitalization stands at $99 billion (compared with $75 billion and $169 billion for Compaq and IBM, respectively).

Inspired by such raw statistics emulators have come thick and fast. In an effort to keep ahead, Compaq has introduced programs which offer the ability to have PCs built-to-order. Crucially, they are still sold through intermediaries. The trouble for established companies like Compaq is that once the middlemen are in place it is very difficult to ease them out of the picture. Another Dell competitor, Gateway, has opted for a halfway house approach – it has introduced "Country Stores" to provide potential customers with a physical site to learn about products in person – the equivalent of a car showroom and test drive.

Emulation is the purest form of desperation as well as flattery. Dell's insight was, after all, blissfully simple. "There is a popular idea now that if you reduce your inventory and build to order, you'll be just like Dell. Well, that's one part of the puzzle, but there are other parts, too," Dell has said. He explains the company's success as "A disciplined approach to understanding how we create value in the PC industry, selecting the right markets, staying focused on a clear business model and just executing."

While the notion of selling direct is appealing, companies which do so are only as good as their ability to deliver. Dell's model creates a

Dell, Michael

direct line to the customer which the company has proved highly adept at maximizing. Direct knowledge of the end consumer builds a satisfied customer base – increasing Dell's brand strength, lowering customer acquisition costs, and boosting customer loyalty. The result is "mass customization" as opposed to the traditional method of broad market segmentation.

Dell, the interloper which has cut out the money grabbing middleman, has a strong rapport with its customers – in a way that Microsoft, for example, has manifestly failed to achieve. "To all our nit-picky – over demanding – ask-awkward questions customers. Thank you, and keep up the good work," read one Dell advertisement. "You actually get to have a relationship with the customer," explains Michael Dell. "And that creates valuable information, which in turn allows us to leverage our relationships with both suppliers and customers. Couple that information with technology and you have the infrastructure to revolutionize the fundamental business models of major global companies."

Dell has proved highly efficient in utilizing the full power of modern technology to create reliable logistic and distribution systems. It is among the pioneers of selling by the Internet. "The Internet for us is a dream come true," says Dell. "It's like zero-variable-cost transaction. The only thing better would be mental telepathy." Dell's online sales alone exceed $3 million a day and, during Christmas 1997, Dell was selling $6 million worth of products every day online.

The company's Web site is expected to manage half of Dell's transactions by the year 2000.

The beauty of the Dell model is that it can be applied to a range of industries where middlemen have creamed off profits. Its low overheads also mean that Michael Dell has no need to mortgage the business to expand. This year's model, may be around for some time.

SEE: ECOMMERCE
MORE INFO: www.dell.com
SOURCES: Stan Davis & Chris Meyer, *Blur*, Capstone, 1998; Richard L.
            Brandt, "Dell Computer Corp's Michael Dell," *Upside*, March 12,
            1998

Dell, Michael

Company:
Dell Computer Corporation

Address
One Dell Way, Round Rock, TX 786682–2244 USA
Phone: 512–338–4400
Fax: 512–728–3653
http://www.dell.com

Business
Computers, Office Equipment

Statistics, Fiscal Year End January

Employees	1998	16,000
Annual sales (million)	1998	$12,327.0
Annual results (million)	1998	$944.0
Other facts	World's #1 direct-sale computer vendor.	
	The company's Web site is expected to manage half of Dell's transactions by the year 2000.	
Hoover's 500	# 139	
Fortune 500	# 125	

Demos

Politics is the art of the possible, the science of practical achievement. But every political movement, every bandwagon, requires the high-octane fuel of theory. Theory is the justification and, when needs be, the fall guy. Politics without theory is inconceivable. Theory without politics is a vacuum.

Sometimes the two worlds click. Theorists and practitioners are at one. It tends not to last long. Demos is the theoretical power behind the practitioners of the UK's Labour Party. Their "Manifesto for changing Britain's insular image," researched by Mark Leonard, is the bible of Cool Britannia.

SEE: COOL BRITANNIA

derivatives

Derivatives are financial arrangements between two parties derived from the future performance of underlying assets such as currencies, debt bond shares and commodities. The market is huge – the Chicago Mercantile Exchange handles $200 trillion worth. Between 1995 and 1998 turnover in the over-the-counter derivatives market increased by 85 percent.

The size of the risks is matched by the size of some of the losses. The mining, metals and industrial group Metallgesellschaft was one of Germany's top companies. Derivatives disasters led to losses for 1993 of DM2 billion. By March 1994 the company had total debts of Dm 9 billion. More dramatic tales continue to unravel.

SEE: SPREAD BETTING

discontinuity

Continuity happened in the past. In the 1950s and 1960s and even the early 1970s, there was a feeling of security, moving inexorably in the right direction. Now, we are told, such halcyon continuity and confidence is the past; discontinuity – with surprises around unknown corners – is the new reality. But what reality?

SEE: CONNECTIVITY

Disney

Under Michael Eisner, family entertainment became Disney's guiding light once more. The result was that Disney moved from being a $1.5 billion company in 1984 to a $22 billion company in 1997. "If you could have great entertainment and not as great profits, or great profits and not as great entertainment, I'll take the great entertainment every time," says Eisner in an unconvincing attempt to sound like Walt Disney himself. The reality is that great entertainment leads to great profits (and, of course, great salaries – Eisner's total income from Disney Corp. in 1993 exceeded $200 million.)

The Disney company is now the second largest entertainment company in the world. Its theme parks continue to attract vast numbers of people. Walt Disney World brings in 32 million visitors a year; Disneyland 14 million; Disneyland Paris 3 million; and Disneyland Tokyo 5.2 million. The 1995 acquisition of Capital Cities/ABC for $19 billion cemented its place among the entertainment elite.

Even so, complacency would be dangerous for its 108,000 cast members. Its 1997 operating profit was $1.03 billion (down by a worrying 31 percent) on revenues of $6.5 billion. With competition from DreamWorks – creator of the movie hits Antz and Prince of Egypt – Disney's heartland of children's entertainment is under fire as never before.

SEE: DISNEY UNIVERSITY
MORE INFO: www.disney.com

Disney University

The entire concept of Disney University is ridiculous, and ridiculously successful. Disney U, complete with ubiquitous ears on the coat of arms, is not Ivy League or Oxbridge. From training Disney staff, Disney U now offers broader programs and executive development.

The Disney approach is simple: Disney is a successful global company with a unique culture; this is how we do it. Basically, Disney University presents its own corporate case study concentrating on corporate culture, motivating and coaching employees, team working and customer service. It has no pretensions to a broader approach, but argues that its success is built on universal managerial skills. As case studies go, it is impressive. Walt Disney World may not be a hallowed hall of academia but it does employ over 40,000 people ("cast members" in Disney jargon). It is all ears. And more.

SEE: CORPORATE UNIVERSITIES; MICHAEL EISNER
MORE INFO: www.disney.com

diversity advantage

Historically, companies tried to recruit the same sort of people time and time again. The thinking was simply that people of the same sort were much easier to control. The end result was companies filled with loyal and dutiful employees, who wouldn't have recognized a bright idea if it exploded out of their desk. More of the same people produce more of the same work. While this was acceptable in the past, the emphasis is now on innovation, speed and flexibility. Managers have to be able to think differently, work with different people and thrive on the difference.

Diversity is a competitive weapon. Diversity advantage is real. If companies accept difference, they are likely to be more responsive to changes in their business environment. They will be more flexible, open-minded and quicker to react. A Swiss multinational with ten nationalities on the board including six women, and the ability to make global teams work, will have a diversity advantage over an American widget maker from Cleveland with a board entirely populated by white middle-aged men who believe that Canada is the international market.

While in the United States, diversity is regarded as a racial issue, in Europe it is cultural. Multi-cultural European role models abound – from soccer teams to entire countries. One outstanding European role model is Switzerland which is highly successful, multi-ethnic and multi-religious. It is notable that some of the most successful and international of companies are Swiss – companies like Nestlé, Ciba-Geigy and ABB appear to handle diversity more easily and positively than others in Europe. Indeed, the Swiss-Swedish conglomerate, ABB, is often held up as the epitome of the modern organization and is a fervent champion of thinking global, acting local. International teamworking is central to making ABB work successfully. It thrives on

diversity advantage

diversity and requires that its managers "have an exceptional grasp of differing traditions, cultures and environments." ABB's supervisory board of eight includes four nationalities, while its executive committee goes one further with five. Its former chief executive Percy Barnevik argues that: "Competence is the key selection criterion, not passport."

Other multinationals are similarly diverse as they discover the twin challenges of globalization and teamworking. After its merger, SmithKline Beecham boasted a management group of 13 which included seven nationalities.

Before long it is likely that diversity advantage will be measured using some highly complex and ultimately useless formula. This will create a lucrative business for consulting firms in proving what companies should already know.

Even so, diversity advantage is a useful phrase to use when in the presence of widget makers from Cleveland – "But tell me, where do you see your diversity advantage coming from?" Once you are feeling confident, you can abbreviate the phrase to DA. This may cause further confusion among Americans who envisage the immediate arrival of law enforcement teams to check on how many Afro-Americans are middle managers.

SEE: ASEA BROWN BOVERI; FONS TROMPENAARS
MORE INFO: Fons Trompenaars, *Riding the Waves of Culture*, 1993

division of mental labor

Booz-Allen & Hamilton consultants, Charles Lucier and Janet Torsilieri, argue that a process-driven model of management has dominated our minds ever since Adam Smith. We have been engaged in maximizing the efficiency of our processes whether we are widget-makers or McDonald's. Efficient, lean processes with cost-efficient overheads have become regarded as the quickest route to profit heaven.

According to Lucier and Torsilieri, good intentions have not been matched by reality. "Overhead in major corporations is not decreasing," they note. One contributory factor to this is the rise of the knowledge worker. As Peter Drucker has jokingly lamented, "knowledge workers are abysmally unproductive."

This calls for a division of mental labor rather than an over-riding emphasis on creating processes to divide physical labor. The route to this requires a number of steps. First, routine work – a depressing 80 percent of what we do – needs to be standardized. This means giving people more responsibility, cutting out middlemen. Second, Lucier and Torsilieri suggest that companies "outsource the most complex (often most critical) decisions to the real experts." "Outsourcing the most complex decisions significantly increases both the quality of decisions and level of service," they say. The end result will be lower costs (though only slightly). "Companies will both eliminate expertise-driven overhead and better manage the productivity of knowledge workers," say Lucier and Torsilieri. They fail to add the most obvious side effect of outsourcing such work: a boon for management consultants.

As an adjunct to the idea of the division of mental labor, Peter Drucker argues that the management's great achievement of the century was to increase the productivity of manual workers fifty-fold. While this cannot be underestimated, it is not the great challenge of the next century. This, according to Drucker, is to increase the productivity of knowledge workers – dauntingly he estimates that the productivity of some knowledge workers has actually declined over the last 70 years.

SEE: PETER DRUCKER
MORE INFO: www.bah.com
SOURCES: Charles Lucier & Janet Torsilieri, "The end of overhead,"
              Strategy & Business, second quarter, 1999

DreamWorks SKG

Put together three geniuses in their own field of entertainment and do you have a sure-fire success on your hands? Throw in a starting fund of $250 million and it would seem a sure thing. It ain't necessarily so. After all, the Titanic was unsinkable.

DreamWorks SKG was founded in October 1994 by Steven Spielberg, Jeffrey Katzenberg, and David Geffen. The name "SKG" is merely the initials of the three founding partners' last names. Spielberg, a world-famous filmmaker, Katzenberg, a former chairman of Disney Studios (with something to prove to Michael Eisner), and Geffen, a giant in the music industry, were widely viewed as a potent combination, and the company immediately announced plans to launch film, music, software, and television projects.

DreamWorks has been criticized for not fulfilling the expectations surrounding the high-powered partnership. To date, DreamWorks' most well-known television project is the weekly situation comedy, *Spin City*, starring Michael J Fox, although another comedy, *Ink*, starring Ted Danson, failed miserably. DreamWorks' first major music release was aging pop idol George Michael's 1996 album, *Older*, which sold only moderately well. And it was not until the end of 1997 that DreamWorks released its first film, *The Peacemaker*, starring George Clooney and Nicole Kidman. The best may be yet to come. (The downside could be that stupendously wealthy people are not the hungriest entrepreneurs.)

Trevor Merriden

SEE: DISNEY

Drucker, Peter

It is ludicrous to include a nonagenarian in any listing of movers, shakers and zeitgeist breakers. Peter Ferdinand Drucker (born 1909) is old, but he remains the pre-eminent business thinker of our age.

"In a field packed with egomaniacs and snake-oil merchants, he remains a genuinely original thinker," observed the *Economist*. Prolific, even now, Drucker's work is all-encompassing. There is little that executives do, think or face which he has not written about.

Take the political fashion of the 1980s for privatization. It was Drucker who first introduced the idea of privatization – though he labeled it "reprivatization." This was energetically seized upon by politicians, though their interpretation of privatization went far beyond that envisaged by Drucker.

Alternatively, take the contemporary fixation with knowledge management. "The knowledge worker sees himself as just another *professional*, no different from the lawyer, the teacher, the preacher, the doctor or the government servant of yesterday," wrote Drucker in his 1969 classic *The Age of Discontinuity*. "He has the same education. He has more income, he has probably greater opportunities as well. He may well realize that he depends on the organization for access to income and opportunity, and that without the investment the organization has made – and a high investment at that – there would be no job for him, but he also realizes, and rightly so, that the organization equally depends on him."

Drucker was exploring the implications of knowledge being both power *and* ownership thirty years ago. If knowledge, rather than labor, was to be the new measure of economic society then Drucker argued that the fabric of capitalist society must change: "The knowledge worker is both the true *capitalist* in the knowledge society and dependent on his job. Collectively the knowledge workers, the employed educated middle-class of today's society, own the means of production through pension funds, investment trusts, and so on."

Far sighted and always opinionated, Peter Drucker was born in Austria where his father, Adolph, was the chief economist in the Austrian civil service. (Freud had lectured in psychiatry to his mother.) His early experiences in the Austria of the 1920s and 1930s proved highly influential.

Drucker worked as a journalist in London, before moving to America in 1937. His first book, *Concept of the Corporation* (1946) was a groundbreaking examination of the intricate internal working of General Motors, and revealed the auto-giant to be a labyrinthine social system rather than an economical machine. (In the UK the book was retitled *Big Business* as, Drucker explains, "both Concept and Corporation [were] then considered vulgar Americanisms.")

His books have emerged regularly ever since – and now total 29. Along the way he has coined phrases and championed concepts such as *Management By Objectives*. Many of his innovations have become accepted facts of managerial life. He has celebrated huge organizations and anticipated their demise. (This has led to suggestions of inconsistency – though this is a rather hollow criticism of a career spanning over sixty years.) His 1964 book *Managing for Results* was, Drucker says, the "first book ever on what we now call strategy;" *The Effective Executive* (1966) was "the first and still the only book on the behavior being a manager or executive requires." As Drucker's comments suggest, he is well aware of his influence – Drucker is not modest; but he doesn't have much to be modest about.

The coping stones of Drucker's work are two equally huge and brilliant books: *The Practice of Management* (1954) and *Management: Tasks, Responsibilities, Practices* (1973). Both are encyclopedic in their scope and fulsome in their historical perspectives. More than any other volumes they encapsulate the essence of management thinking and practice.

The genius of Drucker is that he has combined quantity and quality while plowing a thoroughly idiosyncratic furrow. He has resolutely pursued his own interests, and the dictates of his considerable intellect, rather than the dictates of the dollar. In an age of thinkers as media personalities, Drucker refuses to be distracted. Disturbers of his Californian retreat receive a preprinted message assuring them that he "greatly appreciates your kind interest, but is unable to: contribute articles or forewords; comment on manuscripts or books; take part in panels and symposia; join committees or boards of any kind; answer questionnaires; give interviews; and appear on radio or television."

Drucker has not shunned the world. He is not J.D. Salinger. But he is focused – as he has observed: "The single-minded ones, the monomaniacs, are the only true achievers. The rest, the ones like me, have more fun; but they fritter themselves away. The monomaniacs carry out a *mission*; the rest of us have *interests*. Whenever anything is being accomplished, it is being done ... by a monomaniac with a mission."

Drucker's book production has been supplemented by a somewhat low key career as an academic and sometime consultant. He was Professor of Philosophy and Politics at Bennington College from 1942 until 1949 and then became a Professor of Management at

New York University in 1950 – "The first person anywhere in the world to have such a title and to teach such a subject," he proudly recalls. Since 1971, Drucker has been a Professor at Claremont Graduate School in California. He also lectures in oriental art, has an abiding passion for Jane Austen and has written two novels (less successful than his management books). As if to prove that he is multi-dimensional, in *Who's Who* Drucker lists mountaineering as one of his recreations. He is the ultimate free thinker.

MORE INFO: Peter Drucker, *Management*, 1954; www.pfolf.org
SOURCES: *The Economist*, December 25–January 7, 1994; Peter Drucker,
            The Age of Discontinuity, 1969; *The Economist*, October 1, 1994

Drudge, Matt

Matt Drudge (born 1967) is the man at the keyboards in his LA office controlling the Drudge Report. He styles himself as a kind of Woodward and Bernstein on the Internet; investigative journalist, gossip monger, techno-newshound. Drudge will go down in history as the man who broke the Monica Lewinsky story – if the sordid tale ever reaches the history books.

"I live in the moment. I don't know what I'll be doing two weeks from now. The Internet gives you the freedom to go at your own pace," says Drudge, the techno-innocent abroad. He protests too much. Research by *Brill's Content* found that of 51 stories Drudge claimed as exclusive, only 31 were actual exclusives and in a third of these he got the facts wrong. Drudge may need a fact-checker, but he can cover the marketing vacancy himself.

SEE: BRILL'S CONTENT
MORE INFO: www.drudgereport.com
SOURCES: *Guardian*, October 31, 1998; www.brillscontent.com

Duffield, David

David Duffield is president, CEO and chairman of PeopleSoft. He is also its founder. He collects job titles.

Before founding PeopleSoft, Duffield established two mainframe application software companies. He was president, chairman and chief product architect of Integral Systems a California-based vendor of the first DBZ-based HR and accounting system. He also co-founded Information Associates which developed systems for the higher education market. Further back in his crowded history, Duffield was a marketing representative and systems engineer at IBM. He has an MBA and BS in Electrical Engineering from Cornell.

MORE INFO: www.peoplesoft.com

dumbing down

The belief that in many areas of the media and entertainment industries, content is increasingly catering to the lowest common denominator of human taste. In this regard, reference is made to tabloid newspapers ("Zip me up before you go-go," The *Sun*'s headline after George Michael's arrest); violent movies; moronic advertising; soap operas; sound-bite politics; the Jerry Springer Show; among many other sins.

Dumbing down is undoubtedly true, but it was always thus. Politicians have been peddling pithy placebos for centuries. Business people have been crassly chasing markets, by any means, for centuries. The good news is that there is also dumbing up – witness Oprah Winfrey's book club. This, too, has been happening for a while.

SEE: OPRAH WINFREY

Dyson, Esther

According to the *New York Times*, Ms Dyson is "the most important woman of the electronic age." She is a journalist and securities analyst who, since 1982, has edited the monthly newsletter, *Release 1.0*. Her company, Edventure, has seven employees. Her work appears throughout the world – and now includes the book, *Release 2.0*. "The Net is no place for propaganda, but it's great for conspirators," she cheerfully observes.

SEE: ECOMMERCE
MORE INFO: www.edventure.com
SOURCES: *New World*, February 1998

Dyson, James

The story of James Dyson (born 1947) and his "dual cyclone" vacuum cleaner is the stuff of business legend. In true David and Goliath style, Dyson beat near bankruptcy to establish his factory in Malmesbury, Wiltshire, and became the UK market leader. Today, he is regarded as one of Britain's leading entrepreneurs, but his unorthodox management philosophy is less well known.

As with most overnight successes, it has been a long journey for Dyson. He invented the bag-less "dual cyclone" vacuum cleaner in 1978, when flared trousers were in fashion the first time round. Five long years and 5127 prototypes later, his idea became a working model. But it was another ten years before the product reached the market.

In between, Dyson tried to get backing from the leading manufacturers. It was an eye-opening introduction to the world of big business. One multinational company, he says, would only agree to meet him if he signed over the rights to anything he might reveal to them in advance. Another wanted to license the product but refused to put anything in writing, saying that he would have to "trust" them.

Dyson very sensibly declined both offers. But his brush with the corporate world gave him important insights into the sort of management culture that prevailed in some large companies. He was determined that his own firm would be different.

When it was finally launched in 1993, from the coach house at the family home, Dyson's first product, the DC01 turned the UK market for upright cleaners on its head. Just 23 months after its launch, his invention became Britain's best selling vacuum cleaner, overtaking sales of Hoover, Electrolux, Panasonic and Miele. It was followed in 1995 by the DC02, the company's cylinder cleaner, which achieved similar results.

The company now employs 1050 staff and produces 10, 000 of the eponymous cleaning machines every day. The brand has more than half of the UK market by value and about a third by volume. Profits have jumped from £200,000 in 1993 to £19 million.

Today, the distinctive yellow, gray and purple vacuum cleaners are to be found in homes the length and breadth of the country. Other vacuum cleaners may still be referred to generically as "Hoovers," but a Dyson is a Dyson.

The company's management style also stands out from the crowd. The UK factory operates according to principles laid down by its founder. Employees must follow two rules: no smoking and no ties. (Dyson once told the board of a company on America's East Coast that ties make you go deaf in your old age – "Wearing a suit strait-jackets you," he also says.)

Despite his success, Dyson remains wary of the corporate mindset. Memos are banned. According to Dyson, they are "just a way of passing the buck. He has an even lower opinion of e-mail. 'The graphics are so appalling I just can't get interested enough to read them," he says.

To this day, the company has a slogan that says: "We should be human beings not business people." Dyson employees do not wear suits and ties, and many are recruited straight from university because their minds are open to new ideas and working methods. Half of the senior management are female, including the managing director Tracy Ebdon-Poole.

Hierarchy is frowned upon. Every new employee – as the former trade minister Richard Needham discovered when he joined the company as a non-executive director – spends the first day assembling one of the famous dual cyclone machines which they can then buy for £20 and take home for their own use. Familiarity with the product, the company believes, means that employees are more committed.

Individuality is also a strong feature of the company's culture. Dyson employees are encouraged to be different as a matter of principle – it's part of what Dyson calls his anti-brilliance campaign. "Very few people can be brilliant. And they are over-valued. It's much more exciting to be a pioneer. Be a bit whacko and you shake people up. And we all need shaking up."

Dyson, James

Talented people are also given responsibility at a young age. The marketing manager was appointed when just 23 years old, the head of engineering at 28, and the head of graphics at 27. The average age of Dyson employees is 25.

Product quality is jealously guarded. All final assembly is done by hand (except for a machine that applies the sealing tape to the packaged cardboard boxes ready for dispatch). The Dyson Overnight Courier Service (DOCS) means that customers' cleaners are collected from their homes free of charge, repaired and returned the next day. The idea is that customers are buying not just a single product but a complete service.

As one might expect, research and development are also key to the Dyson philosophy: a quarter of the entire workforce are design engineers, and the company is constantly striving to find better working and better looking designs. "Design is not just about how something looks, but how it works," James Dyson insists.

The company has also shown itself to be adept at design-led marketing – producing special edition models of its upmarket vacuum cleaners that command an additional price premium.

At the Dyson factory, everything from engineering, design, production and servicing is done under one roof – something the company believes encourages staff ideas and the cross-fertilization of activities. The company is currently working on a new product line – possibly a washing machine or dishwasher.

He has already shown that he can do it once, why not again? His example has given British designers a huge lift. "What we have done, that nobody thought we could do, is to take on the multinationals and beat them in a very short space of time, which I hope gives other people heart."

Des Dearlove

SEE: BRANDS
MORE INFO: www.dyson.co.uk
SOURCES: Interview; James Dyson, *Against the Odds*, Orion, 1997

Dyson, James

easyJet

easyJet is one of the most interesting and bravest of entrepreneurial adventures. The airline began life at the end of 1995 from the UK's Luton Airport. In Summer 1997 easyJet owner Stelios Haji-ioannou signed a deal with Boeing for 12 new aircraft costing $500 million.

The easyJet story is one of imagination and no little bravery. The lessons for the fledgling entrepreneur are many. Most notably, find a role model. Haji-ioannou flew with Southwest Airlines in the US and was converted. Southwest is renowned for its thrills free service and remarkable corporate culture. This was the basic model.

Rather than exporting the Southwest model wholesale, Haji-ioannou introduced various adaptations. For example, he cut out travel agents – easyJet is reliant on direct sales. He also had a very clear idea of who his potential customers would be. The market, he decided, was travelers who were cost conscious. These were split into three groups: travelers visiting relatives, leisure travelers making brief trips and managers and executives form small firms. Then easyJet worked at making the process of purchasing a ticket and traveling as simple as possible. Booking a seat was simple – no tickets, no assigned seats, minimum check-in times. The company concentrated on supplying the planes, cabin crew and pilots, and sales and marketing. Other activities were outsourced with suppliers being rigorously rated against a matrix.

Now, comes the hardest part. Competition is increasing with a flood of direct competitors. Keeping the entrepreneurial spirit alive is demanding. "All I need to do now is find six million people a year to fly on my new planes," Haji-ioannou has reflected.

SEE: MICHAEL DELL
MORE INFO: www.easyjet.co.uk
SOURCES: Don Sull, "easyJet's $500 million gamble," *European Management Journal*, Vol. 17, No. 1, 1999

ecommerce

By the year 2002, Price Waterhouse calculates that the value of goods and services traded on the Web will be some $434 billion. Datamonitor reported online retail shopping as being worth $108

Value of ecommerce	1998 ($ b)	1999 ($ b)	2000 ($ b)	2002 ($ b)
Manufacturing	8	17	41	116
Wholesale/ business retail	6	18	48	168
Utilities	2	3	5	10
Services	1	3	11	33

Source: Forrester Research

million in 1997; anticipating $465 billion in 2002. New predictions are published every day. The only conclusion is that the future is unknowable and the potential of ecommerce unbounded.

"Histories will look back on the 20th century as a century of niche competition and the 21st century as a century of head-to-head competition."

SEE: AMAZON.COM; E*TRADE

Eisner, Michael

The Disney CEO (born in 1942) remains one of the most interesting top execs. Things seem to happen. Under his control, Disney's market value has increased from $2 billion to $75 billion. But a $100 million payout to Mike Ovitz, the Jeffrey Katzenbach debacle and protests about the lesbian Ellen have provided a succession of troublespots – not to mention Eisner's salary. For a hugely successful man, Eisner attracts more than his fair share of trouble and detractors.

SEE: DISNEY
MORE INFO: www.disney.com; Michael Eisner, *Work in Progress*, 1999

Ellison, Larry

People have opinions about Larry Ellison. "Larry plays a zero sum game – you have to destroy your competition. It's quite Darwinian. The concept of firing a token shot is alien to Larry's mentality. If he's going to take a shot at you, he's going to go for the heart, or the head, or the dick. He's not going to try to wound you," said Ellison's biographer Mike Wilson. *Upside* magazine labeled him "the consummate press junkie" (though this could be a complement). One fact remains unquestioned: Lawrence Ellison is chairman and CEO of the second largest software company in the world, Oracle.

SEE: KNOWLEDGE UNIVERSE
MORE INFO: www.oracle.com

e-mail

At Sun Microsystems 1.5 million internal messages come and go every day. That's 120 per employee. Tom Peters believes that email leads to a branding question: "When everybody has email and anybody can send you email, how do you decide whose messages you're going to read and respond to first – and whose you're going to send to the trash unread? The answer: personal branding. The name of the email sender is every bit as important a brand – is a brand – as the name of the Web site you visit. It's a promise of the value you'll receive for the time you spend reading the message."

Signs are that the first rush of enthusiasm for email may be waning. One big company in the computing industry is considering banning emails in the afternoon. It found that its people had stopped talking to one another.

SEE: MOBILE INFORMATION

SOURCES: Tom Peters, "The brand called you," *Fast Company*, August–September 1997

employee value proposition

The race is on to become an employer of choice. And the race has to be led from the top. Recruitment and retention could become full board responsibilities, as prospecting for executive talent becomes a business imperative.

If managing talent is a top corporate priority, companies must create and refine an employee value proposition. Senior management must have a persuasive answer as to why a talented employee should work for their company rather than a competitor.

For example, Wal-Mart's manager of executive recruiting, John Hughes, maps out the company's value proposition with practiced ease: "We offer a great deal. We are an international company – that's a strong selling point especially because we're expanding internationally – with a great culture. Our leadership is down-to-earth, approachable and open-minded. More folks are now looking at that total picture rather than simply considering finance. They don't just look at the job but at what they can grow into. People aren't as loyal. We have an extremely strong culture and that is a great retention tool." Why should people work for you?

SEE: WAL-MART

SOURCES: Interviews

empty market-share

The accusation levelled against Eckhard Pfeiffer when he was ousted as CEO of Compaq Computer was that he mistook size for success. He established, said one commentator, "empty market share" – the company became bigger and bigger without organizing itself to reap the economies of scale its size required. Lesson: profits come before size.

SOURCES: "Eckhard's gone but the PC rocks on," *Fortune*

Ernst & Young

Consulting firm Ernst & Young's latest advertising campaign trumpets a service that takes clients "From thought to finish" and invests in full page ads which invite readers to "Connect the dots" – the dots are helpfully labeled "Problem," "85,000 minds" and "Solution." Ernst & Young's objective is, according to chairman and CEO Philip Laskawy, "seamless global integration."

Integration comes with a $100 million budget. Stephanie Shern, Ernst & Young's vice chair of marketing, is one of the architects of the firm's global brand vision and marketing strategy, responsible for the consultancy's brand image in 132 countries. The firm has just unleashed a multi-stranded branding strategy that includes a print and TV advertising blitz.

"There's a lot of noise in the marketplace right now" says Shern. "It's the same in any category where there's a lot of noise. It's no different to what the financial services companies are doing. Everyone is trying to break through the clutter. Some are succeeding. The big consulting firms are all doing it; now it's a case of who breaks through. The most successful will be those with the best messages – or more of it." E&Y begins with more of it, whether quantity equates with quality will soon be seen. For those in the consulting business the big question must be how to build a brand effectively. E&Y's Stephanie Shern acknowledges that it's too soon to tell whether the firm's mass market approach will work. "By late summer [1999] we will have had some months of this continuous messaging. By then we should know whether we have moved the needle at all."

Des Dearlove

SEE: BRANDING CONSULTING FIRMS
MORE INFO: www.ey.com
SOURCES: Interviews

E*Trade

The online brokerage service E*Trade is the best known of its type – a bewildering array of ecompetitors have now emerged. "When you reinvent a global industry by putting power and choice back into the hands of individuals, the world takes notice and great things happen," says chairman and CEO Christos Cotsalios. The great things are 1999 revenues of $621 million (up 85 percent); over 1.5 million accounts; and customer assets of $28 billion. The small drawback? A net loss in the 1999 fiscal year of $54.4 million. Can't have everything.

SEE: ECOMMERCE; AMAZON.COM
MORE INFO: www.etrade.com

executive churn

The turnover of senior executives is accelerating. The upper-middle reaches of US corporations are coming to resemble a game of musical chairs where the music gets faster and faster, and chairs are left emptier for longer.

95

Research carried out by the Center for Creative Leadership in Greensboro, NC, and the executive search firm Manchester Partners International, found that 40 percent of newly hired executives fail within the first 18 months. A daunting two out of every five newly recruited managers don't make it past the first year and a half – "being terminated for poor performance, performing significantly below expectations, or voluntarily resigning from the position."

zeitbite#17
Ricardo
Semler

"Democracy has yet to penetrate the work place. Dictators and despots are alive and well in offices and factories all over the world."

SEE: CEO AGENCY

executive shortages

One major public organization anticipates that it will lose 60 percent of its executives within the next thee years. Another talks of 40 to 50 percent walking through the door never to return. Once upon a time, an orderly line of ready-made replacements stood in the wings. Now, the corporate corridors are empty. Thanks to downsizing, tomorrow's leaders are already yesterday's men.

William C. Byham is president and CEO of Bridgeville, PA-based Development Dimensions International which specializes in HR issues. He is blunt: "There will be a shortage of executive talent. Demographics mean that there are a lot of people nearing retirement age. Downsizing has meant that companies no longer tend to have developmental roles, like assistant or deputy jobs, from which people were traditionally promoted. At the same time, the experience, qualifications and skills needed to become a senior executive have increased."

Trends suggest that this talent shortfall may be no mere blip on the radar; the problem could be with us for decades to come. Three trends, in particular, threaten to exacerbate the situation in the next few years.

First, and in many ways most serious, demand for executives appears to be moving in the opposite direction to supply. Remember the demographic time bomb? Back in the 1980s everyone was talking about it. But it didn't go away when the magazine articles halted. It just kept on ticking and may be about to detonate. Demographic predictions suggest the number of 35–44-year-olds s in the US will fall by 15 percent between 2000 and 2015 while numbers of 45–54-year-olds will rise.

The second factor in the escalating talent shortage is that the demands companies place on executives are increasing. Complex global markets require more sophisticated management skills, including international sensitivity, cultural fluency, technological literacy, entrepreneurial flair and, most critically, leadership. The proliferation of business school educated managers, especially MBAs, suggests that executives are better trained than ever before. The trouble is that business schools are good at turning out business analysts, but have a more questionable record in producing leaders.

The third factor is the rise of many high potential small and medium-sized companies. For the first time, large companies have to compete with – and provide career opportunities and earnings on a par with – their smaller brethren. A host of high-tech start-ups, especially internet-based businesses, are likely to draw off a growing proportion of the high-fliers who might otherwise have joined the blue chips. Who wants to work for a faceless corporation when you can earn more and have more fun working for an exciting upstart?

There appears little doubt that it will become much harder for established companies to attract the brightest and the best. "There will continue to be, for the foreseeable future, greater demand than supply of the best people – the most knowledgeable, skilled, innovative, experienced, entrepreneurial, creative, risk taking super talent," says Bruce Tulgan of Rainmaker Thinking Inc., an influential think tank studying changes in the workplace. "Every business leader and manager in every organization I talk with says that they are spending more time, energy and money on recruiting at all levels."

Leadership guru Warren Bennis, distinguished professor of leadership at the University of Southern California and co-author of *Co-Leaders*, has first hand experience of the problems now encountered. "I've recently been helping out a high powered research center to find a president. The salary is $500,000 plus a house, car and driver, all the perks and they can't find anyone who the researchers feel is adequate scientifically and who wants to manage," Bennis laments. "The more we move into knowledge-based, technically-based organizations – which we clearly are – the scarcer the top leadership talent."

The demographic alarm bells are ringing. The stats don't lie. And they begin with the post-war baby boom. The boomers are growing old. This led to a surplus of middle managers in the late 1980s and is now creating an aging workforce – and an aging executive population. By 2000 there will be more US workers in their late forties than in their late 20s. In 1990 there were 53 million 40–59-year-olds in the U.S. By 2000, there will be 73 million, and in 2010 about 83 million. Add in factors like a booming stock exchange boosting retirement nest eggs and there are an awful lot of people eyeing condos in Florida.

"The American labor force will shrink in the middle," says Paul Wallace, author of *Agequake* (Nicholas Brealey Publishing, 1999), a new book examining demographic trends. "The baby-boom echo and immigration mean that the US does not face youth deficits. Even so, the bulging portion of the labor force will consist of people over 50. If companies are increasingly looking to younger executives there will be a problem."

The numbers don't look good. Broad demographic statistics are backed by research and surveys. In 1998 research by the management consultants McKinsey & Co. covered nearly 6000 managers in 77 companies and concluded that the battle to recruit talented people was already intensifying. The McKinsey report, appropriately entitled "The war for talent" concluded: "Many American companies are already suffering a shortage of executive talent." It found that "Three-quarters of corporate officers surveyed said their companies had 'insufficient talent sometimes'" or were "chronically talent-short across the board."

SEE: EXECUTIVE CHURN
MORE INFO: Paul Wallace, *Agequake*, 1999
SOURCES: *Management Review*, August 1999

executive search

Research from the Economist Intelligence Unit (EIU) indicates that the global executive search market is now worth in the region of $7 to $8 billion. Nancy Garrison Jenn, market expert and author of *Executive Search in Europe*, predicts that if the market continues to grow at its current rate it will exceed $10 billion by 2000 – just about the time that executive shortages will really start to bite.

Heidrick & Struggles, the world's second largest headhunter, has a grandstand view of the international executive talent market. The company operates at the top end of the market, mostly at board level and just below. Recent successes include placing Ray Lane as president of Oracle. According to Richard Wall, managing partner responsible for European Investment Banking: "We are already seeing a shortage of future leaders. That is clear right now. There are not that many people who are able to operate across continents and right across organizations. We are finding more and more companies have to go global with their searches."

Fishing in foreign ponds where the demographic impacts are less dramatic is likely to increase. As shortages persist, there will be a knock-on effect in other countries. In the end, recruiting from outside the US is at best a short-term solution. Aggressive poaching leads to soaring salary levels, and there is little incentive to invest in staff development when that investment is likely to walk out the door.

SEE: CEO AGENCY; CORE COMPETENTS
MORE INFO: www.h-s.com

faculty free agents

Business schools now scour the world in search of academic superstars who will enhance the reputation and standing of any school they work for. The battle for quality faculty has never been more intense.

Fueling the competition is a dearth of talented teachers and researchers. Massive expansion in the numbers of programs and schools means that demand has never been higher. In some areas, including finance, accounting and marketing, shortages are particularly acute – academics in these areas are particularly tempted by higher salaries in the non-corporate world.

The business school stars – people like Michigan's C.K. Prahalad, Harvard's Michael Porter and Rosabeth Moss Kanter – are in the driving seat. They can, for example, specify how they want to spend their time. Often this means that they do not teach on MBA programs. Instead, they can be found teaching on flagship short programs where the profit margins are attractive, or on executive MBA programs where students are senior managers with real corporate power.

The UK's Research Assessment Exercise has simply added to the to-ing and fro-ing as schools seek to bolster their expertise in specific areas to achieve a better rating. Highly rated researchers and their teams can decamp from one school to another to boost research ratings. The increasing transfer market – more of a meat market according to some – raises a number of important issues for business schools. First, there is the problem of management. Hiring an American professor is clearly something of a snub to home grown marketing experts. Long-serving faculty are likely to feel overlooked – at the very least. To this is added financial complexity. British business school professors are, by comparison with their American counterparts, poorly rewarded. Importing a foreign star often means that business schools break the salary system. "If you are willing to pay you can get people," says Professor David Norburn, director of Imperial College Management School. "But where does that leave the other faculty? Alternatively, you could pay all faculty the same, in which case you would fail to attract people."

To attract superstars, business schools have a number of lures. They sometimes offer a package which involves little in the way of teaching. Clearly, this shifts the burden to other faculty. The second lure is the offer of a free rein when it comes to research. Again, this is flawed by its unfairness. More attractive is the offer of consulting opportunities. Traditionally, business school academics are allowed to work as consultants – usually for one day per week. This is highly lucrative. Superstars may be tempted by the offer of two, three, perhaps even four days of consulting per week. The downside to this is that they may never actually see a student. "Schools must ask what contribution a superstar actually makes," says Jonathan Slack, chief executive of the Association of Business Schools. The bottom line for schools must be whether having a guru-in-residence actually attracts new students or adds to the experience of existing students.

Imperial's David Norburn acknowledges that attracting high quality faculty without breaking the bank is fraught with difficulty, but not impossible. "We have succeeded in bringing in some big names because we have a very flat hierarchy, no pompousness and because we laugh a lot. It sounds romantic but we have a better culture. We compete on the basis that this is an enjoyable and fulfilling place to work." Norburn approaches the matter of recruiting faculty with the persistence of a Premier League talent scout. "You court people over a number of years," he says. "You may not be able to get the big stars of today, but who is their brightest PhD student? We have a database of UK academics working abroad who may, at some point, be interested in returning to the UK."

Jonathan Slack of the Association of Business Schools suggests that part of the problem is that UK academics are poor at promoting their research. "American business schools are much better at promoting their faculty in a PR sense," he says. "There are a lot of good people doing a great deal of interesting research at UK business schools, but often you haven't heard of them."

Perhaps the most encouraging thing for European business schools is that the trend increasingly seems to be for international business stars to spend some time in Europe. Recent times have seen a number of high profile business school names make the move to the UK. Cambridge's Judge Institute secured the services of leading strategist George Yip from UCLA's Anderson School. Influential MIT thinker Ed Schein has spent time at Henley Management College. Perhaps the best known move has been that of John Quelch from Harvard Business School to become dean of London Business School. LBS is one of the few business schools with deep enough pockets to be able to compete. Its faculty includes Sumantra Ghoshal, recruited from INSEAD, and young Americans such as Jeff Sampler and Don Sull forging careers from Europe rather than their American homes.

"Schools may need to collaborate if they are to satisfy demand for international faculty," says Professor Stephen Watson, dean of Lancaster University Management School. "Lancaster has a productive association with the strategy guru Henry Mintzberg who is based both at McGill University and at INSEAD. We have together created the innovative international masters program in practicing management, working with the Indian Institute of Management Bangalore and Japanese universities."

Of course, in the final analysis, the solution for schools may well lie in nurturing their own talent.

SEE: BUSINESS SCHOOLS
MORE INFO: Stuart Crainer & Des Dearlove, *Gravy Training*, Capstone, 1998
SOURCES: Interviews

Fast Company

The magazine for its times, the bible of free agency. *Fast Company* is a must read for the legions of free agents. Its niche is clear, though becoming more crowded – the thirty-something free agent with little interest in the academic prose of the *HBR* and not corporate enough for *Business Week*; someone who talks in projects rather than full-time jobs. After a high impact opening, there is the feeling that ennui is already creeping into the *Fast Company* formula. It can appear to be written for a small group of West coast freelancers. The stories tend to the positive and gushing. Nothing wrong with that, but world weary cynicism becomes appealing after a while.

SEE: FREE AGENTS, BRILL'S CONTENT
MORE INFO: www.fastcompany.com

feminizing the boardroom

Dream on. Despite all the talk about the softer side of management and the need to recruit more women to utilize their soft skills and sensitivity, women are notable by their absence from the world's boardrooms. Research from the Kelly School of Business, for example, shows that the number of women with executive positions in the U.S. is now lower than it was ten years ago. In 1987, there were 11 female directors at Fortune 500 companies, but by 1997 there were just eight. The number of women CEOs was two in 1987 and was still two a decade later. It is tempting to say that if corporate America continues to recruit from less than half of the total population then it deserves to be held to ransom.

So, take a bow Golden West Financial Corp, Avon Products, Beverly Enterprises, and publishing group, Gannett. From the Fortune 500, these are the four companies with (nearly) as many women as men on their boards.

The rest perform lamely. A total of 188 of the 500 have no women on their boards. In total 11.2 percent of board seats are held by women.

SEE: EXECUTIVE SHORTAGES
SOURCES: Catalyst Research 1998

Feuerstein, Aaron

Executives aren't renowned for occupying the moral high ground. They prefer the security of the bottom line. Aaron Feuerstein is one of the few business people of recent years to put his conscience where his money is – and vice versa.

Malden Mills was already a pretty unusual company prior to December 11, 1995. In an age of diminishing loyalty and relentless downsizing, it stood for traditional corporate values. Loyal employees worked alongside trusting management. Customer retention and employee retention both registered a staggering 95 percent. The company, based in Lawrence, Massachusetts had remained steadfastly – some said foolishly – loyal to its home base. Founded in 1906, it moved to Lawrence in 1956 rather than following its competitors and many more textile companies in their migration down south.

Feuerstein, Aaron

Malden Mills stayed stoically put. Its loyalty seemed misplaced when, in the early 1970s, it made a disastrous move into fake fur. By 1980 it was in Chapter 11. Malden Mills struck back with the development of Polartec, a lightweight fleece which proved more successful – and tasteful – than fake fur. By 1995 it had sales of $400 million.

Then a fire ripped through its factories leaving over a dozen people hospitalized and the company, it seemed, in ruins.

Malden Mills chief, Aaron Feuerstein, the grandson of the company's founder, immediately announced that with no production capacity and no immediate hope of producing anything, he would continue to pay the company's 2400 employees and pay their healthcare insurance. It was estimated that paying the company's employees for 90 days, and their healthcare for 180 days, cost Feuerstein $10 million.

In the end, Malden Mills was back to virtually full capacity within 90 days. A total of $15 million was invested in a new infrastructure. The committed and grateful workforce worked so well that productivity and quality shot up; before the fire 6 to 7 percent of the company's production was "off quality" – this reduced to 2 percent after the fire. Feuerstein said that the company's employees paid him back nearly ten fold.

SEE: REPUTATION MANAGEMENT
MORE INFO: www.polartec.com
SOURCES: *Hemispheres*, October 1999

Firth, David

There's always one joker. David Firth revels in the role. He spent eight years running the theater company, Lords of Misrule. Now, his company is called Treefrog and his book, *The Corporate Fool*. His current project is the Fool School. "Fools have existed in all world cultures throughout history; now it is time to bring them into modern business," he says. "Fools speak out against those who have power, question accepted wisdom, embody controversy and taboo, cast doubt in the face of certainty, bring chaos to order, point out the obvious, throw a spanner in the proverbial works, turn the world upside down." Great job description.

But, there is a serious side to Firth's various activities. He works with companies on a variety of aspects of organizational life – including communication, building trust, creativity and "learning communities." His clients include some equally serious big names, including British Airways and Unilever. Firth's *The Fool Show* mixes a traditional business conference with multimedia and theater. To prove that business really is the new rock and roll, Firth is touring throughout the world; the end piece – or should it be cod piece – comes at the Melbourne Comedy Festival in Australia.

zeitbite#19
Richard
Pascale

"If it ain't broke, break it."

SEE: JOB TITLES
MORE INFO: David Firth, *The Corporate Fool*, Capstone, 1998

Fitzgerald, Niall

According to one newspaper the CEO of Unilever is the "nearest thing the detergent industry has to a visionary." Niall Fitzgerald (born 1945) is an Irishman who has maintained a low profile in one of the top European corporate jobs. Interviews are few and far between. He appears only willing to break shelter to speak out on behalf of the single European currency.

SEE: BRANDS
MORE INFO: www.unilever.com

free agents

We have been told for years that the nature of work is changing. Yet, despite all the hype about homeworking and greater independence, there appears more hype than reality. It has been calculated that there are 14 million self-employed Americans. There are 8.3 million "independent contractors," and a further 2.3 million who work for temporary agencies. This adds up to around 25 million free agents – who have been described in their bible, *Fast Company*, as "people who move from project to project and who work on their own, sometimes for months, sometimes for days."

Research and experience suggests that people who have escaped the corporate world, (and that is how they tend to regard it,) actually find greater security in self-employment. The dramatic downsizing and restructuring of recent years means that being on your own no longer holds the fear it once did. A marketing consultant told how a bank was dubious about giving a loan to someone without a real job. "If one of my clients goes away, I'm still going to make my payments," she explained. "But if I'm employed by Apple and they let me go, I'm out on the street." The worm has turned.

"Listening to other companies' customers is the best way to gain market share, while listening to the visionaries is the best way to create new markets."

Central to the entire trend is a Dilbert-like cynicism about corporate life. "Much of what happens inside companies turns out to be about nothing," notes one free agent. Most of the others concur. The worry is the degree of flakiness attached to the concept. People talk too easily of finding themselves. "Companies do not exist. Countries do not exist. But the team exists. This is the summer of love revisited, man!" says one. Yet, ignore the Zen clichés, and the experiences and views of the free agents represent a considerable challenge to traditional business world. The corporation has become the great institution of the twentieth century, but there is no reason to assume that this will continue in the new millennium. "The economics of free agency relate to a basic psychological shift, a tremendous San Andreas Fault between employee and employer," says futurist Stan Davis. The question must be whether the corporate world has the will or the imagination to bridge the gap.

SEE: *FAST COMPANY*
SOURCES: Daniel H. Pink, *Fast Company*, Issue 12

Fritz, Robert

In management guru terms, Robert Fritz has a lot going for him. There are his handful of successful books. These include *The Path of Least Resistance;* the pithily titled, *Creating,* which unveils the world of creativity and promises access for all; and his most recent, *Corporate Tides: The Inescapable Laws of Organizational Structure.*

In the late seventies, Fritz joined Peter Senge (the MIT academic and author of *The Fifth Discipline*) and Charlie Kiefer as founders of the consulting company Innovative Associates. Senge and Fritz remain close.

Fritz's background lies in music. No dilettante, he trained at the Boston Conservatory of Music and was on the faculty of the New England Conservatory of Music and Berklee College. He still composes music for films, television and opera. He has also played with jazz great Dave Brubeck and recorded for various record labels. On top of that, Fritz has his own consulting company – the Fritz Group. The company, among other things, markets STPro, charting software designed by Fritz for strategic planning and project management.

Fritz's big idea is the decidedly unsexy one of structure or, in Fritzese, the *structural approach*. Luckily this is not structure in any conventional sense of unmoving, dust gathering hierarchies and the like. This is *structural dynamics*. The roots of the world, according to Fritz, can be traced back to the 1970s when he began to train people in creativity and personal effectiveness. He discovered what he called the *macrostructural pattern* which describes the long-range pattern in people's lives. We are all unique, but Fritz determined there were two general types of pattern in people's lives: oscillating and resolving or advancing. According to Fritz, advancement means moving from where we are to where we want to be; oscillation means moving from where we are toward where we want to be, but then moving back to the original position.

Fritz argues that structure is key to organizational success and to individuals being personally successful within organizations. A small change in structure can yield major benefits. Inevitably, in reality, companies are addicted to making huge structural changes which yield few benefits.

Fritz develops similarities between the creative process in music and the art of management. Music, he says, teaches us a number of important lessons. First, it builds from contrasts. The jazz soloist can be completely at home in a big band. The second element is truth. The artist – whether a painter or a musician – has to live with the truth of their own performance. A bum note is a bum note and can't be covered up. The artist shrugs and hopes to learn enough and to work hard enough to get it right. In contrast, the harried executive is as likely to cover up the truth as reveal it. Truth, in the corporate world, can be construed as weakness.

Fritz's third line of comparison is that of tension. He says that structural tension is "the basis for great leadership." The fourth point is the need for discipline. Fritz observes that the great artists are

Fritz, Robert

"We are
watching the
dinosaurs die,
but we don't
know what
will take their
place."

dedicated to their own development. They are addicted to the discipline of experimentation.

Finally, there must be an overall sense of long-term objectives. Being preoccupied with the short-term is the route to endlessly tedious solos rather than overall excellence.

SEE: **NEW PIG CORPORATION**
MORE INFO: www.realresults.net

Fritz, Robert

Game Theory

The poker tables of Ivy League Princeton and Harvard in the 1930s are an unlikely source for a business theory. Useful business ideas usually emerge from exhaustive studies or initiatives in obscure factories. But, while the well-heeled and well-educated were frittering away their trust funds, they were being watched by John Von Neumann, a mathematical genius rather than a gambler.

The result of Von Neumann's observations was Game Theory, a unique mathematical insight into the possibilities and probabilities of human behavior. Game Theory is based on the premise that no matter what the game, no matter what the circumstances, there is a strategy which will enable you to succeed. If you are playing poker, negotiating salaries or bidding in an auction, rules are at work, however elusive and intangible they might be. Game Theory is the ultimate in rationality, mathematically-proven and beloved of economists.

While Von Neumann went on to apply his genius to the development of the US's nuclear arsenal and the first computer, Game Theory developed its own Zen-like language of dilemmas and riddles. (And if there is anything managers like less than the equations of economists it is abstract theorizing.) The most famous of these is the Prisoner's Dilemma.

Invented by Princeton's Albert Tucker in 1950, the Prisoner's Dilemma is an imaginary scenario. Two prisoners are accused of the same crime. During interrogation in different cells they are each told that if one confesses and the other does not, the confessor will be released while the other will serve a long prison sentence. If neither confesses, both will be despatched to prison for a short sentence and if both confess they will both receive an intermediate sentence.

Working through the possibilities, the prisoners conclude that the best decision is to confess. As both reach the same decision, they receive an intermediate sentence.

And herein lies the problem. Game Theory is rational; reality is not.

Companies which have expressed an interest in Game Theory tend to be from tightly regulated industries – such as power generation; ones where there is limited competition or cartels. With a limited number of players, playing by accepted rules and behaving in a rational way, Game Theory can make sense of what the best competitive moves may be.

zeitbite#22
Edwin Artzt

"Brand loyalty is very much like an onion. It has layers and a core. The core is the user who will stick with you until the very end."

Broader interest was re-ignited in 1994 when the Nobel Prize for economics was awarded to three renowned game theorists – John Nash, John Harsanyi and Reinhard Selten. Each has taken Game Theory forward, making theoretical sense of the situations people find themselves in. Harsanyi has shown that even if players in a particular game are not well informed about each other, the game can still be analyzed in the same way as other games. The precociously brilliant Nash has carved the most notable academic furrow and is the creator of Nash's Equilibrium, an idea developed in his PhD thesis – delivered at the youthful age of 22. The Nash Equilibrium is the point when no player can improve his or her position by changing strategy. Players in a game will change their strategies until they reach equilibrium. (In the Prisoner's Dilemma the Nash Equilibrium is reached when both prisoners confess – they can no longer improve their situation by changing their strategy as this would send them to prison for a longer period.)

The key lesson from this and other scenarios explored by Game Theory is, simply, that the interactions of companies and other organizations are interdependent. What you do interacts, or impacts, on the possible choices of others in your situation or industry. Success depends not only on what you do, brilliantly calculated though it may be, but on how others respond and act.

SEE: COOPETITION
MORE INFO: www.mayet.som.yale.edu/coopetition

The Gap
The Gap was one of the great retailing success stories of the 1980s. The brand appeals to consumers who want to be trendy without being fashion victims. To some extent, the Gap secret is the clever presentation of unexceptional but high quality casual clothes in an aesthetic package that is pleasing to the customer at a number of

levels. These include easy outfit coordination, a wide choice of color, and non-threatening store design.

A key part of the brand appeal is a sense of timeliness. The message is: the Gap helps you create a casual, comfortable look that moves with the times. The Christmas 1996 Gap slogan – "Every color – only Gap" – was the antithesis of Henry Ford's "Any color you like as long as its black."

Founded in 1969, more than just about any other brand, Gap is all about being contemporary, without trying too hard. For a number of years it was content to sell Levi's jeans and identify itself with the lower case gap logo. In the 1970s and early 1980s, the enclosed mall shopping concept was really taking off and creating a recognizable retail outlet was a sensible strategy. But as the look of clothes retailing changed in the early 1980s, Gap began to look dated. Other retail stores had copied the Gap formula, using similar store design and selling look-alike products. Multicolored T-shirts and sweat shirts were piled high in many clothes stores which replicated the Gap feel and atmosphere. The original had to do something to preserve its position.

The company's CEO Millard "Mickey" Drexler realized it was time for The Gap to stop thinking of itself as a retailer and start thinking like a brand. The result is the creation of one of the star brands of recent years.

The company's turnaround under Drexler was impressive. In 1983, the company changed its logo to long, clean-limbed upper-case letters to become The GAP. So different was the new corporate identity that commentators have observed that the old logo seems to belong to a different company altogether.

By 1991, it had reinvented itself, dropping the Levi line altogether. But the Gap stores are only one part of the story. In the US, The Gap Inc. also revitalized Banana Republic – acquired in 1983, tired by the 1990s, since rejuvenated. Gap Inc. also introduced Old Navy Clothing stores in 1994, with a warehouse feel to the outlets.

In effect, the company fashioned three distinctive identities targeted at different market segments. At the top end, there is Banana Republic; at the lower end is Old Navy; and occupying the upper-middle ground is the Gap brand. Key to the brand offering in all three cases is freshness. The company is constantly introducing new colors and rotating its offerings to ensure that whatever the season or the latest fashion, you can walk into its stores and find something that is entirely contemporary. The styles change far less frequently, and the average shopper knows that Gap purchases are solid purchases with a good wardrobe shelf life.

The company has successfully integrated marketing and advertising supported branding into its merchandising operation. The clean, uncluttered look that is the hallmark of the Gap brand image works just as well across age groups. With more than 1000 stores in the US, Canada, France, Germany, Japan and the UK, plus over 550 GapKids and BabyGaps, creatively, all the Gap branding has the same feel, and the same simple clothes designs.

Drexler's insight proved prescient. Since, 1994, when some commentators were writing the company off as a "mature business," sales have rocketed. "They made their name into a brand," notes one leading retailing analyst. "They are one of the few retailers who have that luxury."

Once bitten by the branding bug, Drexler is said to have immersed himself in information about the world's leading brands, especially Coca-Cola. It is no coincidence that Sergio Zyman, a senior marketing executive from Coca-Cola, was invited to join the Gap board of directors. "The Gap accelerated to the point where the brand was on fire," the partisan Zyman has observed. "There is no competitor who has a kind of brand essence that can pose a threat."

The company is taking no chances. It is pouring advertising money into its brand strategy like gasoline to keep the flames high. In 1996, the company spent around $100 million; in 1997, it spent $150 million.

In 1995, recognizing the strength of its brand appeal, the Gap added a line of personal care products packaged with an upbeat stainless steel look that complemented the brand aesthetics and the no-nonsense feel of its stores. The new product line smacked of quality, but affordable quality. It was designer design, without designer prices.

The management style of the company is also important. The corporate culture encourages a degree of risk taking, and mistakes are considered a learning opportunity. The company prides itself on its ability to make fast decisions without lots of management layers. "We decide, 'is it the right thing for the business?'" one executive at the company observed. "When the Gap decides to do something, we do it. That's a rare thing in a company."

The company also has a flair for PR. In September 1997, it organized the "Gap at Work" event. Executives from the company rang the opening bell of the New York Stock Exchange. The exchange has a shirt and tie dress code, but it allowed floor workers to wear the khaki chinos and blue shirts the Gap handed out.

In recent years, too, the company has shown a willingness to move with the times, embracing Internet shopping.

While there is a retro feel to the advertising that harks back to traditional American values, Gap appears to have learned from its crisis in the early 1980s of the dangers of becoming outdated. What customers get at a Gap outlet, as well as some pretty good clothes in a wide variety of colors, is the brand's unspoken promise not to be left behind – a second time. It is a triumph of conservatism over the fashion industry. The Gap brand promise is one of safe, comfortable clothes that will never embarrass the wearer. More than this, the company has successfully exported classic American style to parts of the world that had previously managed to resist it. It is not unusual, for example, to find teenagers in Rome, Paris or London dressed in Gap baseball caps and US style sweats.

Above all, it is easy shopping. Stores offer easy access and garments are color coordinated for customers. The company's first major TV advertising campaign in 12 years, was kicked off by rap artist LL Cool J. The rap? "How easy is this?"

Des Dearlove

SEE: BRANDS
MORE INFO: www.gap.com
SOURCES: Alice Cuneo, "Marketer of the Year: The Gap," *Fortune*,
            December 1997

The Gap

Company:
The Gap, Inc.

Address:
One Harrison St. San Francisco, CA 94105 USA
Phone: 650-952-4400
Fax: 650-427-2795
http://www.gap.com

Business:
Specialist retailer – clothing.

Statistics, Fiscal Year End January

Employees	1998	81,000
Annual sales(millions)	1998	$6507.8
Annual results (millions)	1998	$533.9
Other facts		c. 2300 casual clothing stores in Canada, France, Germany, Japan, the UK and the US
Hoover's 500		#285
Fortune 500		#249

Gates, Bill

William Henry Gates III is a computer executive based in an office on the second floor of building number eight of his company's headquarters in Redmond, CA. He hasn't strayed far. Gates was born in Seattle, Washington, on October 28, 1955. His parents nicknamed him Trey from the III in his name and members of the family never called him anything else.

Gates was precociously brilliant. He read the family's encyclopedia from beginning to end at the age of eight or nine. (His company would later create the first CD-ROM encyclopaedia in the world, Encarta). But his real gift was for mathematics, at which he excelled.

At Lakeside, the elitist Seattle private school which attracts some of the brightest students on America's West Coast, his love of mathematics became an obsession with computers. Even at gray matter filled Lakeside, Bill Gates stood out as a bright kid.

By his junior year, Gates was something of a computer guru to the younger Lakeside hackers. Gates and some of his computer friends formed the Lakeside Programmers Group, which was dedicated to finding money-making opportunities to use their new found computer programming skills. Already a pattern was emerging. As Gates observed later: "I was the mover. I was the guy who said 'Let's call the real world and try to sell something to it.'" He was 13 years old.

It was at Lakeside that Gates met Paul Allen. Though Allen was two years Gates' senior, they developed a remarkable technical rapport. Allen's role in the Microsoft story, and that of a small coterie of Lakesiders recruited by the company is often understated. Gates, Allen, Kent Evans and Richard Weiland – two other members of the Lakeside Programmers Group – would often spend the whole night hooked up, first to a minicomputer owned by General Electric, and later to one at the Computer Center Corporation, sometimes not getting home until the early hours.

Gates' high IQ and massive personal drive ensured him a place at Harvard University. He arrived at America's most respected seat of learning in Cambridge, Massachusetts in the fall of 1973, all brain with no real sense of direction. Later, he would say that he went to Harvard to learn from people smarter than he was ... and was disappointed. The comment probably says as much about Bill Gates opinion of himself as it does about Harvard.

Listing his academic major as pre-law, Gates might have been expected to follow in the footsteps of his lawyer father. In reality, however, he had little interest in a career in law, and his parents had little doubt that their headstrong son would steer his own course.

As it turned out, a degree from Harvard was not on the cards. In 1975, while still at the university he teamed up with Paul Allen once more to develop a version of BASIC, an early computer language. Fired up with the new world at his finger tips, in 1977 Gates decided to drop out of Harvard to work full-time at a small computer software company he had founded with his friend. The company was called Microsoft.

Since the early days of Microsoft, Gates has pursued his vision of "a computer on every desk and in every home." (Interestingly, the original slogan was "a computer on every desk in every home, running Microsoft software," but the last part is often left off these days as it makes some people uncomfortable).

The rise of Microsoft has been both rapid and relentless. Gates soon proved that he combined a bone-deep technical understanding with superb commercial instincts. When ill health forced Allen to leave Microsoft, Gates position as leader was confirmed. In the second half of the 1980s, Microsoft became the darling of Wall Street. From a share price of $2 in 1986, Microsoft stock soared to $105 by first half of 1996, making Gates a billionaire and many of his colleagues millionaires.

The secrets which lie behind Microsoft's uninterrupted spiral of success have been dissected from every possible angle. What can be said is that the company hires very bright, creative people and retains them through a combination of excitement, constant challenge, and excellent working conditions. The odd stock option helps,

Gates, Bill

It's what you do with it, Bill

Gates is the richest man in the world today. In September 1998, his fortune was estimated at $60 billion based on his 22 percent stake in Microsoft. But he ranks only fifth in the list of the wealthiest tycoons of all time.

Forbes magazine has recalculated the fortunes of past and present businessmen by comparing the Gross National Product (GNP) in their lifetimes with the size of their bank balances. On this measure, Texas oil baron John D. Rockefeller amassed a fortune of $190 billion, more than three times that of Gates' pile. In the number two slot is Andrew Carnegie, the steel baron, who would be worth $100 billion today. Cornelius Vanderbilt, the railroad and shipping magnate comes third on $95 billion; followed by John Jacob Astor, the real estate and property tycoon, on $79 billion.

Gates, however, is still in his early forties and is likely to move up the league table. If Microsoft continues to grow faster than the American GNP, he will pass Andrew Carnegie.

Des Dearlove

MICROSOFT'S GROWTH

Year	Revenue $	Employees
1975	16,005	3
1976	22,496	7
1977	381,715	9
1978	1.3 million	13
1979	2.3 million	28
1980	7.5 million	40
1981	16 million	128
1982	24 million	220
1983	50 million	476
1984	94 million	608
1985	140 million	910
1986	197.5 million	1,153
1987	345 million	1,816
1988	590 million	2,793
1989	804 million	4,037
1990	1.183 billion	5,350
1991	1.84 billion	8,226
1992	2.75 billion	11,542
1993	3.75 billion	14,430
1994	4.6 billion	15,257
1995	5.9 billion	17,801
1996	8.6 billion	20,561
1997	11.3 billion	22,276
1998	14.8 billion	27,320

too. At less than eight percent, labor turnover is extremely low for the IT industry.

Microsoft's own encyclopedia Encarta says that "Much of Gates' success rests on his ability to translate technical visions into market strategy, and to blend creativity with technical acumen." What sets Bill Gates apart from any other business leader in history is probably the influence that he wields over our lives. Whereas the power of earlier tycoons was usually concentrated in one sector or industry, through the power of software, Microsoft extends its tentacles into every sphere of our lives.

Des Dearlove

SEE: **PAUL ALLEN**
MORE INFO: **www.microsoft.com**
SOURCES: *Context* magazine, December 1997; *BusinessWeek*, August 25, 1997; James Wallace, & Jim Erickson, *Hard Drive: Bill Gates and the making of the Microsoft Empire*, 1992; *Forbes*, September 1998; *The Observer*, October 18, 1998

Gateway 2000

Not much generally happens in Iowa, but the year 1985 proved an exception: Gateway 2000 was started in a farmhouse in the state by Ted Waitt, now chairman and CEO, and business partner Mike Hammond, now senior vice president, manufacturing. They formed the company with one goal in mind – to offer PC buyers an alternative to the high mark-ups, limited choices and inadequate support common in the retail PC market.

Waitt and Hammond sold hardware add-ons and software to owners of Texas Instruments PCs. By placing ads in computer-related publications and selling their products directly, they generated sales of $100,000 in their first four months of business. Realizing they were onto a good thing, Waitt recognized another relatively untapped market of clients – people who would buy completely configured PCs, sight unseen, if offered a good price. Gateway designed and assembled its own fully configured PC systems for direct sale – and the company flourished. So much so that by 1997, Gateway reported revenues of $6.3 billion and employed more than 13,000 people worldwide, with headquarters in North Sioux City, South Dakota, and manufacturing facilities in the United States, Ireland and Malaysia. Gateway became a publicly traded company in 1993, and entered into the S&P 500 in April 1998.

Trevor Merriden

SEE: MICHAEL DELL
MORE INFO: www.gateway.com

Gee, David
"Part of our job is to shake up the status quo. We want to get in trouble. We bend the rules," says David Gee. And he works for IBM! Whether Thomas Watson Sr. would have given him the same job description is unlikely. Gee is Worldwide Program Director for alphaWorks and Java Marketing at IBM's Software Solutions Division.

SEE: INTERNATIONAL BUSINESS MACHINES
MORE INFO: www.alphaworks.ibm.com

General Electric
Of the great smokestack brands, General Electric (GE) is one of the few survivors. It has survived – and prospered as never before – because it learned how to leverage its brand. The GE of the new millennium is a creator and maximizer of brands. Its brands feed on, and feed from, each other.

The modern GE began life in December 1980, when Jack Welch was announced as the new CEO and chairman of GE. It was a record breaking appointment. At 45, Welch was the youngest chief the company had ever appointed. Indeed, he was only the eighth CEO the company had appointed in 92 years.

He took over a company which was a model for American corporate might and for modern management techniques. GE had moved with the times – though usually more slowly. When Welch became top man, GE's net income was $1.7 billion. By most measures, the company was growing at a healthy rate – by nine percent in the

zeitbite#23
Warren
Buffett

"Your premium brand better be delivering something special or it's not going to get the business."

123

General Electric

previous year. Everything seemed rosy. More plain sailing was anticipated as the new chief got used to the job.

But, plain sailing was not on Jack Welch's route map. During the 1980s, Welch put his dynamic mark on GE and on corporate America. GE's businesses were overhauled. GE's workforce bore the brunt of Welch's quest for competitiveness. GE virtually invented downsizing. Nearly 200,000 GE employees left the company. Over $6 billion was saved.

Stage one of life under Jack Welch was a brutal introduction to the new realities of business. Perhaps Welch was too brutal. But, there is no denying that by the end of the 1980s GE was a leaner and fitter organization. Any complacency which may have existed had been eradicated. Having proved that he could tear the company apart, Welch had to move onto stage two: rebuilding a company fit for the twenty first century. The hardware had been taken care of. Now came the software.

Central to this was the concept of Work-out which was launched in 1989. Welch has called Work-out, "a relentless, endless company-wide search for a better way to do everything we do." Work-out was a communication tool which offered GE employees a dramatic opportunity to change their working lives.

Welch the destroyer became Welch the empowerer. Work-out was part of a systematic opening up of GE. Walls between departments and functions came tumbling down. Middle management layers had been stripped away in the 1980s. With Work-out, Welch was enabling and encouraging GE people to talk to each other, work together and share information and experience. At first surprised, they soon reveled in the opportunity.

The next stage in Welch's revolution was the introduction of a wide ranging quality program. Entitled Six Sigma, it was launched at the end of 1995. Six Sigma basically spread the responsibility for quality. Instead of being a production issue it was recast as an issue for every single person in the company.

Back in 1981, as Jack Welch began life as CEO, GE had total assets of $20 billion and revenues of $27.24 billion. Its earnings were $1.65 billion. With 440,00 employees worldwide, GE had a market value of $12 billion.

By 1997 GE's total assets had mushroomed to $272.4 billion and total revenues to $79.18 billion. Around 260,000 employees – down a staggering 180,000 – produced earnings of $7.3 billion and gave the company a market value of $200 billion.

GE now operates in over 100 countries, with 250 manufacturing plants in 26 countries. Its workforce totals 276,000, with 165,000 in the US. The company's 1997 revenues were $90.84 billion, with net earnings of $8.203 billion. The company's market value (according to the 1997 annual report) was the highest in the world: $300 billion. As a total entity, GE was ranked fifth in the most recent *Fortune 500*. Nine of GE's businesses would be in *Fortune*'s top 50 if ranked independently. GE remains a corporate giant. And now, it appears to be big in all the right places.

Jack Welch has said that "Our job is to sell more than just the box." He has moved the company from industrialized service to customer intimacy. When he took over, GE's attitude to customer service was typical of a traditional manufacturer. "At one time, GE executives spent more time on company politics than they did on actual business. People said that GE operated with its face to the CEO and its ass to the customer," Welch quipped.

Welch has turned things round. He has done so in a number of ways. First, GE has moved from being a manufacturer to a manufacturing and service business. In 1998 more than two-thirds of GE's revenues came from financial, information and product services. Central to this has been the development of its financial services operation.

As a new service, GE Capital has made the most of GE's strengths in other channels. By using the company's triple-A credit rating it has gained financial power its competitors can only dream of. Its base remains GE customers; retailers and end consumers. From providing financing for GE equipment customers, GE Capital has become the largest issuer of private label credit cards for retailers and

- Aircraft engines: In 1996–97, GE won 70 percent of the world's large commercial jet engine orders. It is the world's largest producer of large and small jet engines for aircraft.
- Appliances: GE Appliances sells over 10 million appliances in 150 world markets, including refrigerators, freezers, ranges, cooktops, wall ovens, dish washers and washing machines. Its brands include the Monogram, GE profile, Hotpoint, RCA and private label brands.
- Capital services: GE Capital is the star in GE's firmament. From being a side line it has become a high performing diversified financial company.
- Industrial systems: Circuit breakers, switches, transformers, switchgear, meters etc.
- Information services: Business-to-business electronic commerce solutions. GE manages the world's largest electronic trading community with more than 40,000 trading partners.
- Lighting: From halogen lamps to outdoor lighting, GE supplies lighting for consumer, commercial and industrial markets.
- Medical systems: Medical diagnostic imaging technology – including x-ray equipment.
- Broadcasting: GE owns the US television network NBC which has, among other assets, the US rights to the Olympics until 2008. Various other operations including CNBC and MSNBC.
- Plastics: Engineered plastics for a variety of industries including building and computing.
- Power systems: The design, manufacture and service of gas, steam and hydroelectric turbines and generators. And, controversially, nuclear fuels and services.
- Transportation systems: Locomotives and similar products. GE makes more than half of the diesel freight locomotives in North America.

Company:

General Electric Company

Subsidiaries Include: National Broadcasting Company, Inc; GE Capital services/GE Aircraft Engines

Address:

3135 Easton Tpke. Fairfield, CT 06431-0001 USA

Phone: 203-373-2211

Fax: 203-373-3497

http://www.ge.com

Business:

Electronics, Electrical Equipment

Statistics, Fiscal Year End December

Employees	1997	276,000
Annual sales(millions)	1998	$100,469.0
Annual results Net Inc. (millions)	1998	$9296.0
Other facts		GE is the only company listed in the Dow Jones Industrial Index today that was also included in the original 1896 index; GE topped Fortune's survey of America's most admired companies both in 1998 and 1999.
Hoover's 500		# 5
Fortune 500		# 5

others. "We're trying to develop a culture that says the world is the marketplace – don't make distinctions by country. The distinction remains the type of customer, not the country," said former GE Capital chairman, Gary Wendt. "The private label credit card business is really a marketing arm for retailers – we spend as much time dissecting customers' buying habits as their creditworthiness."

In the not too distant future, it is possible that GE Capital, which finances everything from washing machines to jet engines, will make more money than all the rest of the company's businesses combined. "GE Capital could get to be 50 percent-plus of the company," Welch has said.

In 1996, GE Capital made after-tax profits of $2.8 billion on revenues of $33 billion. Of US financial services businesses, only Citicorp, the American International Group and Bank America earned more.

The second element to this is that GE has worked hard at sustaining a variety of customer channels. It has developed better means of servicing, and meeting the needs of smaller retail outlets to make their businesses sustainable, in the face of intensifying competition from big retailers such as Circuit City.

In order to make smaller retailers more viable, GE developed a distribution system involving five different mixing warehouses and 76 locations, where products can be delivered to the retailer or end user. Its logistics network means that there is a one to two day delivery service. This allows retailers to reduce inventory so they only need display models. For the retailers this is a major leap forward as inventory usually ties up most of their assets. In addition, retailers are given the opportunity to take advantage of business loans, store remodeling kits as well as software, to help them manage their stores more efficiently.

GE has effectively positioned itself as the retailer's partner rather than simply a supplier and has made the small retail sales channel viable and sustainable. By providing quicker service it has made the channel more economically attractive and split the gains with the retailers.

General Electric

Finally, GE has explored changing customer expectations in great depth. GE's customer service help desk, the GE Answer Center, has been used to help gather valuable market research on evolving product and service preferences.

The result of all this is that internal and external perceptions of GE have changed. Once upon a time, GE sold boxes. You went to your friendly retailer and bought a washing machine. That was that. Now, the washing machine is only a lure to get you into the GE empire of service. One brand leads to another and all come with the GE guarantee of quality. You buy the washing machine with credit from GE's very own credit company in a store kitted out at GE's expense. Your numbers and details are fed in. You walk out with the hardware while GE's software cranks into action. The box is increasingly incidental. Long live the smokestack as service.

Georgina Peters

SEE: GRASSROOTS LEADERSHIP; ORGANIZATIONAL AGILITY
MORE INFO: www.ge.com
SOURCES: General Electric Annual General Meeting, 1990; Tim Smart, "Jack
              Welch's encore," *Business Week*, October 28, 1996; Noel Tichy &
              Stratford Sherman, *Control Your Destiny or Someone Else Will*,
              Currency Doubleday, New York, 1993; Richard Waters, "Too big
              for its booties," *Financial Times*, October 9, 1997

Generation X

"Gen X is proving to be the flexible, independent, technoliterate, information savvy, entrepreneurial workforce that management experts and business leaders say is necessary if organizations are going to continue increasing productivity," says Bruce Tulgan of Rainmaker Thinking. It is easy to dismiss the entire notion of Generation X as journalistic invention, one of those neat phrases which are of little practical use or relevance. We all know who they are. Reared on a diet of MTV and Nirvana albums, Generation Xers are skeptical thirty somethings. The big question must be how can they be managed and how do they manage?

Jay Conger, of the Leadership Institute of the University of Southern California, is among those who have examined the reality behind the mystique. Conger contends that Generation Xers (born between 1965 and 1981) exhibit four important characteristics. First, they seek to achieve a balance between their working and private lives. They are far removed from the corporate beings of previous generations whose personal lives were subsumed by the body corporate. Their second characteristic is that they are fiercely independent. This is partly attributed by Conger to the impact of the right wing politics of the eighties which emphasized personal responsibility rather than collective responsibility.

The third characteristic of Generation Xers is their appetite for technology. They are the witnesses to – and often the instigators of – the IT revolution. Finally, Xers prefer to see companies in terms of communities. Conger points out that the organizational model of companies such as Microsoft, Nike and Sun Microsystems, is the college campus as much as the traditional organization. The message is simple: ignore Generation X at your peril.

SEE: FREE AGENTS
MORE INFO: Bruce Tulgan, *Managing Generation X*, Capstone, 1995

Ghoshal, Sumantra

With his film-star cheekbones, piercing eyes, hawkish intensity and intellectual brilliance, Sumantra Ghoshal (born 1948) is an intimidating figure. Working along with Harvard Business School's Christopher Bartlett, he has become one of the most sought after intellectuals in the business world.

Ghoshal first came to prominence with the book *Managing Across Borders* (1989), which was one of the boldest and most accurate pronouncements of the arrival of a new era of global competition and truly global organizations. The 1997 book, *The Individualized Corporation*, marked a further step forward in the thinking of Ghoshal and Bartlett. Ghoshal joined London Business School in 1994 and was formerly Professor of Business Policy at INSEAD and a visiting professor at MIT's Sloan School.

Ghoshal has mapped and recorded the death of a variety of corporate truisms. He insists that his questions have remained the same, but the answers have changed: "I am a plain-vanilla strategy guy. What does strategy mean is where I started."

Today's reality, as described by Ghoshal, is harsh: "You cannot manage third generation strategies through second generation organizations with first generation managers." Even the perspectives from "successful" companies appear bleak. "Talk of transformation and you get the same examples," he says. "Toshiba in Asia Pacific, ABB, GE. If you listen to managers of those companies you will detect great skepticism about achieving victory. The battle ahead is far more complex."

Despite such a damning critique of corporate reality, Ghoshal is not totally discouraged. "Look at today and compare it to years ago. The quality of the strategic debate and discussion has improved by an order of magnitude," he says.

The shift in emphasis in Ghoshal's work is from the cool detachment of strategy to the heated complexities of people. While *Managing Across Borders* was concerned with bridging the gap between strategies and organizations, Ghoshal and Bartlett's sequel, *The Individualized Corporation*, moved from the elegance of strategy to the messiness of humanity.

One of the phenomena Ghoshal has examined is the illusion of success which surrounds some organizations like a well burnished halo. "Satisfactory underperformance is a far greater problem than a crisis," he says, pointing to the example of Westinghouse which is now one seventh the size of GE in revenue terms. "Over 20 years, three generations of top management have presided over the massive decline of a top US corporation," says Ghoshal. "Yet, 80 percent of the time the company was thought to be doing well. Westinghouse CEOs were very competent and committed. They'd risen through the ranks and did the right things. Yet they presided over massive decline."

The explanation he gives for this delusion of grandeur is that few companies have an ability for self-renewal. "You cannot renew a company without revitalizing its people. Top management has always said this. After a decade of restructuring and downsizing, top management now believes it. Having come to believe it, what does it really mean?"

Ghoshal, Sumantra

zeitbite#24
Tom Peters

*"We are
CEOs of
our own
companies:
Me Inc."*

Ghoshal contends that revitalizing people is fundamentally about changing people. The trouble is that adults don't change their basic attitudes unless they encounter personal tragedy. Things that happen at work rarely make such an impact. If organizations are to revitalize people, they must change the context of what they create around people.

"The oppressive atmosphere in most large companies resembles downtown Calcutta in summer," says Ghoshal. "We intellectualize a lot in management. But if you walk into a factory or a unit, within the first 15 minutes you get a smell of the place."

The way out of the smog is through

- *purpose* – "the company is also a social institution;"
- *process* – "the organization as a set of roles and relationships;" and
- *people* – "helping individuals to become the best they can be"

Undoubtedly these factors are less hard and robust than the three Ss of strategy, structure and systems, but Ghoshal believes they are the way forward.

SEE: HUMAN CAPITAL

MORE INFO: Sumantra Ghoshal & Christopher Bartlett, *The Individualized Corporation*, 1997; www.lbs.ac.uk

SOURCES: International Management Symposium, London Business School, November 11, 1997

ghostwriting

The acknowledgments pages of business books are prone to gushing sentimentality. They contain more gratuitous thanks and tributes than an awards ceremony and most appear as sincere. But, beneath the sugary sentiments, often lies the true story of a book's creation and the figure of a ghostwriter.

From the point of view of publishers, ghostwriters are useful because they mean that it is likely that a manuscript will be delivered more or less on time – journalists meet deadlines; academics tend not to; and consultants are usually too busy making money – and that it will be more or less readable. These are highly persuasive factors. For publishers, ghostwriters often represent no additional expense or risk.

Of course, ghostwriting is nothing new. Sports stars have been using ghosts for years and the recent flurry of celebrity novels proves that the fictional ghost is alive and well. The process which lies behind ghostwriting is far removed from the traditional publishing process, where someone has an idea for a book and approaches a publisher. "There are parallels with the film industry. You get the star and build the project around the star," says Dr Timothy Clark of King's College, London, who has studied the guru industry. "We are moving away from the origins of management books – the Peter Drucker-style academic – into the entertainment industry." Indeed, the idea for a book can play a secondary role to the marketing plan.

What happens once a ghost has been identified differs from case to case. "A ghost will interview the author and write a first draft of the material, possibly then writing a second or third draft as well, and then helping with final edits," says Art Kleiner (ghost to Peter Senge and many more). "But it varies. Different authors prefer different types of working relationships. Many times ghosts will not do research or vice versa."

The matter of how and where the ghost is credited is significant. Many get their name on the cover – though it is usually in much smaller typeface than the more famous name. This is understandable. Big names sell books. While some ghosts make the cover but miss out on the promotional tour of Alaska, others have their name on the inside title page or buried at the bottom of the dust jacket. It is increasingly common to find ghostwriters included in lengthy lists of acknowledgments. There is, therefore, an art in discovering if a book has been ghostwritten. Euphemisms abound.

It should be emphasized that there is nothing illegal with any of this. Ghostwriting is legal – yet another service in a service society. But is it decent? The ethics of ghostwriting provide an interesting area for debate. The obvious point of departure is whether the person credited on the cover is actually the author in any shape or form. Stories are recounted of authors who have never actually read their book, and of a well-known management academic who produced a book simply by dictating onto tapes for 20 hours, and then handing the tapes over to

ghostwriting

a ghost. Given such stories – and not all are apocryphal – some suspect that the point of no return has been passed. "The problem with ghostwritten books," says Tom Brown, who collates a top ten book list, published on the Management General web site, "is that they often camouflage or misrepresent the ideas of the author. In the best case, such books are often rhetorically enhanced, so that the name on the book cover sounds much more provocative, savvy or deep than he or she really is. In the worst case, the book actually presents the ideas of the writer instead of the author – so whose book is it really? And which person should be making speeches around the world on its behalf?

"At least a book that lists a name on the cover *with* another name as writer makes it clear to the reader that, if in doubt, either person can be approached and interviewed. But a full-hidden ghostwritten book does a disservice first and foremost to the person who finds himself the author of a bestseller and is, because of that, tongue-tied in more ways than one."

SEE: WORDWORKS; ART KLEINER; KEN SHELTON; BUSINESS BOOKS;
            BOOK BUYING
MORE INFO: www.well.com; www.fieldbook.com

Giel, Elwin

Elwin Giel (born 1968) is the Dutch managing director of Power Leisure, the largest leisure group in the Netherlands. His company includes a string of nightclubs, a disco consultancy, and an export business for "electronic cloakrooms." Giel started his first business at the age of 12 – a mobile disco.

Later, he attended the European Business School in London where he ran a basement disco. He worked for First Leisure in London and as the UK tour manager for Miss World. Giel is the innovator of the "drinks stockmarket," a concept which he has franchised around the world. Customers are able to influence the price of their drinks through what they buy. They're also allowed to bulk buy and resell their drinks, and to take advantage of engineered crashes.

Global Business Network

Thanks to the Global Business Network (GBN), it's rare these days to find a top executive who fails to drop the words "scenario planning" into his or her smooth patter within minutes of meeting you. Members of the GBN's staff and network originated the said art at Royal Dutch/Shell back in the 1970s; and since its foundation by Peter Schwartz, Stewart Brand *et al*, in 1987, GBN has been keeping the flame burning brightly.

Based in Emeryville, CA, in a former tractor factory, GBN has around 100 clients including the government of Singapore as well as big corporations. (Its members are predominantly American: approximately 60 percent have headquarters in North America, with another 30 percent in Europe and 10 percent in Asia, Africa and Latin America.)

"Basically, GBN does two very different, though related kinds of things," explains Peter Schwartz. "One is to help people get information about leading edge change. Particularly, what we're interested in are those things that come in from the fringes, from left field as it were – the things that are likely to cause great surprise and that, by definition, companies are not going to see by looking at the mainstream sources of information. Secondly we try to give our client companies a process, a tool – namely scenario planning – that offers a more rigorous approach to thinking about the future."

Small fry need not apply. Corporate membership costs $35,000 annually and individual members are invited to join only if they can "contribute remarkable insights, provocative ideas and deep experience"; Henry Kissinger, in other words. In return for their membership cards, thrusting executives get the chance to hobnob with each other at seminars and conferences, picking up lots of fresh ideas and perspectives on the way. The GBN also provides consulting services for individual firms, although scenario planning remains the focus of its work to this day. Indeed, scenario planning is mentioned sixteen times over only three pages of the GBN Web site.

GBN "associates" include hipper personages than Henry Kissinger, including Brian Eno, Laurie Anderson, Paul Saffo, Peter Senge,

Esther Dyson and Kevin Kelly.

Trevor Merriden

SEE: **ESTHER DYSON**
MORE INFO: **www.gbn.org**
SOURCES: **www.businesstech.com**

zeitbite#25
Harry
Quadracci

*"People think
the president
has to be the
main
organiser.
No, the
president is
the main
dis-organiser.
Everybody
manages
quite
well;
when-
ever
anything goes
wrong, they
take immedi-
ate action to
make sure
nothing'll go
wrong again.
The problem
is, nothing
new will ever
happen, ei-
ther."*

136

golden hellos

According to fashionable theorists, the motivational power of money has never been weaker among the executive elite. There is a great deal of discussion of employability and values, of working for organizations whose objectives you truly believe in. Meanwhile, business schools proudly trumpet the salaries enjoyed by their MBA graduates. Their message is that an MBA increases your earning power. Money continues to talk.

Indeed, there is a constant war among business schools to establish that their graduates earn more than those who emerge from the competition. The average starting salary for full-time MBAs graduating from London Business School (LBS) in 1998 was £54,695. One LBS 1998 graduate moved into a job with a salary of £100,750. "We publish salary figures chiefly for the benefit of incoming students," says Lesley Aylward, director of LBS's Career Management Centre. "If we stopped doing so, I think they would be alarmed." Other schools follows suit. Graduates from the MBA program at Madrid's Instituto de Empresa, average salary increases of 147 percent – giving them salaries of just over $84,000; MBAs from Imperial College Management School can look forward to an average starting salary of £40,000 (1997); and so on.

In the United States, the salary battle is at constant fever pitch. Top of the pile is Harvard Business School where MBA graduates can anticipate average salaries of $145,000. Stanford MBAs can look forward to average salaries of $138,000 and students at Philadelphia's Wharton School average post-MBA salaries of $125,500. These figures are put into context when set against average pre-MBA salaries of $60,000 (Harvard); $55,000 (Stanford); and $50,000 (Wharton).

golden hellos

Clearly, such figures are good news for MBA graduates. Salaries remain high and it appears that the "golden hello," popular in the 1980s, has made something of a comeback. A total of 76 percent of the 1998 LBS graduation class received a signing-on bonus. Commonly, this involves companies paying off the debts amassed by the students during their MBAs. "Bonuses are almost the norm and can be anything from £2,000 to £25,000," says LBS's Lesley Aylward.

The downside is that some MBAs may price themselves out of the market. While consulting firms and banks can offer substantial packages, smaller organizations simply cannot compete or have to develop more imaginative remuneration packages. Electronic commerce companies, for example, are among those who commonly offer an equity share rather than a substantial starting salary.

The salary wars beg a number of questions. First, there is the accuracy of the information. While most people are cagey about the exact details of their salary package, MBA graduates seem unusually open and precise. Skeptics might suggest that they are unlikely to play down their salaries. MBAs have a tendency to use the figure for their "total package" – including such things as their signing-on fee, expected bonus, and the value of their health plan or company car – rather than the straightforward amount of their salary. In the self-perpetuating world of business schools, large salaries attract students and increase the prestige of the business school. MBA graduates have a vested interest in talking up salaries for MBA graduates. The schools insist that their figures are generally accurate – checks are made between the known salaries offered by employers and those claimed by employees – and lament the fact that rankings of schools inevitably and prominently include salary details.

The second question is whether there is more to doing an MBA than money. While bellowing salary figures from every rooftop, business schools are keen to emphasize that their MBA students are not simply financially driven. "MBA graduates are not as financially oriented as they were ten years ago. Now, they are more likely to ask a recruiter about its contribution to society and to consider the lifestyle implications of a particular job," says John Mapes, director of

golden hellos

the full-time MBA program at Cranfield School of Management. "In the main, people who do MBAs believe that they have the ability to make it in senior management. They like the idea of making a difference. If they were really money-driven they would go straight into the City or management consulting."

SEE: BUSINESS SCHOOLS
MORE INFO: www.mbaplanet.com

Goleman, Daniel

Daniel Goleman is the author of the best-selling *Emotional Intelligence*. He has created an industry – the touchy-feely world of emotional intelligence – in which executives are encouraged to get in touch with their feelings as well as their balance sheet. "The qualities of leadership and the qualities of the heart ... are largely the same," Goleman writes, going on to explore the importance of the emotional dimension in determining the effectiveness of leaders.

Goleman argues that in demanding jobs, where above average IQ is a given, superior emotional capability gives leaders an edge. At senior levels, emotional, rather than rational intelligence marks the true leader. This is supported by studies of outstanding performers which show that about two thirds of the abilities that set star performers apart are based on emotional intelligence. Against this, only one third of the skills that matter relate to raw intelligence (as measured by IQ) and technical expertise.

"Our emotions are hardwired into our being," he explains. "The very architecture of the brain gives feelings priority over thought." In reality, it is impossible to entirely separate thought from emotion. "We can be effective only when the two systems – our emotional brain and our thinking brain – work together," says Goleman. "That working relationship, which encompasses most of what we do in life, is the essence of emotional intelligence."

The good news is that emotional intelligence can be learned. There are five dimensions to this, he says, each of which is the foundation for specific capabilities of leadership. These are:

Goleman, Daniel

- *self-awareness* – we seldom pay attention to what we feel. A stream of moods runs in parallel to our thoughts. Our moods and previous emotional experiences provide a context for our decision making;
- *managing emotions* – all effective leaders learn to manage their emotions, especially the big three of anger, anxiety, sadness. This, in the self-improvement argot, is a decisive life skill;
- *motivating others* – according to Goleman, the root meaning of motive is the same as the root of emotion: to move;
- *showing empathy* – the flip side of self awareness is the ability to read emotions in others;
- *staying connected* – emotions are contagious. There is an unseen transaction that passes between us in every interaction that makes us feel either a little better or a little worse. Goleman calls this a "secret economy." He, however, has unearthed a far more open economy.

SEE: LEADERSHIP RIP
MORE INFO: www.haygroup.com
SOURCES: Daniel Goleman, "The emotional intelligence of leaders,"
            Leader to Leader, No. 10, Fall 1998

139

grassroots leadership

Leadership was once about heroes, indomitable individuals fighting against the odds, leading organizations from the front. Then it all changed. First came the fashion for empowerment. This created a lot of talk about changing leadership roles and skills. But, examples of empowering leaders were usually notable by their absence. Second, uncertainty levels increased through industry after industry. Leaders traditionally thrived on creating certainty. If they didn't know where they were going how was anyone else to know?

As an attempt at squaring the leadership circle comes grassroots leadership, an approach used by Royal/Dutch Shell. This addition to the management vocabulary is attributed to Steve Miller, group managing director of Shell. Miller observed the difficulties the company was experiencing in becoming more creative, innovative and faster moving. It was attempting to transform itself one layer of management at a time. Change quickly became becalmed.

Miller cut out the middlemen and went straight to employees. In small groups, the people from filling stations and the like were brought in for intensive training. Miller concentrated half his time on talking to, meeting with and involving "grassroots" people. "As people move up in organizations, they get further away from the work that goes on in the field – and as a result, they tend to devalue it," he says. "People get caught up in broad strategic issues, legal issues, stakeholder issues. But what really drives a business is the work that goes on down at the coal face. It's reliability, it's producing to specification, it's delivering to the customer." Grassroots leadership is, in essence, another attempt to put management in touch with what really happens in their organizations.

SEE: LEADERSHIP RIP
MORE INFO: www.shell.com
SOURCES: Richard Pascale, "Grassroots leadership," *Fast Company*, April/
            May 1998

groups

Staggeringly, the world of business theory only discovered the power and potential of teamworking in the 1990s. (The long-standing work of Meredith Belbin in this area had been generally overlooked.) Theories on teamworking then emerged at the rate of one a day. Teams were vaunted as the cure to all known organizational ills – based by some on the true but simplistic observation that teamworking was successfully used by software companies and management consulting firms. Amid this ludicrous clamor, teams took on a Dilbertian ring, just another word for committee. As a result, it is now preferable to talk of groups – carefully selected individuals working together to a common, often short-term, goal. Groups sound like teams for grown-ups.

SEE: FREE AGENTS
MORE INFO: www.belbin.com

Grove, Andy

Born in 1936, Andy Grove was educated at City College of New York and the University of California at Berkeley. He worked as assistant to Gordon Moore at Fairchild Semiconductor. He then joined a fledgling company called NM Electronic which was set up in 1968. Its first

zeitbite#26
Charles B.
Wang

"The natural human inclination for conspicuous consumption is a poor reason to invest in technology for business. If we are not cautious, we will find ourselves, at the end of the day, with technology investments that might be great fun but are not really serving any legitimate purpose."

140

year's revenues were less than $3000. The company became Intel, one of the most successful corporations in history.

With Grove as CEO, Intel became the world's largest semiconductor manufacturer. Revenues rose from $1.9 billion in 1987 to $25.1 billion in 1997. Its investment in the future remains prodigious – in 1998 it spent $5 billion on new plants and equipment; and nearly $3 billion on R&D. Big ideas cost big bucks. But the pay-offs keep rolling in – in 1997, Intel recorded a 20 percent increase in revenues and a 33 percent increase in profits.

"Grove calls the shots in the high-tech world. Every company in the PC, software, network and Internet universe must interact with Intel's chips in some way. A monopoly? Sure, but it looks to us like he won it fair and square," said *Upside* magazine.

In 1998 Grove stepped down as CEO to be replaced by Craig Barrett.

SEE: BILL GATES
MORE INFO: www.intel.com
SOURCES: *Upside's* 1997 Elite 100

141

Grove, Andy

Hamel, Gary

In 1978 Gary Hamel (born 1954) left his job as a hospital administrator and went to the University of Michigan to study for a PhD in International Business. At Michigan, Hamel met his eventual mentor, C.K. Prahalad. Twenty years on, Hamel has established himself at the vanguard of contemporary thinking on strategy. Hard hitting and opinionated, Hamel summarizes the contemporary challenge as "separating the shit from the shinola, the hype from the reality and the timeless from the transient."

As well as being visiting professor of strategic and international management at London Business School, California-based Hamel is a consultant to major companies and chairman of Strategos, a consulting company. His reputation has burgeoned as a result of a series of acclaimed articles in the *Harvard Business Review* – including "Strategic intent," "Competing with core competencies," and "The core competence of the corporation" – as well as the best-selling, *Competing For the Future.* (All co-written with Prahalad.)

Along the way, Hamel has created a new vocabulary for strategy which includes strategic intent, strategic architecture, industry foresight (rather than vision) and core competencies. (Hamel and Prahalad define core competencies as "the collective learning in the organization, especially how to coordinate diverse production skills and integrate multiple streams of technologies" and call on organizations to see themselves as a portfolio of core competencies as opposed to business units.)

Hamel argues that there are three kinds of companies. First are "the real makers," companies such as British Airways and Xerox. They are the aristocracy; well managed, consistent high achievers. Second, says Hamel, are the takers, "peasants who only keep what the Lord doesn't want." This group typically have around 15 percent market share – such as Kodak in the copier business, or Avis.

Third are the breakers, industrial revolutionaries. These are companies creating the new wealth – and include the likes of Starbucks. "Companies should be asking themselves, who is going to capture the new wealth in your industry?" he says.

He argues that there are four preconditions for wealth creating strategies.

1   A company must have "new passions." People inside the organization must care deeply about the future.
2   Wealth creation requires "new voices." In many companies Hamel observes "a lack of genetic diversity. Young people are largely disenfranchised from discussions of strategy. We need a hierarchy of imagination, not experience."
3   There is a need for "new conversations." Instead of having the same five people talking to the same five people for the fifth year in a row more people need to become involved in the process of strategy creation.
4   There is a need for "new perspectives." "You cannot make people any smarter but you can give them new lenses," says Hamel. "Only non-linear strategies will create new wealth."

It cannot be assumed that Hamel is universally popular. Bill Gates is not a fan. Indeed, Gates said of *Competing for the Future*: "The authors are two smart guys. They're probably as good as there is in the field. So what examples did they pick? General Magic – Yeah – they understood the future. Apple Computer? Every example they gave, with the exception of Hewlett-Packard was a total joke!"

SEE: SUMANTRA GHOSHAL; COMPETENCY TRACKING
MORE INFO: www.strategosnet.com
SOURCES: *Context* magazine, December 1997

Handy, Charles

Charles Handy (born 1932) is a best-selling writer and broadcaster. In his quiet and undemonstrative way, Handy has brought major questions about the future of work and of society onto the corporate and personal agenda.

Handy worked for Shell until 1972 when he left to teach at London Business School. He spent time at MIT where he came into contact with many of the leading lights in the human relations school of thinking, including Ed Schein.

Handy's early academic career was conventional. His first book, *Understanding Organizations* (1976), gives little hint of the wide-ranging, social and philosophical nature of his later work. It is a comprehensive and readable primer of organizational theory which was written as much to clarify Handy's own perspectives on the subject. From there Handy moved on to the more idiosyncratic, *Gods of Management* (1978).

It was in 1989 with the publication of *The Age of Unreason* that Handy's thinking made a great leap forward. Suddenly the world mapped out by Handy became an uncertain and dangerous one. He predicted a future of "discontinuous change" (a phrase which has now entered the mainstream).

In practice, Handy believes that certain forms of organization will become dominant. These are the type of organization most readily associated with service industries. First and most famously, what he calls "the shamrock organization" – "a form of organization based around a core of essential executives and workers supported by outside contractors and part-time help."

The second emergent structure identified by Handy is the federal one. It is not, he points out, another word for decentralization. He provides a blueprint for federal organizations in which the central function coordinates, influences, advises and suggests. It does not dictate terms or short-term decisions. The center is, however, concerned with long-term strategy. It is "at the middle of things and is not a polite word for the top or even for head office."

The third type of organization Handy anticipates is what he calls "the Triple I" – Information, Intelligence and Ideas. In such organizations the demands on personnel management are large.

As organizations change in the age of unreason so, Handy predicts, will other aspects of our lives. Less time will be spent at work – 50,000 hours in a lifetime rather than the present figure of around 100,000. Handy does not predict, as people did in the 1970s, an enlightened age of leisure. Instead he challenges people to spend more time thinking about what they want to do. Time will not simply

Handy, Charles

be divided between work and play – there could be "portfolios" which split time between fee work (where you sell time); gift work (for neighbors or charities); study (keeping up-to-date with your work); and homework and leisure.

Handy has become a one-man case study of the new world of work he so successfully and humanely commentates on. At a personal level, he appears to have the answers. Whether these can be translated into answers for others remains the question and the challenge.

SEE: FREE AGENTS
MORE INFO: Charles Handy, *The Age of Unreason*, 1989

Healtheon Corporation

An estimated $1 trillion was spent in the US on healthcare in 1997. One of those on the tail of big bucks is Healtheon. Helping it make a more convincing case than most in the healthcare fray is Jim Clark – ex-Silicon Graphics and Netscape.

Founded in 1996, Healtheon was backed by Kleiner Perkins Caufield and Byers. Its first three years brought in revenues of $47 million, though overall $73 million was lost. The company aims to use technology to bridge gaps in healthcare and to simplify healthcare. The promise is a "universal health data platform."

SEE: ECOMMERCE
MORE INFO: www.healtheon.com

Helios Consulting

Analytically exceptional, Chicago-based consulting firm Helios was launched in 1998. Its first year revenues passed the magical $1 million mark. The Helios founders are Chris Lederer and Sam Hill. Hill is the former head of worldwide strategic planning and business development at D'Arcy Masius Benton and Bowles. Hill spent 15 months with the ad agency in an experiment to see whether his analytical vigor could be brought to bear on the ad world. Previously Hill had been with management consultants Booz-Allen & Hamilton – he was the brains behind the firm's move into thought leadership and

Home Depot

Company
The Home Depot, Inc.

Address
2455 Pace Ferry Rd, Atlanta, GA 30339–4024 USA
Phone: 770–433–8211
Fax: 770–384–2337
http://www.homedepot.com

Business
Specialist Retailer – home improvement

Statistics Fiscal Year End January

Annual sales (millions)	1998	$24,156.0
Annual results (millions)	1998	$116.0
Other facts		More than 770 stores. Largest home-improvement retailer in US
Hoover's 500		#48
Fortune 500		#44

the launch of its award winning magazine *Strategy & Business*. Hill is also co-author of *Radical Marketing*.

SEE: BRANDING CONSULTING FIRMS
MORE INFO: Sam Hill and Glenn Rifkin, *Radical Marketing*, 1999

Home Depot
DIY with management that has combined the high tech with common sense. (See chart for further information.)

human capital
First came personnel. This evolved into an administrative function, an extended exercise in paper shuffling and wage differentials. Personnel was impersonal. Then came the current incarnation, human resources (HR). This is personnel with added strategic ingredients. HR is the big picture: careers, training, employment trends. The trouble, some now suggest, is the second word – *resources*. This is redolent of another age when people were fodder in the industrial machine, mere raw materials. HR has been hit by PC. A more accurate and appropriate description could be human capital. This encapsulates the concept of people as a vital corporate investment and source of future profits. It also embraces the idea of intellectual capital – human capital includes all workers regardless of whether they wield a pickaxe or a laptop. Order your new business cards now.

SEE: CORE COMPETENTS

Ikea

Ikea is one of the great retail brands of our times. The Swedish furniture company has endeared itself to younger, price-conscious home makers in the 130 or so countries it operates in. To them, Ikea – with its DIY assembly from flat-packs – represents stylish design at affordable prices. To the loyal customers who fill its stores Ikea is self-assemble chic.

Rising from its humble origins in Small-land, a rural area of Sweden, Ikea has grown from a tiny mail order business to a $5.8 billion furniture giant. The brand is driven by the philosophies of its founder Ingvar Kamprad – from whose initials the company partly derives its name.

Ikea now operates more than 140 stores in 28 countries and employs about 35,000 people. The "Ikea way" enshrines a set of values that have ensured an almost unrivalled communion with its customers. A simple white lacquered bookshelf called Billy, has been selling well for 20 years. Such lucrative simplicity is testimony to the fact that Ikea knows the minds of its customers.

In recent years, however, the darling of the 20 and 30 somethings, has received a rough ride from the media. Revelations about Kamprad's past – his Nazi sympathies and drinking habits – did little to enhance the brand's wholesome appeal. In these more forgiving days, however, even billionaire entrepreneurs are allowed a few skeletons in the closet.

The Ikea story began in the 1930s. The company grew out of the vision of one extraordinary man, Ingvar Kamprad, the company's founder and chairman. That vision – created years before Anita Roddick's Body Shop and other New Age brands – remains the guiding principle for the business today.

It is summed up in a mission statement: "To contribute to a better everyday working life for the majority of people, by offering a wide range of home furnishing items of good design and function, at prices so low that the majority of people can afford to buy them."

Born in the barren country of Small-land in Sweden, Kamprad grew up during the Great Depression of the 1920s. He took the qualities of resourcefulness he saw around him to heart. The thrifty, hard working ideals of his Swedish homeland were applied to the retail business. Starting with matches he moved onto furniture and ended up as one of the largest furniture retailers in the world. Now in his seventies, he refers to the values he instilled in Ikea as the "testament of a furniture dealer."

Building on its early experience in Sweden – when a visit to an Ikea store could involve a day's travel – the company has developed a distinctively integrated approach to retailing which aims to make shopping an enjoyable experience rather than a chore.

Cynics may question whether its folksy, for the people, philosophy can truly survive the transition to a big business, but the Ikea employees are genuinely committed to it. According to one senior Ikea executive at the company's headquarters in the Swedish town of Almhult: "The only way of keeping the customer long-term in our vision is that he has a benefit from coming to Ikea. The product and price quality that we offer must be the best. We even say that we must have better prices than our competitors as one of our operating principles. That is basic to our long-term success."

"From there we say how can we make a visit to Ikea a day out. Ikea should be a day out. That started in the first store here in Almhult. In the old days to come to our store they had to leave early in the morning. The journey would usually take a couple of hours and many of our customers had small children." Hence the family restaurants and crèche facilities that have become a feature of Ikea stores (on weekends and holidays, the company even employs clowns and magicians to entertain the kids).

The same sort of egalitarian principles apply to the management culture. Ikea permits no status symbols and refers to all employees as co-workers. The philosophy is reinforced by the example of Anders Moburg, the company's current President, who was hand-picked by Kamprad. When travelling on business, for example, Moburg is famous for flying economy class, and refuses to take taxis when public transport is available. True to its small company roots, too, Ikea carries out relatively little customer research into new products, relying instead on a feel for the market.

Ikea

In recent years, Ikea has also succeeded where many European retailers have failed, successfully taking its formula to North America. The experience, however, was not without lessons. Puzzled at first by poor sales of beds and other lines, it quickly learned that although Americans liked the simplicity of its designs they wanted furniture to match their larger homes. The answer? Bigger furniture.

In 1997, Ikea introduced a new line of children's furniture and toys, and the company continues to invest in new stores. There are plans to expand extensively in Eastern Europe; ten stores in Poland by 2000 as well as stores opening in Bulgaria, Romania, and Russia. Next stop Asia.

With a $10 million investment to date in Shanghai, China, and $130 million on retail and distribution networks in Taiwan and Hong Kong, the only potential cloud on the horizon is the issue of succession. With Kamprad now in his seventies it seems certain that he will take a step back and allow his chosen successor to step into his shoes. Whether the company can continue its success without the idiosyncratic touch of its founder remains to be seen.

But the omens are good. Despite prices up to 30 percent cheaper than rivals, in 1997 sales were up 21 percent for the year. Somehow Ikea continues to squeeze increasing returns from its retail units; it has been estimated that sales per square meter are twice the industry's average. Analysts say Ikea's stores generate about $43 million a year in revenues and $3 million a year in cash. With such low debt and strong cash flow, Ikea is able to finance expansion from its own pockets.

Ikea remains privately owned. Its capital has been estimated at £2.69 billion and, sometimes, more. "Ikea itself is a money machine," concluded Stellan Bjork, author of a book about the company.

Des Dearlove

SEE: BRANDING
MORE INFO: www.ikea.com

Ikea

iMac

Launched in August 1998, the iMac was the Apple Mac for the next generation. "For everyone who thinks computers are too costly, too complicated or too beige," said its advertising. In the US the iMac received 150,000 orders in the first week. Elsewhere, orderly queues formed outside stockists. The iMac, a vision in translucent blue, sold 278,000 units in the first six weeks, an achievement that had *Fortune* magazine describing it as "one of the hottest computer launches ever." Wall Street, too, seemed to recover its confidence in Apple – the company's share price doubled in less than a year.

"The iMac is a return to the design of the original Macintosh and its descendants ... a cute, simple, all-in-a-box design which helped Apple became the first computer company to reach $1 billion in sales," said *Wired*.

Being Apple, there is unseemly squabbling about who is the architect of its (perhaps brief) renaissance. The spurned CEO, Gil Amelio, claims that Steve Jobs – who returned to the company in 1996 – stepped in at just the right time, and that he, Amelio, took on a moribund company and turned it around. The Amelio angle is that he bequeathed a re-energized Apple, with $1.5 billion in the bank and a number of stunning new product lines including the iMac.

The Jobs fans say the once and future king of Apple came in and saved the day. His actions since becoming self-styled "interim CEO" include dumping the NeXT operating system that he sold to Apple, dumping loss-making licensing contracts, and spotting the potential of the iMac.

Whatever the sordid corporate machinations behind it, the new machine is the embodiment of everything Jobs believes in: eye-catching design, and simple operation. The iMac is also the product of a different vision of the computer industry. It doesn't have a disk drive – because Jobs believes they have been superseded by external storage devices such as Zip drives. Nor does the Apple CEO subscribe to the common view that the PC and TV are moving together. Whether Jobs or his nemesis Bill Gates proves correct on this could determine the future of both companies.

In the meantime, the iMac looks the best chance to restore Apple's fortunes. Apple owners have always been passionate, fierce even, in their belief that Jobs builds a better mouse trap. Brand loyalty has always been high. The best news of all for Apple is that some 40 percent of iMac sales are to new customers. This suggests that the iconoclast Apple brand can seduce a new generation of computer buyers.

Des Dearlove

SEE: STEVE JOBS
MORE INFO: www.apple.com
SOURCES: "Edsel or etch a sketch," *Wired*, August 13, 1998

Imus, Don

The radio host Don Imus is among the most listened to voices in America. His show is syndicated to over 90 stations and televised on MSNBC. In similar vein to Oprah Winfrey, Imus has created the Imus American Book Awards with four prizes worth $250,000. There is more to Imus than mouth.

SEE: OPRAH WINFREY
SOURCES: *The Economist*, October 17, 1998

increasing returns

Santa Fe Institute star, W. Brian Arthur (see separate entry) is among those arguing that the classic economic law of diminishing returns has been turned on its head to produce the law of increasing returns. This means that under certain circumstances companies can quickly come to totally dominate a market. Such is the power of increasing returns that the power of market forces appears negated – indeed, for a while it is. The invisible hand of market forces is "a little bit arthritic" notes Arthur.

"High technology operates under increasing returns, and the degree modern economies are shifting toward high technology, the different economics of increasing returns alters the character of competition, business culture, and appropriate government policy in these economies," says Brian Arthur.

"The blur of businesses has created a new economic model in which returns increase rather than diminish; supermarkets mimic stock markets; and you want the market – not your strategy – to price, market, and manage your offer," write Stan Davis and Chris Meyer.

SEE: BRIAN ARTHUR
MORE INFO: www.santafe.edu
SOURCES: W. Brian Arthur, *Increasing Returns & Path Dependence in the Economy*, University of Michigan Press, Ann Arbor, 1994

ineffective habits

Stephen Covey's book, *The Seven Habits of Highly Effective People* has sold over 6 million copies. People like its sugary admonitions to self-improvement. They appear to thrive on its mixture of old-fashioned common sense (vintage 1950s) and holistic self-help (vintage 1990s). It makes them feel good. Of course, whether this makes them better managers or better people is difficult if not impossible to determine.

The success of the book flies in the face all of corporate reality. Everyone in the corporate world knows that plain, unabashed inefficiency stalks the corridors of power. Sugary sentimentality is usually in short supply as the knives are drawn. There may be a profusion of effective people in Salt Lake City, Utah, home to the Covey industry, but in reality bad habits abound. Of course, people are not quite as keen to buy books about bad habits as they are to buy books which promise success on a bald pate.

This is a pity because identifying the seven habits of highly ineffective people is potentially more useful. Cut away the dross and you will be a better manager and person. Eliminate your bad habits and you are automatically better. It is like giving up smoking. You feel warm and virtuous (though you would exchange the life of your grandmother in return for a single puff). Take Covey's route and you are always going to be disappointed – perfection is the preserve of the select few (your boss, for example).

The first habit of ineffective people is that they are *reactive rather than proactive*. This is understandable. You walk through the office door every morning and your in-tray is filled with things that need

157

sorting out today. You receive 25 e-mails demanding an explanation as to why you didn't finish what you were sorting out yesterday. Ineffective people are firefighters. Trouble is they are bit players in the *Towering Inferno* and there is no Steve McQueen to save the day. The building is burning and the e-mails are still coming in.

This habit can be easily cured. Simply, put your feet up and gaze out of the window. When you are asked why you're not putting the fire out on the fifth floor, explain that you are taking a more strategic view. Becoming a Strategic Firefighter is a new job title and a beginning. Start by imagining where the fires are going to break out tomorrow. Soon, you will be able to completely ignore the immediate demands on your time. This is because in all likelihood you will be unemployed.

A more useful approach is to come to terms with your bad habit. Okay, so you are always reacting to events rather than dictating what happens. So what? Being reactive is not necessarily such a bad thing – it depends on the speed of your reactions. Go with the flow, but pass the habit on by peppering youthful colleagues with urgent demands and impossibly tight deadlines. If everyone is reactive there can be nothing wrong in being reactive. The proactive strategist becomes a freak.

Being reactive leads naturally to the second habit of ineffective people: *they begin with the beginning in mind.* If goldfish could hold senior executive positions this is how they would behave. Forget the past (too awful); do not contemplate the future (potentially worse). If you get through the next day or two everything will be alright.

Ineffective people do not respond to long-term objectives, mission statements or visions. They should, perhaps, be congratulated for their insight. Words of carefully honed wisdom on specially laminated cards mean nothing to them. Grandiose objectives are wasted. This means that ineffective people are cheaper and easier to manage. There is no need for the board to decamp to a stately home to contemplate the organization's objectives. All they have to do is tell the ineffective people what they need to do today. This is jigsaw management. The trouble is that though the pieces may seem to fit together, the picture keeps changing.

ineffective habits

Then there is the flip side. Ineffective habit number three is *to start at the end and forget about the beginning*. Management fads and fashions usually bring out this ineffective habit most successfully. Here is what happens. The chief executive reads a business book. This is worrying. The chief executive likes the book and buys the top management team copies. (Of course, the company pays.) The chief executive is then interviewed by a journalist. Stuck for something to say, and anxious to give the impression that the recent disastrous downturn is a momentary blip, the chief executive blurts out that the company is now a total quality organization; re-engineering itself; instigating leading edge interpretations of intellectual capital; or some such phrase culled from the book. The chief executive has done a great job. The journalist didn't know about the blip and is pleased to understand some of the interview. As a result, the company is successfully repositioned as thoughtful and fashionable. Everyone feels good.

Of course, in an efficient and orderly world, the chief executive would then have to tackle the thorny problem of making this happen. In inefficient reality, the chief executive has no such concerns. A few months later, you can guarantee that the chief executive will be heard to say that management is about making things happen rather than theorizing. Re-engineering? Unworkable nonsense dreamt up by people with no idea of what life is really like at the sharp end of Inefficient Inc. The end is forgotten before how to begin to get there is even considered.

Ineffective habit number four is *to make sure that you win, no matter what*. Forget everyone else. Forget win-win. Teamwork is for wimps. Think of doing things which make you look good. If your decisions cause factories in distant lands to close down, so be it. If colleagues turn their backs when you stroll into the Corporate Arms after work, so be it. That is the price you must pay for your craven inefficiency. To achieve this you have to eschew all divisional or corporate targets. Instead you must invest all your time and energy in taking credit for the achievements of others; ensuring that colleagues look bad; and massaging the system to your own benefit. Total inefficiency should soon result.

The surly and unpleasant stepchild of habit number four is habit number five: *do not acknowledge anyone else in the organization.* There is a great deal of talk about synergy, about sharing knowledge and information. Don't believe any of it. Knowledge networks are just another chance for the corporate thought police to follow your every inefficient move. The joy of sharing is easily outweighed by the joy of possession. Why give someone else the glory? Keep the ideas to yourself. If another unit is performing woefully it is not a cause for concern but for celebration: the worse it does, the better your performance appears.

If there is any suggestion of cross-company cooperation, stamp on it firmly but subtly: "My concern is that they don't really understand our marketplace"; "I'm not sure if they share our long-term objectives"; or "Our cultures just aren't compatible: we are an empowered, action-oriented group; they are hierarchical and ponderous. You risk ruining everything we have strived for."

All this keeps the ineffective manager very busy indeed, which leads to ineffective habit number six: *an addiction to action.* This brings in many elements of ineffective habits numbers one and two. The truly ineffective manager is addicted to action. Give them a problem and they will immediately leap up from their desk and run around making things happen. Obviously, there isn't the time to consider whether the things that are happening are a good idea. Managers afflicted with this ineffective habit, fire and then, eventually, aim.

Signs of this form of ineffectiveness are easily observed. Managers who openly brag about the number of hours they work are probably afflicted – "I counted it up and it was 98 and a quarter hours in one week." Likewise those who have copious "to do" sheets, which list every single activity undertaken during the day, should be treated with fear. There is a thin line between healthy enthusiasm and unhealthy obsessional behavior.

The final habit of ineffective people is *to call a meeting.* Managers who spend their lives in meeting rooms can be spotted by their deathly pallor, and their interest in which pens work best on whiteboards. They wear dark glasses and mutter Sasco Year Planner like a mantra when they venture outside.

ineffective habits

Meetings are the melting pot of inefficiency. Ineffective nirvana can be achieved at meetings in which all six other habits of ineffective people are displayed. Meetings are a parade ground for bad habits. Like oversexed peacocks, executives can strut around, brazenly demonstrating their mastery of the full quota of bad habits. If in doubt call a meeting. Ideally, you can fill your entire day with meetings. No need to do anything. No need to decide anything. Just indulgent inefficiency. Stephen Covey is probably in a meeting right now.

SEE: STEPHEN COVEY

intellectual capital

"Business is not about bunches of shareholders who buy machines and employ labor to make things, but bunches of knowledge workers who get together to do something which others cannot do," says Fortune's Tom Stewart.

Capital used to be viewed in purely financial terms. Corporate balance sheets explained all. During the last decade, however, balance sheets have increasingly had to reflect intangible corporate assets. Now, the quest is on for greater understanding and, who knows, valuation of the most intangible, elusive, mobile and important assets of all: intellectual capital.

Intellectual capital can be crudely described as the collective brain power of the organization. The concept is irrevocably bound up with the notion of the knowledge worker and knowledge management. In some hands, the terms are used virtually synonymously.

Their root, as with so many other ideas, lies in the work of Peter Drucker. His 1969 book, *The Age of Discontinuity*, introduced the term "knowledge worker," to describe the highly trained, intelligent managerial professional, who realizes his or her own worth and contribution to the organization. The knowledge worker was the antidote to the previous model, corporate man and woman.

If you wish to go further back, you still encounter Drucker. The foundations of the idea can easily be seen in Drucker's description of Management By Objectives in his 1954 book, *The Practice of Management* where the worth, motivation and aspirations of the executive are integral to corporate success. The individual is not an unthinking functionary valued for an ability to do what is demanded, but an independent and committed force.

Drucker recognized the new breed, but key to his contribution was the realization that knowledge is both power *and* ownership. Intellectual capital is power. If knowledge, rather than labor, is the new measure of economic society then the fabric of capitalist society must change: "The knowledge worker is both the true 'capitalist' in the knowledge society and dependent on his job. Collectively the knowledge workers, the employed educated middle class of today's society, own the means of production through pension funds, investment trusts, and so on." Thinkers of the world unite.

The information age places a premium on intellectual work. There is growing realization that recruiting, retaining and nurturing talented people is crucial to competitiveness. Intellectual capital is the height of corporate fashion – prompting, among other things, three books bearing the title *Intellectual Capital*. The challenge is that talent, or intellectual capital, is a scarce and therefore highly prized resource (one explanation for booming executive pay).

The rise in interest is understandable and, perhaps, woefully late in the evolution of industrial life. "Of course, knowledge has always mattered, but two things have changed," argues Tom Stewart, author of one of the major books on the subject. "First, as a percentage of the value added to a product, it has grown to be the most important thing. Costs used to be 80 percent on material and 20 percent on knowledge – now it is split 70–30 the other way. Second, it is increasingly possible to manage knowledge."

Intellectual capital is, in many ways, simply concerned with fully utilizing the intellects of those employed by an organization. "If Hewlett-Packard knew what it knows we'd be three times more productive," reflects Hewlett-Packard chief, Lew Platt. In the year 2000, it is calculated that the UK will have 10 million people who could be termed knowledge workers and seven million manual workers. In the US, despite the downsizing epidemic, the numbers of managerial and professional workers has *increased* by 37 percent since the beginning of the 1980s.

intellectual capital

Having identified intellectual capital as important, the next question is inevitable: how can it be measured? After all, what gets measured gets done. Intellectual capital is increasingly codified as part of corporate life. The Swedish company, Skandia, has a "director of intellectual capital" and others are following suit – with job titles at least. Skandia's Leif Edvinsson is one of the thought leaders in this field; he has developed a model for reporting on intellectual capital based around customers, processes, renewal and development, human factors and finance.

The trouble is that turning bland statements about knowledge and intellectual capital into reality is a substantial challenge. Intellectual capital is good, but how do you create it? Here, companies can hit a wall. Research by Booz-Allen & Hamilton consultants, Charles Lucier and Janet Torsilieri, found that most knowledge management (or equivalent) programs have limited results. Indeed they estimate that "about one sixth of these programs achieve very significant impact within the first two years; half achieve small but important benefits; and the remaining third – the failures – have little business impact."

Amid the hype and hyperbole, as well as the plethora of conferences and publications, such research makes for salutary reading. For all the talk, successfully harnessing intellectual capital remains a formidable challenge which few corporations can claim to have overcome.

SEE: **CORE COMPETENTS**
MORE INFO: Leif Edvinsson & Michael Malone, *Intellectual Capital*, 1997;
Thomas Stewart, *Intellectual Capital*, Doubleday, 1997
SOURCES: *Management Skills & Development*, October 1997

International Business Machines
At one point, IBM earned 70 percent of the worldwide computer industry's profits. Then came one of the most dramatic collapses in corporate history. IBM's gross profit margins fell from 55 percent in 1990 to 38 percent in 1993. The IBM brand was ranked third in the world in 1993, and by the 1994 league tables was rated as having a negative value.

At the beginning of the 1990s, IBM stared over the corporate precipice. Big Blue, the symbol of American corporate might recorded massive losses and seemed too out of touch with the marketplace to make a comeback.

Then it recruited former McKinsey consultant and turnaround master, Lou Gerstner as CEO. When he became CEO in 1993, Gerstner decided not to split IBM – something which previous CEO, John Akers had prepared for. The company's revitalization owes a great deal to this decision. Gerstner also reflected that IBM had been through "an economic shock the equivalent of an earthquake."

Under Gerstner, IBM has made a surprisingly strong recovery. It has got back in touch. Take its role in Internet development. In 1993, long-serving IBMer, John Patrick was arguing that everyone at the company should have their own e-mail address and that the company needed a web site. "Connect with other people. If you become externally focused, you can change the whole company," said Patrick. What is interesting is that Patrick's call to arms was basically a return to the company's first principles – get in touch with customers and communicate internally. The only difference was that Patrick was championing the latest technology to do so.

As proof that IBM's culture has changed, forces were mobilized in a way the slow moving monolith of the past never even contemplated. In 1995 only two of the company's 220,000 employees were working on Java. By 1997, 2400 scientists and engineers through-out the world were doing so. Indeed, such is the cultural change that parts of IBM more resemble Microsoft. There is talk of breaking rules, using small eccentric groups to tackle problems from different angles, to bring fresh thinking.

Lou Gerstner stalks in the background, pulling the strings, exerting pressure when needed. In fact, his behavior appears to be a textbook example of modern leadership – empowering and coaching rather than controlling. At the same time, his feet appear firmly planted in commercial reality. Says Gerstner: "My view is you perpetuate success by continuing to run scared, not by looking back at what made you great, but looking forward at what is going to make you ungreat, so that you are constantly focusing on the challenges that keep you humble, hungry and nimble."

Typically, when Gerstner was shown the Internet for the first time his reaction was "This is great, this is a new channel for business. How do we make it real for customers? How do we make money on it?" The order of these priorities – customers and then profit – is perhaps the vital lesson from IBM's renaissance and the rise, fall and rise of the IBM brand.

SEE: BILL GATES
MORE INFO: www.ibm.com
SOURCES: Eric Ransdell, "IBM's grassroots revival," *Fast Company*,
              October/November 1997; Louise Kehoe, "Big Blue-eyed boy
              makes good," *Financial Times*, April 22, 1995

The Internet

"The Internet is ushering in a set of changes that are unstoppable," says Jim Clark. He may well be right, but the commercial possibilities of the Internet remain, for most businesses, tantalizing rather than real.

First comes the temptation: one prediction estimates that the number of people online will expand from 57 million in 1997 to 377 million in 2000; another calculates that 2.5 million people have already bought products or services on the Web; and a market research company predicts that Internet-based sales in the US will jump from $518 million in 1997 to $6.6 billion by 2000.

It is surprising, therefore, that relatively few companies have joined the bandwagon. Some, such as the virtual bookshop, Amazon.com, have been highly successful. Others report decidedly mixed fortunes. "People looking back five or ten years from now may well wonder why so few companies took the online plunge," writes Mark Hodges in *Technology Review*.

The reasons for this are many and varied, but security and privacy remain central issues for both customers and companies. Fears about privacy mean that customers can be unwilling to divulge financial details over the Internet. There is also confusion on the other side. Around 20 companies have software packages offering payment or security solutions. Hodges notes "the lack of compatibility between methods of processing Web transactions." As a result, it can be difficult for companies and customers to agree on a method of payment or to confirm each other's identity. "We're well down the path to digital anarchy," says one industry spokesman, calling for "a universal protocol between any wallet and any merchant." Until this is achieved, bandwagon boarders beware.

SEE: ECOMMERCE; EMAIL
MORE INFO: .com

Iridium

Motorola's Iridium Project is setting the pace in space. Its seven-star logo is now well known thanks to a $180 million advertising and direct mail campaign. The aim is satellite phones for the people, for 5 million people by 2002 in fact. The chief competition is Globalstar, a consortium hardly off the launch pad and a year behind Iridium. Taking your time, however, may not prove to be such a bad strategy.

SEE: MOBILE COMMUNICATION
MORE INFO: www.motorola.com

job titles

In the past, executives were addicted to introducing the word "strategic" into job titles at the slightest opportunity. One would have thought in the hierarchy-free age of Generation X and virtual organizations, job titles would have slipped off the executive agenda. Not so. The magazine, *Fast Company*, has a regular feature on job titles and they seem as loaded and important as ever.

Two approaches are popular. First, there are companies which are eliminating job titles. Disney, Harley-Davidson, Bloomberg, Microsoft and Silicon Graphics are among those reported to be dropping job titles. (It's names only at Bloomberg; Harley has abolished executive VPs, as well as machine operators and machine inspectors.) Then there are others which have allowed their imaginations to run riot with job titles with bells and whistles attached; fanfares for common men and women whether they are chief of strategic sourcing; chief quality officer; leader of change; or chief learning officer. All these job titles share one thing: you have no idea what they might involve. This is deliberate and undeniably useful.

"Technological developments and dynamic business processes certainly are the driving forces," says Louisa Wah of *Management Review*. "A new generation of workers, a new workplace culture and a break from tradition all call for a rethinking of job functions and the titles that reflect them." Some go the whole hog with titles including Vibe Evolver; Master of Madness and Pied Piper of Promotion. These say more about the lure of alliteration than anything else.

More seriously, job titles are signposts to corporate culture. They signal what the organization considers to be important. Appointing a Vice President of Diversity makes it clear that the company is dedicated to fair employment opportunities. Similarly, Chief Knowledge Officer is a statement of intent as much as a new job. After all, companies have been gathering and utilizing knowledge since time immemorial. The job title sends a message.

"There has got to be a change in the titles to show that employees do not belong to the old paradigm, but to a new paradigm," says one executive. "The important thing is that these titles must convey the true meaning they are used for. It's very important to make them compatible with the level of knowledge and the type of culture of the organisation." To work, job titles must describe the job. They must be meaningful to communicate.

SEE: **FREE AGENTS**

SOURCES: *Management Review*, June 1998; *Financial Times*, January 21, 1997

Jobs, Steve

In 1977, Steve Jobs conceived the Apple 1, regarded by many as the first real personal computer. Jobs and his technically brilliant partner Steve Wozniak built the first machine in a garage. They founded the Apple company. The Apple 2 followed, and then the Apple Macintosh with which it planned to conquer the world.

Instead of writing commands in computerese, Macintosh owners used a mouse to click on easily recognizable icons – a trash can and file folders, for example. Suddenly, you didn't need a degree in computer science to operate a personal computer. Other companies followed where Apple led – most significantly Microsoft. But while Apple remained the darling of the creative world, Bill Gates and crew never achieved the same iconoclast status.

One newspaper described Jobs as a "corporate Huckleberry Finn" (begging the question who was the corporate Tom Sawyer?), and said his early business exploits had already made him part of American folk history. The fairy tale story came to a sticky end in 1987 when former Pepsi chairman John Sculley, who had been brought in to add some corporate know-how to the wilting Apple, removed Jobs.

Sculley himself was booted out in 1993 after a disastrous period that saw Apple's market share plummet from 20 percent to just eight percent. He was replaced by Michael Spindler, who lasted until 1996, by which time market share had fallen to just five percent. Apple was staring oblivion in the face as its long-term devotees began to switch to the Microsoft-powered PCs.

Spindler was shown the door, and Gil Amelio stepped into the hot seat. After 500 days in post, Apple's market share had fallen to four percent and Amelio invited Jobs to come in and help. (Jobs was a friend and advisor to Amelio.) With two being a crowd, Amelio exited in July 1997 and got down to the real business of writing a book about his experiences – *On the Firing Line: My 500 Days At Apple.*

After a 13 year exile, Jobs was back. The iconoclast who founded the computer company with attitude was now its only hope of survival. The wheel had come full circle. The world has changed in the intervening period, but the Apple brand and the style of its famous founder remain well matched. The launch of the iMac seemed to mark a return to past triumphs. But, with Jobs, the future remains defiantly unpredictable.

Des Dearlove

SEE: **APPLE**
MORE INFO: www.apple.com

Jobs, Steve

Kim, W. Chan

The Korean W. Chan Kim is Professor of International Management at the top French business school, INSEAD. Kim was formerly at Michigan Business School and also studied at the Asian Institute of Management and Seoul National University. He is currently one of those select academics whose intellectual star is in the ascendant. This can be accredited to Kim's work along with Renée Mauborgne which has produced a series of articles and a forthcoming book (in 1999) on managing in the knowledge economy.

With diligent academic work, Kim and Mauborgne inject an air of common sense into the frenzied debate concerning knowledge. Among the concepts they champion is that of "fair process," which contends that "people care as much about the fairness of the process through which an outcome is produced as they do about the outcome itself." Fairness should permeate managerial systems. In a study of 19 companies Kim found that there was a direct link between processes, attitudes and behavior: "Managers who believed the company's processes were fair displayed a high level of trust and commitment which, in turn, engendered active co-operation."

Elsewhere, Kim and Mauborgne argue that successful companies are differentiated from the chasing pack by "the way managers make sense of how they do business." Outsmarting the competition involves challenging industry conditions; not benchmarking against competitors; focusing on what customers value; thinking like a start-up business; and thinking "in terms of the total solution buyers seek."

SEE: GARY HAMEL
MORE INFO: www.insead.fr

Kelsey, Serena

What do actor Nigel Havers, Oasis' Noel Gallagher, and landscape gardener Lord Kenilworth, have in common? The answer is, they all wear Serena Kelsey's clothes. Kelsey was a professional dancer before training as a tailor and designer. Soon she launched her own business, Kelsey Fine Tailoring in 1985. Her first shop opened in 1993, and in 1998 she added a second in the City and launched a ready-to-wear collection. A range of Kelsey-designed evening dresses is now on offer. "I want the Kelsey label to be instantly recognizable everywhere," she proclaims. All men have to lose is their pinstripes.

SEE: ALEX McQUEEN
MORE INFO: www.kelseytailors.co.uk
SOURCES: *Business Life*, December 1998

Kleiner, Art

Art Kleiner is a researcher, writer and educator. He teaches on New York University's Interactive Telecommunications Program. He is best known as the ghostwriter behind a string of successful business books. He worked as a "consulting editor" on *The Fifth Discipline* by Peter Senge, *The Art of the Long View* by Peter Schwartz, *Control Your Destiny* by Noel Tichy, *The Last Word on Power* by Tracy Goss, *The Living Company* by Arie de Geus and other less prominent volumes.

"Many business people don't know how to convert their speaking insights to the printed page," says Kleiner who began ghostwriting in 1989. It wasn't easy – "I felt tainted, like an honest trucker who drifted into contraband" – but well paid.

173

Kleiner's own work includes *The Age of Heretics* and *The Dance of Change*. He has also worked with MIT's George Roth in research examining the phenomena of workplace experience. Experience is one of the great mysteries of organizational life. Kleiner and Roth believe there are means by which companies can actively harness their own experience.

Kleiner and Roth say that "managers have few tools with which to capture institutional experience, disseminate its lessons and translate them into effective action." To do so, they suggest using a tool called the *learning history*: "a narrative of a company's recent set of critical episodes, a corporate change event, a new initiative, a widespread innovation, a successful product launch or even a traumatic event like a downsizing." The histories can be anything from 25 to 100 pages in length and are arranged in two columns. In one column the people involved in the events describe what happened. In the opposite column are comments and observations from grandly titled, "learning historians." These are consultants and academics from outside the organization, though people from inside the corporation may also comment. The commentary draws out the lessons, trends and conclusions which can be drawn from the narrative. The history can then be discussed by groups.

While this may all sound remarkably flaky – Kleiner and Roth believe it is related to ancient community storytelling – the observed benefits are worthy of consideration. The method, say the authors, builds trust. People are asked about their version of events. They can speak out, without fear, on subjects which may have concerned them for years – the contributions are anonymous. Most importantly, learning histories can allow an organization to transfer experience from one division to another. The end result, could be organizations which genuinely learn from experience, and "a body of generalizable knowledge about management."

SEE: GHOSTWRITING; BUSINESS BOOKS; WORDWORKS; STORYTELLING
MORE INFO: www.well.com
SOURCES: *Wired*, October 1998

Knowledge Universe

Knowledge Universe was founded by ex-junk bond king Michael Milken at the beginning of 1996, partnered by his brother, Lowell Milken, and Oracle CEO, Larry Ellison. Targeting the "education products market," Knowledge Universe now has majority interests in seven computer training companies as well as owning Symmetrix, a Boston technology consulting company, The Executive Committee (with 5000 member CEOs) and Children's Discovery Centers of America (20,000 students). Milken – partnered by Donaldson Lufkin & Jenrette – narrowly missed out on buying Simon & Schuster in Spring 1998. The media group, Pearson won that auction, where the prize was Simon & Schuster's educational publishing. Education, Knowledge Universe and others have decided, is where it's at. "The first focus has been on the IT training marketplace, but the end goal is to build a substantial broad-based business in education," said Joe Costella, the company vice-chairman. "IT is a good place to start because you can get the money needed to build the underlying technology, methodology and skills which then can be applied to other

Knowledge Universe

areas, such as K-12 and continuing education, where you couldn't build a business right off the bat."

SEE: MICHAEL MILKEN
MORE INFO: www.knowledgeu.com
SOURCES: *Computer Reseller News*, November 3, 1997

178

Lavelle, James

His life has been lived at such a speed that James Lavelle is now approaching middle age. The hyperactive Brit started his own record label Mo' Wax in 1991. Lavelle was 17. The son of a jazz drummer, Lavelle is a fixture in fashionable magazines and has fingers in a variety of musical pies: DJ; remixer; perfomer with his own group U.N.K.L.E.; and model. Lavelle has also branched out into the clothing business. He plays down the entrepreneur label, pinning his faith on culture rather than capital: "I had an original idea which I built up. I was obsessive about it. I've always been an obsessive person."

SEE: COOL BRITANNIA
MORE INFO: www.fly.co.uk/mowax.htm
SOURCES: *Business Life*, December 1998

leadership RIP

Leadership was once about hard skills – such as planning, finance, and business analysis. When command and control ruled the corporate world, leaders were heroic rationalists who moved people around like pawns. They spoke and the company jumped. Now, if the gurus and experts are right, leadership is increasingly concerned with soft skills including teamwork, communication and motivation. The trouble is that for many executives, the soft skills remain the hardest to understand, let alone master. Old style leadership RIP.

After all, hard skills have traditionally been the ones to get you to the top of the corporate ladder. "The entire career system in some organizations is based on using hard functional skills to progress," says Philip Hodgson of Ashridge Management College. "But when executives reach the top of the organization many different skills are required. Corporate leaders may find that though they can do the financial analysis and the strategic planning, they are poor at communicating ideas to employees or colleagues, or have little insight into how to motivate people. The modern chief executive requires an array of skills."

Indeed, some suggest that we are expecting too much. Renaissance men and women are rare. "Leadership in a modern organization is highly complex and it is increasingly difficult – sometimes impossible – to find all the necessary traits in a single person," says Jonas

Ridderstråle of the Stockholm School of Economics. "Among the most crucial skills will be the ability to capture the attention of your audience – you will be competing with lots of other people for their attention. The leaders of the future will also have to be emotionally efficient. They will promote variation rather than promoting people in their own likeness; they will encourage experimentation and enable people to learn from failure; they will build and develop people." Too much for one person? Dr Ridderstråle thinks so and predicts that "In the future we will see leadership groups rather than individual leaders."

This change in emphasis from individuals towards groups and teams has been charted by the leadership guru Warren Bennis. His latest work concentrates on the power of famous groundbreaking groups rather than individual leaders. His book *Organizing Genius* tells the stories of exceptional groups including Xerox's Palo Alto Research Center, the group behind the 1992 Clinton campaign, Lockheed's Skunk Works, and the Manhattan Project which invented the atomic bomb. "None of us is as smart as all of us," says Bennis. "The Lone Ranger is dead. Instead of the individual problem solver we have a new model for creative achievement. People like Steve Jobs or Walt Disney headed groups and found their own greatness in them."

Bennis provides a blueprint for the new model leader. "He or she is a pragmatic dreamer, a person with an original but attainable vision," he says. "Inevitably, the leader has to invent a leadership style that suits the group. The standard models, especially command and control, simply don't work. The heads of groups have to act decisively, but never arbitrarily. They have to make decisions without limiting the perceived autonomy of the other participants. Devising and maintaining an atmosphere in which others can put a dent in the universe is the leader's creative act."

As Professor Bennis' comments suggest, the role of the new model leader is ridden with paradox. For example, the leader has to be decisive and yet empower others to make decisions. "Paradox and uncertainty are increasingly at the heart of leading organizations," observes Robert Sharrock of business psychologists YSC. "A lot of leaders don't like ambiguity so they try to shape the environment to resolve the ambiguity. This might involve collecting more data or narrowing things down. These may not be the best things to do. The most effective leaders are flexible, responsive to new and emerging situations. If they are particularly adept at hard skills, they surround themselves with people who are proficient with soft skills. They strike a balance."

While flexibility is clearly important in this new leadership model it should not be interpreted as weakness. The two most lauded corporate chiefs of the last decade have been Percy Barnevik of Asea Brown Boveri (ABB) and Jack Welch of General Electric. Somewhat surprisingly perhaps, they share a number of characteristics. Both are incessant communicators with the capacity to endlessly repeat the same message to different audiences. Barnevik estimates that he spends one tenth of his time deciding on the strategy, and the rest communicating it.

Both Barnevik and Welch also dismantled traditional bureaucratic structures filled with strategists and overseers. They are adept at soft and hard skills. They continually coach and cajole, as well as command and control.

The leader as coach is yet another of those phrases more readily seen in business books than in reality. Acting as a coach to a colleague is not something which comes easily to many executives. Indeed, there appears growing demand for support for corporate leaders. Says Robert Sharrock: "It is increasingly common for senior executives to need one-to-one coaching and mentoring. They need a sounding board to talk through particular decisions – particularly people-related decisions – and to think through the impact of their behavior on others in the organization."

In the past such support may have been construed as weakness. In the era of macho, heroic leadership, support was for failures. Now, there appears growing realization that leaders are human after all and that leadership is as much a human art as a rational science. "Today's leaders don't follow rigid or orthodox role models, but prefer to nurture their own unique leadership style. They don't do people's jobs for them or put their faith in developing a personality cult," concludes Ashridge's Philip Hodgson. "They regard leadership as drawing people and disparate parts of the organization together in ways that make individuals and the organization more effective."

MORE INFO: www.funkybusiness.com

Leahy, Terry

Terry Leahy (born 1956) is the UMIST educated CEO of retailing group Tesco. Leahy is a mover and shaker within the Labour government – he is a member of the influential Demos think tank.

Tesco is one of Europe's most innovative and successful retailers. It is in the midst of a £500 million program building 22 new stores and creating 10,000 new jobs. It holds 15 percent of the UK market and, during his first year as CEO, Leahy oversaw a 9 percent increase in profits.

SEE: WAL-MART
MORE INFO: www.tesco.co.uk

Ledecky, Jonathan

Jonathan Ledecky is the founder of the multi-billion dollar corporation, US Office Products, and now heads Consolidational Capital Corporation and USA Floral Products. Before founding US Office Products, Ledecky spent 15 years in venture capital, merchant banking and corporate investment partnerships. He is a graduate of Harvard College and Harvard Business School.

MORE INFO: www.usafp.com

Lee, Kam-hon

Professor Kam-hon Lee holds one of the most intriguing academic positions in the world. He is Dean of Business Administration at the Chinese University of Hong Kong, a post resonant with geographical importance, political complexity, and the ideological paradox of studying capitalism in a communist country. "The 21st century is the Asia-Pacific century," Lee predicts. "Among Asia-Pacific countries, China is set to play an especially prominent role in that new order. Hong Kong will become of paramount importance in China. It serves, and will continue to serve, as the regional headquarters of business

zeitbite#28
Michael Dell

"It's easy to decide what you're going to do. The hard thing is figuring out what you're not going to do."

181

Lee, Kam-hon

operations in the region and is universally regarded as the business gateway to China."

Lee is also Professor of Marketing and has an impressive marketing pedigree. He has a PhD in the subject from Northwestern University, home of the doyen of marketing thinkers, Philip Kotler. Northwestern has close and developing ties with China – it has recently launched an executive MBA program with the Hong Kong University of Science and Technology (also run by a Northwestern alumni).

Lee's research focuses on cross-cultural marketing, strategic marketing and marketing ethics and has been featured in academic journals worldwide. Lee has also worked with the World Bank, the Hang Seng Bank, and Western giants including Coca-Cola and Proctor & Gamble. His influence may also be broadened with the development of the Asia Academy of Management which was set up in 1997, and in which the Chinese University of Hong Kong plays a central role.

"There are useful gener-alizations, but in manage-ment, con-text, timing, personality and history are every-thing. The challenge lies in developing judgement, knowing which tool to use rather than reaching for the ham-mer every time."

SEE: BUSINESS SCHOOLS

182

Levin, Mark

Mark Levin is a chemical engineer and biotech pioneer. Levin has worked for Miller Brewing and Genentech. He has also spent time as a project manager, in marketing and as a venture capitalist. His current aim is to boost the productivity of drug discovery by 50 percent. *The Economist* noted "the obvious omission from his curriculum vitae is time spent getting his hands dirty at the laboratory bench."

Levin's company, Millennium Pharmaceuticals (a name whose kitschness is only matched by its money raising powers) is based in Cambridge, Mass and was set up in 1993. It broke even by the end of the first five years – akin to turning an immediate and large profit in any other business. Now it employs 600 managers, technicians and scientists – it began life with 30. Millennium raised $1 billion, mostly through alliances with pharmaceutical giants. In 1998 it announced a $465 million agreement with the German drugs company, Bayer (giving Bayer a 14 percent stake in Millennium).

Levin, Mark

MORE INFO: www.mlnm.com

SOURCES: *The Economist*, September 26, 1998

Lexus

Toyota is now the third biggest car maker in the world (behind GM and Ford). It sells five million vehicles a year (1.3 million in North America, 2 million in Japan and 0.5 million in Europe). In Japan it has nearly 40 percent of the market. Its 1998 sales were $88.5 billion with a net income of $3.5 billion.

Toyota's production philosophy, and the carefully developed strength of its brand, reached its high point in 1990 with the launch of the Lexus. The Lexus was initially greeted as a triumph for Japanese imitation. Media pundits laughed at the company's effrontery – "If Toyota could have slapped a Mercedes star on the front of the Lexus, it would have fooled most of the people most of the time."

With the Lexus, Toyota moved the goalposts. It out-engineered Mercedes and BMW. Toyota is keen to tell you that the Lexus took seven years; $2 billion; 1400 engineers; 2300 technicians; 450 prototypes; and generated 200 patents. Its standard fittings include a satellite navigation system and much more. Toyota made great play of the fact that the car was tested in Japan on mile after mile of carefully built highways which exactly imitated roads in the US, Germany or the UK. Toyota even put in the right road signs.

183

While the product stood up to scrutiny, where Lexus really stole a march on its rivals was through the Lexus ownership experience. Even when things went wrong, the service was good. An early problem led to a product recall. Lexus had dealers call up people personally and immediately. Instead of having a negative effect it strengthened the channel. Lexus screwed things up like everyone else, but then they sorted the problem out in a friendly, human way. With the Lexus, Toyota proved that its capacity to stay ahead of the pack remains undiminished.

SEE: SATURN

MORE INFO: www.lexus.com

Lexus

LG

LG is another one of those Korean conglomerates that seems to have been involved in just about every shape and form of business in its 51 year history. Established in 1947 by Koo In Hoi as the Lak Hui Chemical company it started to manufacture cosmetics, while also developing a nice sideline in soaps and detergents. It followed that with a dabble in the plastics market which resulted in, among other things, the first domestically produced tube-form toothpaste. Then in 1958 it made a major move into the Korean electronics industry under the name of Goldstar and in another twist it also moved heavily into financial markets in 1969 with the formation of LG Securities.

In 1974, the name for the whole group was changed to Lucky Group (hence LG). The story ever since has been that of remorseless advances in foreign markets, and a burgeoning reputation for research and development breakthroughs in diverse products as robots, antibiotics, wide screen TVs, CD players and human growth hormones. Whether through luck or good judgement, the group is now a $73 billion business with 126,000 employees located in over 120 countries.

Trevor Merriden

SEE: DAEWOO
MORE INFO: www.lg.com

Lindahl, Göran

The Swede Göran Lindahl (born 1945) is CEO of the industrial colossus ABB. Lindahl was trained as an electrical engineer at Gothenburg's Chalmers University of Technology. He joined the engineering company ASEA in 1971. "He has a technical breadth and technical depth that far surpass my knowledge," observed his predecessor as CEO, Percy Barnevik. But Barnevik's are big footsteps to follow.

SEE: ABB
MORE INFO: www.abb.com
SOURCES: William Hall, "All the power but none of the glory," *Financial Times*, September 24, 1998

loyalty

During the more stable times of the 1950s and 1960s, the careers enjoyed by corporate executives were built on solid foundations. This was the era of corporate man (there was no such thing as corporate woman at this time). Grey suited and obedient, corporate man was unstintingly loyal to his employer. He spent his life with a single company and rose slowly, but quietly, up the hierarchy.

Implicit to such careers was the understanding that loyalty and solid performance brought job security. This was mutually beneficial. The executive gained a respectable income and a high degree of security. The company gained loyal, hard working executives.

This unspoken pact became known as the psychological contract, a kind of corporate loyalty bond. The originator of the phrase was the social psychologist Ed Schein of MIT. While the phrase is comparatively recent, blind corporate loyalty is longstanding. "The most important single contribution required of an executive, certainly the most universal qualification, is loyalty [allowing] domination by the organization personality," noted Chester Barnard in *The Functions of the Executive* (1938). (The word "domination" suggests which way Barnard saw the balance of power falling.) While loyalty is a positive quality, it can easily become blinkered. What if the corporate strategy is wrong or the company is engaged in unlawful or immoral acts? Also, there is the question of loyal to what? Thirty years ago, corporate values were assumed rather than explored.

Loyalty meant that executives were hardly encouraged to look over the corporate parapets to seek out broader viewpoints. The corporation became a self-contained and self-perpetuating world supported by a complex array of checks, systems, and hierarchies. The company was right. Customers, who existed in the ethereal world outside the organization, were often regarded as peripheral.

Clearly, such an environment was hardly conducive to the fostering of dynamic, risk-takers. The psychological contract rewarded the steady foot soldier, the safe pair of hands. It was hardly surprising, therefore, that when she came to examine corporate life for the first time in her 1977 book, *Men and Women of the Corporation*,

Rosabeth Moss Kanter found that the central characteristic expected of a manager was "dependability."

The reality was that the psychological contract placed a premium on loyalty rather than ability and allowed a great many poor performers to seek out corporate havens. It was also significant that the psychological contract was regarded as the preserve of management. Lower down the hierarchy, people were hired and fired with abandon. Their loyalty counted for little.

As the use of the past tense suggests, recent years have seen radical changes to the psychological contract between employers and employees. The rash of downsizing in the 1980s and 1990s marked the end of the psychological contract.

Expectations have now changed on both sides. Employers no longer wish to make commitments – even implicit ones – to long-term employment. The emphasis is on flexibility. On the other side, employees are keen to develop their skills and take charge of their own careers. Employability is the height of fashion.

As a result, the new psychological contract is more likely to be built on developing skills than blind loyalty. The logic is that if a company invests in an individual's development, the employee will become more loyal. The trouble is that the employee also becomes more employable by other companies.

In the age of flexible employment, downsizing and career management, conventional loyalty is increasingly elusive as managers flit from job to job, company to company. Yet, at the same time, some research suggests that free agents, the managers who take control of and responsibility for their own careers, tend to be more loyal to their new employers than their previous employers. The logic behind this is that those who have remained with their employer since 1989 have usually seen a decrease in opportunities and their view of the company has probably suffered a buffeting. Those who left tend, therefore, to feel that their decision was the right one and feel more benevolently towards their current employer.

Georgina Peters

loyalty

SEE: FREE AGENTS

MORE INFO: Ed Schein, *Organizational Culture and Leadership*, 1997; Ed
           Schein, *Organizational Psychology* (3rd edition), 1980

SOURCES: *Sloan Management Review*, Summer 1997

Lynton, Michael

The former Wall Street investment banker who is now CEO of Penguin Books. Educated at Harvard, Lynton (born 1960) became Penguin chief in 1997. His task was to bring his branding expertise to what he called "the only brand in publishing." Formerly with Disney, where he was responsible for *Crimson Tide* and *Mr Holland's Opus*, Lynton has produced a distinctive ad campaign for Penguin as well as moving Penguin into Internet publishing.

SEE: AMAZON.COM

MORE INFO: www.penguinputnam.com

zeitbite#31
Robert Fritz

"Style is not the essence of leadership. The essence of leadership is substance, including wise judgement, strength of character, clarity of purpose, and a generative nature with a strong dynamic urge towards values and aspirations. For the most part, leadership styles are irrelevant."

187

McGee, Alan

British record company exec best known for discovering Oasis. McGee (born 1960) is founder of Creation Records. He also owns the Reaction photo agency, one of the largest in Europe.

SEE: JAMES LAVELLE; COOL BRITANNIA
MORE INFO: www.creation.co.uk

McKenna, Regis

Chairman of the McKenna Group, Regis McKenna has been called the "granddaddy of hi-tech marketing." He would probably not welcome this description (but who would) though it has more than an element of truth.

SEE: MOTIVATIONAL SPEAKERS
MORE INFO: www.mckenna.com

McKinsey & Co

Conservative, a little on the staid side, but incredibly successful, McKinsey & Company remains the thought leader among consulting firms. It has been doing for years what other firms are only now discovering. In particular, it has nurtured its brand with care ever since Marvin Bower and AT Kearney split the company between them in the 1930s and Bower, sagely, took the McKinsey name rather than attaching his own name to the business. The McKinsey brand remains the touchstone for consulting firm brand wannabes. McKinsey has long been the number one choice of employer among top b-school graduates. The brand makes it much easier for McKinsey to attract the best people and the most prestigious clients.

"McKinsey's level of brand recognition and quality means that it is an automatic port of call for any company seeking high-level strategic consultancy services," says London Business School Dean John Quelch. "It achieved this positioning without any significant advertising. Instead, a distinct aim from the outset was to recruit top intellectual talent to be brought to bear on consultancy assignments. That intellectual talent is very important to the brand positioning. There is a strong tradition at McKinsey of encouraging people to write. This helped disseminate the idea of new thinking which is part of the brand positioning. There is also what can be called the IBM effect – no manager ever got fired for hiring McKinsey. The strength of the brand can help cushion management decision making, or even on occasion rubber stamp a management decision that has already been made."

No sign yet that McKinsey's touch has deserted it.

SEE: BRANDING CONSULTING FIRMS
MORE INFO: www.mckinsey.com

McQueen, Alex

The "bad boy of fashion." McQueen (born 1969) was trained at St Martin's School of Art in London. He has been chosen as Designer of the Year with John Galliano. McQueen is now head designer at Givenchy.

SEE: SERENA KELSEY; COOL BRITANNIA
MORE INFO: www.givenchy.fr

Management General

Originally a consulting company owned by Tom and Rita Brown, formerly of the Management Development Center in Honeywell Aerospace. Then began a printed, quarterly newsletter for its clients in the early 1990s. This metamorphosed into an online version, officially launched on January 1, 1997, with a ranking of the top business books and "ezzays" (the medieval essay, transformed for the 21st Century).

One thing led to another, Management General then began to publish e-books – and to get reader response while writing a book – and was reincarnated in early 1999 as the "New Ideas" Web site, publishing once a week. Now averages 35–50,000 hits per week; which translates to 1.5–2+ million hits per year.

SEE: BUSINESS BOOKS
MORE INFO: http://www.mgeneral.com or by e-mail to
response@mgeneral.com.

Manchester United

One of the world's greatest sporting brands outside North America is the British football club Manchester United. United has led the way in turning soccer into a true international and lucrative business. Until the early 1990s, the club was a long-term underachiever. It had failed to win the English championship for over 20 years – despite throwing money at the problem with something approaching abandon. Then its business and playing fortunes were revived. Success on the pitch continued and fed into rapid development of the club's brand. Merchandising – until the early nineties a peripheral activity – became big business. In 1999 the club became European champion for the first time in 31 years.

SEE: BRANDS
MORE INFO: www.manutd.com

marketspace

The INSEAD duo of W. Chan Kim and Renée Mauborgne has produced some of the most interesting work in the area of strategy over recent years. Companies, say Kim and Mauborgne, become mired in taking on their competitors in macho, head-to-head battles. If one company jumps ahead, the others follow by doing the same thing. Competitive advantage is short-lived and insubstantial – an incremental improvement here and there. Breaking free of the competition should be every company's objective. Only by creating its own "marketspace" can a company achieve significant competitive advantage.

To get out; look out. Kim and Mauborgne suggest that it is only by looking across industries rather than within industries that companies can develop the necessary insights to break free. They point to the example of Home Depot (as do virtually all business writers at the moment). Home Depot looked more broadly at the home improvement needs of its consumers and recognized that different consumers have different needs.

Kim and Mauborgne suggest that companies look at buyers within their industry, similar and complementary products, as well as "across the functional-emotional orientation of an industry." By looking at old data in new ways, inspirations and insights may arise.

SEE: CHAN KIM
MORE INFO: www.insead.fr

SOURCES: W. Chan Kim & Renée Mauborgne, "Creating new market
space," *Harvard Business Review*, January/February 1999

Mercedes-Benz

"Oh Lord, won't you buy me a Mercedes-Benz," Janis Joplin wailed, "My friends all have Porsches and I want to make amends." The appeal of the Mercedes-Benz brand was immortalized in a song. People understood: they wanted one as well.

At Daimler-Benz, where the illustrious brand resides, they put it slightly differently. "At Daimler-Benz the name 'Mercedes-Benz' is considered a synonym for the production of high-quality and innovative vehicles," the company's Web site proclaims with due solemnity.

But Daimler was not averse to a posthumous endorsement from Joplin. The company used her rendition in a recent advertising campaign. This is the magic of the Mercedes brand: it is a premium quality automobile brand which appeals to a wide range of people. The famous three-pointed star logo is one of the most widely recognized logos the world has ever known.

In a 1997 analysis of the leading global brands, the branding experts Interbrand, ranked Mercedes-Benz seventh, ahead of both Levi Strauss and Marlboro. The consultancy noted: "For many, Mercedes-Benz is the ultimate in status brands, embodying safety, heritage, and longevity."

The marque also has that special quality you can't quite put your finger on; an aura that surrounds the world's top brands. Impossible to describe, Mercedes drivers say, it is something you feel when you sit behind the wheel: a sense of having reached the pinnacle of human achievement in a certain field; a sense of having arrived; that cars really don't get any better than this.

At least, that's what Mercedes would like us to feel. And the company does everything it can to make that intangible experience real for the people who buy its cars.

The business press briefly hailed the company's charismatic chairman Jurgen Schempp as Germany's Jack Welch, the CEO credited with saving General Electric. He was dubbed Neutron Jurgen as he fought to slim down the monolithic Daimler machine into something more economically viable and fleet of foot. But even with a brand as powerful as Mercedes-Benz, the company could not survive alone. The question was who to couple its carriage to. The answer: a reinvented and greatly improved Chrysler in a deal code-named Operation Gamma.

The deal was sealed in early 1998, with a $40 billion merger of the two legendary auto brands. It combined Mercedes' brand muscle in the luxury car market with Chrysler's share of the volume market (attempts by Mercedes to crack the volume market with its own cheaper Mercedes branded offering called the A-Type had run into problems).

The deal was a reality check for many in the car industry. It underlined the dramatic game of survival being played out among the world's leading manufacturers. An editorial in *Fortune* observed: "The result, the largest industrial marriage in history, takes what had been the world's number 6 car company, Chrysler, and stuffs it into the trunk of erstwhile number 15 Daimler-Benz to produce the planet's fifth biggest automobile concern."

Valued at around $40 billion, the new company has 400,000 employees and is expected to generate around $130 billion in sales. Mercedes-Benz purists may mourn the passing of the company's German identity. But the deal guarantees the survival of one of the most famous brands in the world.

Des Dearlove

SEE: LEXUS; SATURN
MORE INFO: www.mercedes.com

MIT Media Laboratory

Deciding what to watch on TV is becoming increasingly complicated. The bewildered can blame the boffins at the Massachusetts Institute of Technology's Media Laboratory. Formed in 1980 by Nicholas Negroponte and Jerome Wiesner, it carries out advanced research into a broad range of information technologies. Aside from its pioneering work in the world of digital television, it is at the forefront of research into holographic imaging, electronic publishing and education.

Only a select few work and/or study there. Senior research staff number only 30 and graduate enrolment totals a little over 150. The Media Laboratory's annual budget is in the region of $25 million per year – more than 90 percent of its funding comes from around 150 corporate sponsors. Cash is allocated to four self-explanatory areas. These are Digital Life, News in the Future, Things that Think and Toys of Tomorrow. About half of the sponsors are from America, with a quarter each from Europe and Asia.

This focus on corporate support has helped the technology transfer of the Media Laboratory's projects into worldwide everyday use. New projects include electronic newspapers and wearable computers.

Trevor Merriden

SEE: **SANTA FE INSTITUTE**
MORE INFO: www.media.mit.edu

Meyer, Chris

For the executive of the new millennium, mountains of information and endless complexity lurk at every corner. Never has so much been so misunderstood and never has there been so much. Chris Meyer is one of those who has taken on the task of breaking through the mire and mythology of the information age. He is a sometime economist and Harvard MBA who has transformed himself into a high-tech consultant and author.

While at Mercer Management Consulting, Meyer founded the company's practice in IT industries. His eyes were soon opened. "Around 1980 I started getting interested in telecoms and IT and worked with NASA and ITT on the new generation of telecoms technology, fiber optics, digital switching and so on. It was a seminal project from my point of view. It taught me how telecoms systems of the world were set to change."

"How do you create strategy in the absence of a map?"

Meyer has been seeking to understand more about the emerging information economy ever since. He joined Ernst & Young in 1995 and heads the firm's Center for Business Innovation – an R&D shop which aims to identify the issues that will be challenging business in the future, and defining responses to them.

Meyer also established the Bios Group, Ernst & Young's initiative to develop complexity-based solutions for management. The entire challenge of making complexity theory understood and practical lies at the heart of Meyer's current work. Forget metaphorical butterflies. "I am interested in moving between the theoretical and the practical. I enjoy ideas but I also enjoy seeing the business world change. At the moment this is an area of huge opportunity because practice is up for grabs," he says. "Complexity, for example, can be applied to operational situations. People understand about the interaction of parts. You don't start with the factory, you start with the machinery. Big things are made up of small things – that's the way the world is."

Meyer is co-author, with Stan Davis, of *Blur*. At the heart of *Blur* are three forces: connectivity, speed, and intangibles ("the derivatives of time, space, and mass"). According to Davis and Meyer, this triad "are blurring the rules and redefining our businesses and our lives. They are destroying solutions, such as mass production, segmented pricing, and standardized jobs, that worked for the relatively slow, unconnected industrial world." The three forces are shaping the behavior of the new economy. They are affecting what Davis and Meyer label "the blur of desires; the blur of fulfillment; and the blur of resources."

The "blur of desires" has two central elements: the offer and the exchange. These were once clear-cut. In the product-dominated age, a company offered a product for sale. Money was exchanged and the customer disappeared into the distance. Now, products and services are often indistinguishable from each other, and buyers and sellers are in a constantly evolving relationship ("mutual exchange") which is driven by information and emotion as well as by money.

The second aspect of the new economic reality is "the blur of fulfillment." As organizations change to meet changing demands so,

Meyer, Chris

too, must the entire theory and practice of competitive strategy. Connectivity produces different forms of organization operating to different first principles.

The third leg to the economic stool is that of resources and the emergence of intellectual capital as the key resource. Hard assets have become intangibles; intangibles have become your only assets.

SEE: CONNECTIVITY
MORE INFO: www.ey.com

Milken, Michael

Michael Milken (born 1946) grew up in the suburbs of Los Angeles. His father was an accountant. He went to the University of California: Berkeley and later joined Drexel, Burnham, Lambert in 1970. He rose to become the king of the junk bonds. His junk habit led to charges of a number of financial transgressions which he admitted in April 1989. Milken was freed from prison in 1993. Since then, Milken has not sought out a comfortable retirement. He could – even after paying a fine of $200 million – afford a comfortable life. Instead, he has speedily returned to deal making. Milken's attentions are now focused on educational businesses and fundraising for cancer research.

SEE: KNOWLEDGE UNIVERSE
MORE INFO: www.knowledgeu.com

mobile information

Back in computing pre-history, there was the mainframe. Mainframes filled rooms. Now, they fill museums. Then mainframes were dramatically superseded by the PC revolution. PCs filled desks. Now comes life – and working life – beyond the PC. In this new business revolution, data constantly shifts, a moveable feast accessible and utilized by far more people than ever before. From being the preserve of the corporate few, data has become the lifeblood of the many.

Computing has moved from being dominated by hardware to a world in which hardware and operating systems matter less and less.

197

"All of our software is made available across every device, every operating system," says Jacob Christfort, director of Product Management and Marketing for Oracle's Mobile and Embedded Products Group. Now, access to the Internet has extended the boundaries of reach and utilization in much the same way as PCs did twenty years ago.

Greater access means more and more information. A trickle has become a deluge and, as executives with 50 daily e-mails to wade through are quick to tell you, more is not always good. In the information business, quantity and quality are rarely synonymous. This has prompted Larry Ellison to bemoan the "irrational distribution of data and complexity." "We're putting databases in hamburger stands, branch offices, and banks – it's all a mistake. A colossal mistake, this irrational distribution of information," warns Ellison.

The message is not that we are in danger of being swamped, but that how you manage the information is, increasingly, the key to competitiveness. How companies manage information can be a vital differentiating factor. A well-managed loyalty program which maxi-mizes data about customers is a potent commercial weapon. The more you know, the more you can customize products and services for individual customers, delivering exactly what you know they want. The opposite is also true: a poorly managed loyalty program is as likely to undermine loyalty as to build it.

Clearly, it is not only the amount of information which is crucial, but its timeliness and accuracy. If information has to be input by someone when they get back to the office or deciphered from notes made when they talked to the customer, it runs the risk of being slow and inaccurate. Yesterday's news on customer expectations and experiences is simply history. Today's news on customer expecta-tions and experiences is tomorrow's profits.

The trouble is that for many years data has been housed in the room with the mainframe or the office with a PC. Companies have made history – but not in the way they would have liked. They have created instant relics. A salesman would visit a customer and dutifully record an order before going back to the office to enter it into the company database; a service engineer would arrive, identify the problem and then depart to order the necessary parts, only returning a few days later when the parts arrived. Once out of the office, factory, warehouse or depot, the humble employee was basically out of touch. Data was often already old when it was recorded.

The case for enabling data to be put into a database speedily and accurately while people are out of their usual place of work is easily made. Allowing people to gain access to corporate data while on the move enables better decisions in the field – no need for that call to HQ to check the figures – and improved customer relations; a customer's needs can be put instantly into the system. The lift engineer can order the parts immediately and receive them within the hour. No need for a cost-consuming and customer-annoying second visit. The salesman can place a customer's order on the spot. No need for the reams of paperwork.

Technology means that the business case can now be made into reality. Armed with small handheld computers, people can access corporate and public information no matter where they are. Mobile information is the new reality. In the US it is estimated that 25 percent of the workforce is mobile and this figure is projected to grow by 75 percent by the end of the year 2000. (In this case, mobile workers are defined as those who spend 20 percent or more of their time away from their desk or make use of mobile communications.)

Of course, network computing was built up as the savior of the working world. While network computers have not become as pervasive as many anticipated, Personal Digital Assistants (PDAs) have emerged in their place. After getting off to a slow start, PDAs have metamorphosed from fashion accessories to genuine business tools. With PDAs in operation, network computing is actually more prevalent than ever before – it is just used in ways not imagined at the outset.

PDAs can now carry a database. This effectively squares the mobile circle: PDAs don't have a hard disc but can still run a database; they combine power, connectivity and mobility. There is also the price. While laptops remain more expensive than desktops, PDAs can cost one tenth of the price of a laptop.

mobile information

All this means that offices are set to become emptier. Mobility beckons.

SEE: FREE AGENTS
MORE INFO: www.oracle.com

Motorola University

Perhaps the best known corporate university, Motorola University ("an instrument of renewal" according to the company) opened in 1981 as the Motorola Training & Education Center. It now has 20 offices in 13 countries on five continents, supplies 550,000 student days a year and costs the company $170 million. Every single Motorola employee – and there are 139,000 – is expected to receive at least 40 hours of training per year. The company has also developed its own international MBA program. Motorola calculates that every dollar invested in training reaps $33. The only difference between the Motorola U and a conventional university is that it doesn't have a football team.

SEE: CORPORATE UNIVERSITIES; DISNEY UNIVERSITY
MORE INFO: mu.motorola.com
SOURCES: *Human Resources*, May/June 1996; mu.motorola.com

motivation

zeitbite#33
Don Sull

"Managers need first-rate Plutarchs, not second-rate Adam Smiths."

If you believed everything you read in the business press, the business world would be entirely populated by jargon-speaking free agents, flitting from project to project, from one interesting assignment to the next. According to the fashionable pundits, corporate loyalty is dead. Today's employee is loyal to no one but themselves.

Perhaps, somewhere in California, working life really is like that. Meanwhile, back in reality, many millions of people continue to work in much the same way, working much the same hours, as they have done for decades.

Sad? Some would say so. The champions of free-agency would suggest that remaining with the same organization for 10, 15, maybe 20 years, is mutually unsatisfactory. The employee becomes jaded, comfortable and complacent; hardly good news for any organization. The bright and ambitious new arrival is surely preferable to the cynical long-term resident with an eye on retirement and a gift for corporate maneuvering.

The flip side of this is that an organization populated by people whose loyalty is at best fleeting and, at worst, elsewhere is hardly likely to take the world by storm. Indeed, it is more likely to be riven with political intrigue, uncertainty and insecurity. Short-term employees have eyes only for the short term; free agents are set on their individual freedom and success rather than team goals. "Mercenaries tend to move on and not become marines. Can you build a company with a mercenary force?" asks Sumantra Ghoshal of London Business School, co-author of *The Individualised Corporation*.

Luckily perhaps, the talk of an army of mercenaries appears overblown. "At its worst the free-agency argument is extremism. We exist in a trading environment. Companies trade flexible hours, decent pay, and working with colleagues, for our loyalty," says Brian Baxter senior partner at organizational development consultants Kiddy & Partners.

Research by Incomes Data Services found that in 1993, 36 percent of men had been with the same employer for ten years or more. This was at the peak of downsizing mania. Interestingly – and surprisingly given the hysterical talk of the emerging promiscuous workforce – in 1968, 37.7 percent of men had been with the same employer for ten years or more.

More research from Business Strategies forecast that 79.2 percent of all employees would be in full-time permanent jobs in 2005 – compared with 83.9 percent in 1986. The revolution has been postponed.

For better or worse, people stick around. Even after downsizing, the flurry of demographic time bombs and talk of Generation X, working life retains a strong element of security. It may be unfashionable to spend thirty years working for a single employer but many people do. Some undoubtedly do so because they have limited opportunities elsewhere, limited ambition or limited abilities. These are facts of life generally ignored by the free-agent propagandists.

motivation

But many choose to stay. They choose to do so presumably because they find their work and working environment stimulating, rewarding or enjoyable. Indeed, some of the corporate titans of our age are devoted company loyalists. Perhaps the best known is GE's Jack Welch. Feted far and wide as the very model of the modern CEO, Welch joined the company in 1960. No one suggests that his loyalty has been misplaced.

With nearly 40 years of service, people like Jack Welch may appear to some as a throwback to a more naïve, even simplistic age. It was never meant to be like that. In the 1970s pundits envisaged the leisure age; in the 1980s they talked of flexible working, a world of teleworkers. Well, the technology now exists and teleworking remains a decidedly minority pursuit. "The failure of teleworking to really catch, on despite the availability of the technology, demonstrates that some sort of a physical relationship is important to people at work. People want to feel part of a team and of something much bigger. They want to be connected," says Gerry Griffin, director of global PR firm Burson-Marsteller and author of *The Power Game*.

Corporate loyalty is engendered by the fact that conventional working life still holds a remarkable attraction. Its immediacy makes business sense. In business, being there remains of crucial importance. "The psychological dynamics of business means that conversations in corridors or over coffee actually move the business forward," says Brian Baxter.

The point is developed by consultant psychologist Robert Sharrock of YSC. "A lot of people are motivated by their social needs and many also like to compartmentalize their home and working lives," says Sharrock. "Perhaps more important is the need managers often have to feel that they are managing. Managers make an impact, make a difference and get results by talking to people, walking around and listening to people. They need to be there and for people to be there."

The reality is that people are loyal to the environment they spend every day in, and to their colleagues. "What corporate life can offer are the benefits of any good community – support, direction and exchanges of ideas and solutions," says Richard Stagg editor-in-chief for business books at publishers Financial Times Prentice Hall. "With

motivation

the right culture, the right structure and the right people, it's easy to behave entrepreneurially within the corporate universe. You can draw on the company's resources and wisdom, while moving quickly all the time. The trouble is that most corporations tend towards sluggishness; trading creativity and risk for conformity and control. That's when independence beckons."

While the traditional attractions of office life remain, it is true that companies no longer have an aura of permanence. They change with accelerating regularity. "The profusion of joint ventures, mergers and acquisitions, means that peoples' roles now change more regularly. In the past, people might have filled two or three roles in 15 years with a company. Now, they are likely to change every three years or so," says Michael Greenspan of Kiddy and Partners. This, perversely perhaps, can actually encourage people to stay. If you want a fast moving, stimulating, constantly changing environment, why move when it is happening all around you and you're a player in making it work? If you stay with a company for ten years or more, change will happen. You either develop your own skills and move forward with the organization or you leave.

All this is not to say that the corporate man of the 1950s and 1960s is alive and well. "Passive obedience was once mistaken for loyalty. The entire notion of loyalty was wrapped up with control. Now, people are not loyal in a slavish sense," says Brian Baxter. "This is based on the realization that you can question the system without being disloyal."

Today's employees are more questioning and demanding. They are loyal but confident enough to air their concerns, grievances and aspirations. If they were customers, we would call them sophisti- cated. (It is perhaps significant that we tend not to.) "People are now more likely to question the action behind the corporate rhetoric. As a result the HR and internal communications functions are much more important," says Burson-Marsteller's Gerry Griffin. Indeed, internal communications has emerged as an industry in its own right, reflecting the need for companies to create communication channels with their own people.

motivation

Central to the demanding nature of employees is the notion of values. In the past, loyalty was basically bought. Job security, gradual progression up the hierarchy and a decent salary were offered by the employer. In return, the employee offered unwavering loyalty and a hard day's work. Now, values determine loyalty. Values motivate. "Every organization needs values, but a lean organization needs them even more," GE's Jack Welch says. "When you strip away the support systems of staffs and layers, people have to change their habits and expectations, or else the stress will just overwhelm them."

A report produced by consultants Blessing/White, "Heart and Soul," studies the impact of corporate and individual values on business. "Values have two critical roles: a company that articulates its values enables potential recruits to apply a degree of self-selection. Values also provide a framework to match individual career goals with the organization's objectives," observes the report.

Among those companies which have sought to nurture a sense of values is Anglian Water. It formulated its vision and a values statement in 1998. The company's senior executives have since been travelling throughout the company to communicate directly with employees. "Stating the values was an acknowledgment of the changing nature of our business and that we needed to change the way we worked," says Anglian Water HR business manager Ian Plover. "We won't and can't do anything without the support and involvement of our employees." Plover – 23 years with the company – admits that loyalty is a question of belief. "I believe in what we do. There is a feeling of camaraderie in doing something for the community and a level of empowerment within the company," he says. "Though the days of a job for life have gone, people need a feeling of safety and of being led. They need to know that their pay is fair and reasonable and that they have a say. They need to feel ownership."

The challenge for organizations is that values are more complex than mere money. Values cannot be simplistically condensed into a mission statement or neatly printed onto an embossed card. "In the past there was a belief in one set of values. Now, in more sophisticated companies, there is an awareness that the uniqueness of the firm comes from multiple values and cultures. Previously,

motivation

people's needs were interpreted as being homogenous. Now there are flexible benefits and working arrangements and recognition that people are motivated by different things. Organisations have to understand what motivates individuals. Money and power don't work for everyone," says Brian Baxter.

With values becoming an increasingly important aspect of motivation, it is little wonder that companies are paying them more attention. Indeed, in the modern world, companies are crucial in identifying and developing the values which shape society. "The corporation is a value creator in modern society. In our secular world, corporations create belief systems, values which people buy into," says Gerry Griffin. Companies are the great institutions of our age. In the past, value systems were created by the church and the state. Now, companies have distinct and strongly defined value systems which we may – or may not – buy into. The choice is ours.

"Companies increasingly resemble tribes," says Jonas Ridderstråle of the Stockholm School of Economics. "Companies have to find people who share their values. Recruiting is now about finding people with the right attitude, then training them in appropriate and useful skills – rather than the reverse. We can no longer believe in the idea of bringing in smart people and brain washing them at training camps into believing what is right."

For the better executives clearly there is a choice. They work for companies which are in accord with their own value systems. If they don't want to work for a polluter, they will not. After all, people want to hold their heads up when they are with their peers. They don't want an embarrassed silence when they announce who they work for. "These days we value a great mission and a great working lifestyle as much as a bigger desk and the prospect of promotion," says publisher, Richard Stagg. "Who gets out of bed in the morning for a distant corporate objective? If a company gives real meaning to people's work, and the freedom and resources to pursue their ideas then it's a good place to be." Values, it seems, are the new route to developing loyalty among employees.

All of this is not to suggest that corporations are workplace nirvana. A healthy strain of skepticism is evident among those who spend their lives within corporations. "It helps to have the power of a big brand behind you and, of course, there's always unlimited coffee, fax paper and internet access," says one manager. "Corporations can be good places in which to learn skills, make mistakes, discover talents, build networks and identify the right personal or market niche before doing your own thing." Motivation must be earned in new and different ways.

SEE: LOYALTY
MORE INFO: www.fastcompany.com

motivational speakers

A handful of individuals have created substantial businesses on the back of their talent to energize the corporate troops. Ken Blanchard, author of *The One Minute Manager*, runs Blanchard Training & Development from San Diego. It has estimated annual revenues of $15 million. The king of them all, business wise at least, is Stephen Covey with his Covey Leadership Institute in Provo, Utah. Covey has turned himself into a one-man industry. His books include *The Seven Habits of Highly Effective People* (six million copies in 32 languages), *Principle Centered Leadership* and *The Seven Habits of Highly Effective Families*. There is also a profitable newsletter, *Executive Excellence*; consulting and Covey's seminars (daily rate $50,000-$75,000).

Of course, the market in motivational speakers is nothing new. Dale Carnegie, author of *How to Win Friends and Influence People* (over 15 million copies and still selling) can probably be credited with its invention. Over 40 years after his death, Carnegie's brand of self-help is still big business. The company bearing his name prospers and his book even reached the German bestseller lists when it was re-released. It is surely no coincidence that Covey studied American "success literature," of which Carnegie is a prime example, before coming up with *The Seven Habits of Highly Effective People*.

The man who really created the modern motivational speaker business is Tom Peters. From being a staid McKinsey consultant, during the 1980s Peters transformed himself into a business equivalent of Billy Graham. His seminars became bigger and bigger events. Sweating profusely and stalking the auditorium, he holds audiences in a spell. He shouts. He implores. He laughs. Like any natural performer, Peters knows exactly what he is doing. "I do pretty good seminars because I know when to screw with people's minds. You can take them to the brink and pull them back," he admits. With no need to work again, Peters (current daily rate $70,000–90,000) continues a hectic schedule of seminars, perennially globetrotting armed with a pack of ever changing slides.

The motivation industry remains thoroughly American. People like Zig Ziglar, "the world famous motivator," are barely known in Europe. Yet Ziglar charges between $30,000 and $50,000 per day for his seminars. Though it is an American-based industry, motivation is a universal issue. This suggests that the market for motivational speakers is here to stay.

Whether they perform a worthwhile service is debatable. After the initial excitement, the willingness to act becomes dissipated among the fogs of corporate ennui and politics. (This is why all the motivational gurus sell books, videos and cassettes – Anthony Robbins cannot be there to help, but listening to him for five minutes might recharge your batteries.)

Undoubtedly, the feel-good factor can be short-lived. Back in reality, bravado can speedily evaporate. It is here that quality becomes an issue. The lazy speakers endlessly – and cynically – repeat the same material. Others are constantly updating and adding to their repertoire. The degree of motivational impact is usually related to the quality of the message. Some motivational speakers can talk all day without actually adding a great deal to the sum of human knowledge. The best combine mastery of the medium with a meaningful and useful message.

SEE: ANTHONY ROBBINS; STEPHEN COVEY
MORE INFO: www.franklin-covey.com

Murdoch, Elisabeth

In an inheritance race not everyone can win, Elisabeth Murdoch (born 1968) looks like being a loser in the race of the Murdoch dynasty. Educated at Vassar College, married at 25 to a Ghanaian (now separated), Elisabeth was dispatched to London to learn about the media business in the sizeable shadow of Murdoch's UK satellite TV chief, Sam Chisholm. Her planned mentor soon departed and as chief executive of BSkyB, Elisabeth has been left to learn the ropes the hard way. She appears to have largely succeeded.

SEE: RUPERT MURDOCH
MORE INFO: www.newscorp.com
SOURCES: *The Economist*, September 5, 1998

Murdoch, Lachlan

Rupert Murdoch is a hard act to follow. This makes the decision of his children to follow careers in News Corporation all the more surprising, ill-advised or brave, depending on your opinion. The question of which of Lachlan, Elisabeth or James was to be Rupert's successor was discussed from every angle. Lachlan (born 1971) is now designated heir apparent; "first among equals," the choice of the children according to their father. Lachlan is cutting his teeth as managing director of the Australian part of the Murdoch empire. He is also on the board of News Corporation. A media empire is his for the taking. The question is when.

208

SEE: RUPERT MURDOCH
MORE INFO: www.newscorp.com

Murdoch, Rupert

Keith Rupert Murdoch – KRM to his employees – is probably the most famous businessman in the world, whose power and influence is only matched by his profits and ambition. The *Washington Post* has called him "the global village's *de facto* communications minister."

Murdoch (born 1931) has referred to the early institutions which formed him: at Toorak Presbyterian Church (his grandfather preached there sometimes); Geelong Grammar School; and Flemington Race Course. Their influence was not necessarily made in that order.

He was educated at Geelong Grammar and was then despatched to England in 1950 to go to Oxford University's Worcester College where he studied economics. He then worked on Fleet Street as a sub-editor at Lord Beaverbrook's *Daily Express*.

In 1952 Rupert inherited the *Adelaide News* and *Sunday Mail* from his father. The *Adelaide News*, as left by Sir Keith Murdoch, was an uninspiringly small newspaper. The Murdoch inheritance was no empire. To it, Rupert brought youthful vigor, and a willingness to embrace the mass market. Murdoch took to business life easily. As the ink dried and the presses whirled, deals were struck. In 1960, Murdoch bought the Sydney *Daily Mirror* and tested the water in the television market. Various deals came and went.

Perhaps the boldest sign of Murdoch's broadening ambitions came in 1964 with his founding of *The Australian,* the country's first national newspaper. However, the first international deal which shaped the media image of Murdoch was the purchase of the British Sunday newspaper, the *News of the World* in 1969. Next, Murdoch began to roll out a brash new form of populist journalism with the purchase for less than £500,000 of another British newspaper, *The Sun*, in 1969.

Others soon followed. Among them was the *New York Post* bought by Murdoch in 1976. His relationship with the *Post* has been a typically complex saga. He lost control of it in 1988 – because he bought a local TV station, WNYW – and then regained control in 1993 when the newspaper was acquired once again by News Corp.

In 1981, Murdoch marked a remarkable new chapter in his career when he bought *The Times*, fighting off bids from the newspaper's editor (William Rees-Mogg) and a group of journalists, as well as from the editor of the *Sunday Times,* Harold Evans, and the inevitable Robert Maxwell.

In Wapping, in the East of London, he built a new printing plant which didn't need union labor. Computers were installed which meant that editorial content could be transferred directly to the page. On January 25, 1986 four million newspapers were produced at Wapping. This precipitated war.

Murdoch, Rupert

Technology

Etak Inc
Fox Interactive
HarperCollins New Media
Kesmai Corp
News Electronic Data

Entertainment

Fox Television Stations (22 stations)
Fox News Channel
Fox Sports Net (part owner)
Family Channel (part owner)
F/X (cable TV)
SF Broadcasting
LA Dodgers
Twentieth Century Fox
Twentieth Television
JSkyB (part owner)
British Sky Broadcasting (part owner)
Star Television
Los Angeles Dodgers

Publishing

HarperCollins
Mirabella
The Times Literary Supplement

Newspapers

New York Post
Weekly Standard (Washington)
News of the World (UK)
The Sun (UK)
The Sunday Times (UK)
The Times (London)
Sydney Sunday & Daily Telegraph (Australia)
Melbourne Herald Sun (Australia)

Over the following months, Wapping became a battlefield. Thousands of pickets, from the print unions and others, attempted to bring printing at the plant to an end. The protests were increasingly violent and raged throughout most of 1986. The end result was complete victory for Murdoch. The printers were paid off with £60 million and disappeared into history. Murdoch was left with a massively more efficient operation and substantially reduced costs. Valuations of News Corp soared from $300 million to $1 billion.

During the 1980s, Murdoch created his empire. Acquisition followed acquisition. His aspirations appeared ever bolder. In 1985 he acquired Fox Studios; seven Metromedia TV stations followed in 1986; and, in 1988, he paid Walter Annenberg $3.2 billion for *TV Guide*.

The spending flurry was impressive but it was built on a mountain of debt which made Robert Maxwell look the very model of financial prudence. The beginning of the 1990s marked a watershed. News Corp's fabulous debts – $7 billion and counting – nearly brought it to its knees. Only a last minute deal at the beginning of 1991 saved Murdoch's empire from ignominious collapse.

Month after month, the deals keep coming. Look at Murdoch's headline making deals during a mere six months in 1998:

- March 1998: bought the LA Dodgers baseball team for $300 million (the previous record paid was $173 million paid for the Baltimore Orioles).
- April 1998: acquired distribution rights to the new series of *Star Wars* films.
- June 1998: sold the 13 million circulation *TV Guide* to TCI's Universal Video Satellite Group for $2 billion.
- July 1998: Murdoch announced that he was floating off 20 percent of Fox group to help reduce News Corp's debts of $6.5 billion.

The end result is a personal wealth now calculated at many billions of dollars – anything from $3 billion to $10 billion depending on what

Murdoch, Rupert

you believe. Murdoch's is a truly global empire – according to *Asia Week*, Murdoch is the fourth most powerful person in Asia. The total assets of News Corp (as of March 1998) were $33.2 billion and the company had total annual revenues of US$13 billion. The News Corp empire includes BSkyB, News International, the Los Angeles Dodgers, HarperCollins, 20th Century Fox, Fox TV, Star TV and many more. Over 780 businesses in 52 countries. It is a huge global business empire which brought us *Titanic* and *The Simpsons* as well as delivering a daily diet of scurrilous gossip. News Corp not only owns many companies, it has shares in many other ventures. These criss-cross the earth and cross political affiliations – for example, News Corp has invested in ChinaByte a joint venture with the *People's Daily* newspaper in China.

In 1997 Murdoch quietly announced that the Murdoch family stake in News Corp now belonged to his children. While the Murdoch family owns 36.2 percent share of the company, it is, to all intents and purposes, Rupert Murdoch's company. News Corp is Murdoch's corporate empire – and what an empire.

Georgina Peters

SEE: ELISABETH MURDOCH; TED TURNER
MORE INFO: www.newscorp.com
SOURCES: *Washington Post*, December 7, 1997

Murdoch, Rupert

National Basketball Association

In 1996, the National Basketball Association (NBA) amassed $1.2 billion from ticket sales and television rights. Ten years previously, the figure was $255 million. Promotions, sponsorships and an array of commercial links brought in $3 billion (against $107 million in 1986).

What is interesting about this is that the actual product is very limited. The NBA has a mere 29 teams. Nor is basketball a universally popular sport. Name a British basketball team or player? Yet, the NBA has succeeded because of its expertise in brand development.

In *Radical Marketing*, Glenn Rifkin and Sam Hill identify a number of elements crucial to NBA's success. First, it has developed line extensions – such as a professional woman's league. Second, the NBA has built and nurtured a plethora of strategic alliances. It has worked closely with retailers and television networks. Third, it has gained visibility while others have footed the bill. When Michael Jordan advertises Nike, he is also advertising the NBA. And, finally, it has a happy knack of keeping its name in the news.

Behind this are a number of other important elements – an astute leader, high quality standards throughout the use of the NBA brand, motivated workers (on the court and off) and a global perspective. The question must be whether this recipe for brand success can outlast the career of the man who did much to ignite it, Michael Jordan.

SEE: BRANDS
MORE INFO: Glenn Rifkin & Sam Hill, *Radical Marketing*, 1998
SOURCES: *Strategy & Business*, Third Quarter 1997

Neuro-Linguistic Programming

Critics of Neuro-Linguistic Programming (NLP) suggest that it is moonie management. They may well be right. NLP is basically the systematic use of language to exert influence over people. It is built on the recognition that voice quality is 38 percent of the total impact of the communication. Control that and you control the result of the conversation.

NLP has yielded an impressive crop of jargon. There is "syntactic ambiguity" (an ambiguous sentence where a verb plus *ing* can serve either as an adjective or a verb – such as influencing) and tonal marking ("using your voice to mark out certain words as being significant.")

SEE: BUSINESS BITES

New Pig Corporation

Despite its name, the New Pig Corp. has to be taken seriously. With more than 300 employees and anticipated sales of $77 million in 1998, New Pig is growing at a healthy annual rate of 10 percent. But then, you don't have to take the company that seriously. After all, its employee cafeteria is called the Pig Trough and its catalog is known to one and all as the Pigalog.

New Pig is not a PR firm with a slick line in irony. It sells a range of 2500 cleaning, absorbent and containment products to manufacturing companies virtually all through direct mail. Items like absorbent socks and mats are neither sexy nor particularly amusing. To each unheralded product, New Pig brings the Pig brand. The New Pig branding is all pervasive. There are boar facts and the catalog even features a Pork Avenue collection of Oink products, including the oinking pig hat and the oink sweatshirt. The company can be called on 800-HOT-HOGS, and its HQ is One Pork Avenue.

There is, New Pig cheerfully admits, nothing clever and strategic behind the New Pig brand. The aim is to draw people in and make dull products fun. It works. There is no doubt that branding the previously unbrandable has given the company a competitive advantage. Imitators have tried to make inroads into the market – there have been snakes and gators – but all have lacked the elan of New Pig.

The consumer catalog, launched in July 1997, is an attempt to move the company into the household products market – worth around $10 billion – where New Pig initially aims for sales of more than $10 million in five years. This is part of a reinvention of the company's business. New Pig UK was launched in 1993, and in 1997 New Pig bought control of the Fritz Group – the training, consulting and software applications part of Fritz's activities.

SEE: ROBERT FRITZ
MORE INFO: www.newpig.com

Nike

zeitbite#36
Bill Gates

"Size works against excellence."

For years Nike's "Just do it" slogan seemed to sum up its whole approach to business. Between 1995 and the first half of 1997, the sports shoe company with the distinctive whoosh logo sprinted from $4.8 billion to $9.2 billion in sales, capturing almost half of the US sports shoe market. At the same time, it continued its expansion around the globe. Since then growth has slowed.

Nike made its name – and much of its money – in basketball and America's jogging boom, both markets that are now saturated. After a hiccup in 1993–94, the company realigned itself: "We decided we're a sports company, not just a shoe company," said CEO Phil Knight.

The new view of itself translated into advertising and sponsorship deals aimed at a wider sports audience. In particular the company promoted a message that we can all be athletes in our own way, and at our own level. Product association was critical to the brand strategy.

In 1997, Nike spent an incredible $5.6 billion on marketing, including $4 billion on sponsorship for individual athletes; Tiger Woods and Michael Jordan are two of Nike's key stars. But with its traditional sports of basketball and jogging running out of puff, the company is looking for other sports fields to play on. To achieve Knight's stated goal – a turnover of $2 billion by 2002 – the company has targeted soccer as one of its core sports.

In the 1998 soccer World Cup, hosted by the eventual winners France, it sponsored Brazilian star Ronaldo, Maldini of Italy and England's Sheringham and Scholes. The company also shelled out $400 million for a ten year deal with Brazil and another $120 million to the US Soccer Federation to sponsor the American team – figuring the sport has to explode there some time.

Nike

The brand's massive advertising spend concentrates on a passion for sport. This has gradually evolved into a metaphor for the aspirations consumers have. Recently, Nike has experimented with a new slogan to augment, but not replace its classic "Just do it." The new slogan is "I can."

Nike is based in Beaverton, Oregon. Its verdant headquarters near the city of Portland, reflects its obsession with sport. CEO Knight views his empire from an office in the John McEnroe building. Such fanaticism is in keeping with a company that began life designing shoes for serious athletes.

Knight launched the company in 1964 with Bill Bowerman, his former track coach at the University of Oregon. The idea for the company came from an MBA project when Knight was at business school at Stanford. Knight believed that by importing shoes, made using cheap labor in Japan, he could undercut the market leader Adidas. He started with running shoes. But one morning Bowerman had a better idea.

According to Nike folklore the sports coach made an outsole by pouring a rubber compound into a waffle iron. Sports shoe technology would never be the same again. Nike was ready to break away from the pack.

This still lends kudos to the brand with aspiring sports stars. Over the years, Nike also cultivated a highly competitive management style which mirrors the spirit of sportsmen and women on the field.

The company went public in 1980. Since then, market capitalization has increased by over $12 billion – from $386 million to $13 billion. On a $100 shoe, the manufacturer's profit is around $20 to $25.

More recently, the mighty Nike brand has looked less sure-footed. Sales dipped by 8 percent in the third quarter of 1997, and the company was left with piles of inventory in its warehouses. The company has had knock backs before. In the mid 1980s Knight tied the company in knots with a misguided expansion plan, and sales also tripped up in 1994.

Nike

But in recent times Nike has also experienced other problems. On October 18, 1997, pressure groups in the US organized a series of demonstrations worldwide against Nike's use of cheap labor in developing economies. Allegations of subsistence-level pay rates, worker intimidation and the use of child labor, which have dogged Nike for several years, culminated in protests in 50 US cities and 11 countries.

Nike reacted to the criticisms with a range of defensive measures designed to refute the claims while also protecting the company's public image. It joined Apparel Industry Partnership, a new group of clothing manufacturers that hopes to eradicate the use of sweat-shops, by enforcing an industry-wide code of conduct in their overseas factories.

It also severed its relationship with some of its contractors in Indonesia because they did not adhere to Nike's code of conduct, and introduced a system of penalties for other factories failing to meet all of the company's standards.

Nike bashing, however, remained a popular sport. Garry Trudeau also lambasted the company in his Doonesbury cartoon strip, and the film *The Big One* featured Knight in its critical examination of corporate America. The company was also accused of treading on toes as it tried to push its way into the soccer market.

The 1998 World Cup involved more than just a clash of playing styles. France 98 brought the marketing teams of Nike and the resurgent European sports shoe brand Adidas into a penalty shoot out for the biggest prize in soccer – $4.5 billion worth of sportswear sales. Nose to nose were two new products. Adidas had its new Predator Accelerator boot, while leading Nike's counter attack was its Mercurial boot – "genuinely designed" by the Brazilian star Ronaldo.

The tussle illustrated the approach that has made Nike such a formidable brand. "Those Nike guys call it war, we call it competition," observed an Adidas spokesman. A Nike manager preferred to see it as a sporting contest: "Emotionally, Nike executives are like top

STATE-OF-THE-ART SNEAKER TECHNOLOGY

1979: The Tailwind – the first shoe to feature Nike-Air cushioning.

1983: The Pegasus

1985: The Epic

1987: The Air Max

1991: The Air 180

1993: The Air Max

1994: Air Max 2

1997: Zoom Air

1998: Air Zoom Citizen

sportsman – very focused, very determined, hardworking ... They want to win."

"Our hope is that Ronaldo plays in the World Cup Final and scores a goal ... wearing our boots." In the event, Ronaldo did play in the final – a mysteriously disappointing appearance that almost caused a riot. He did not look like scoring. Brazil were roundly beaten by the host nation France. (It was also suggested that Nike had somehow put pressure on Brazil to include their star player despite the fact that he was obviously not fully fit.)

"Just do it," however, does not translate easily into French; the result is the French slogan: "Ta vie est à toi" – your life is your own. What does translate is the Nike brand essence, which is all about passion for sport.

Des Dearlove

SEE: BRANDS
MORE INFO: www.nike.com
SOURCES: Ronald Lieber, "Just redo it," *Fortune*, June 23, 1997

Nonaka, Ikujiro

Ikujiro Nonaka's work reached a big audience for the first time with the success of *The Knowledge-Creating Company*, which he co-authored with Hirotaka Takeuchi. Nonaka's prominence culminated in May 1997, with his appointment to the first professorship dedicated to the study of knowledge and its impact on business at the University of California's Haas School of Business. Nonaka is also professor of management at Japan's Hitosubashi University but is no stranger to the University of California from where he has both an MBA and a PhD.

Nonaka and Takeuchi's 1995 book was at the vanguard of interest in managing knowledge. In it the duo argued that Japan's industrial success was grounded on innovation. But why is Japan more innovative than the West? The answer from Nonaka and Takeuchi is that the West emphasizes "explicit knowledge" – things which can be measured and monitored – while the Japanese value "tacit knowledge," the elusive and abstract. The West is hidebound by its faith in rationalism; the East enabled by its "oneness of body and mind." Interestingly, Nonaka and Takeuchi also speak up in favor of middle management. Rather than regarding middle managers as the burdensome masses, they suggest that they are a vital conduit for innovation, a voice of reason below the chaotic creativity of the top.

Nonaka has gone on to write *Relentless* (with Johny K. Johansson), a populist insight into the art of Japanese marketing.

SEE: INTELLECTUAL CAPITAL
MORE INFO: *The Knowledge-creating Company,* 1997

Nordström, Kjell

Your typical business guru is an American academic in a dull suit who runs through a well worn presentation and then collects his check. Kjell Nordström (born 1958) and his partner Jonas Ridderstråle (born 1966) are different. They are Swedish, young and have shaved heads. They do gigs not seminars. They are not Michael Porter. In fact, the only similarity between the Swedish duo and conventional gurus is their jobs – they are academics at the Stockholm School of Economics. In unconventional times, Nordström and Ridderstråle are building up a sizeable following throughout Scandinavia and increasingly beyond. Their seminars are sell outs. Their ideas focus on globalization and innovation. In a world of suits, Nordström and Ridderstråle's message is refreshingly different. A book, *Funky Business,* hopes to bring their ideas – and their shaven heads – to a wider audience.

SEE: CORE COMPETENTS
MORE INFO: www.funkybusiness.com

NPR costs

Companies typically spend 20–25 percent of sales with third party suppliers, for goods and services not directly related to the end product or services of the business. These Non-Product Related (NPR) costs sometimes exceed those spent directly for the end product. NPR goods and services consume considerable budgets and those budgets are usually rising. John Houlihan of consulting firm Booz-Allen & Hamilton is one of the experts in the emerging field looking at the dynamics of NPR sourcing.

zeitbite#38
Bill Gates

"The only big companies that succeed will be those that obsolete their own products before somebody else does."

Its importance is obvious. Typically, NPR goods and services account for over 20 percent of sales. Managed more rigorously, NPR sourcing's hidden value can be substantial. According to Houlihan, often around 25 percent of annual NPR expenditure can be saved with 15 percent achievable within two years. This can be equivalent to around two to four percent of sales – and may exceed this amount.

Among the organizations which have already reaped the benefits of playing closer attention to NPR are a major Dutch bank which realized annual savings of 21 percent on its printed material; a UK government agency which saved 23 percent on its cleaning services; and a German electronics company which saved between 30 and 40 percent on its telecommunications expenditure.

Houlihan emphasizes that there is more to NPR management than mere cost cutting. Managing the purchasing of NPR goods and services more professionally can have a much broader impact, with improved overall organizational effectiveness and enhanced strategic capabilities, as it encompasses such activities as advertising, transport, research services and information systems. The wonder is that apparently well managed companies have overlooked NPR goods and services for so long.

SEE: DIVISION OF MENTAL LABOR
MORE INFO: www.bah.com
SOURCES: John Houlihan, "How to capture hidden value," *Strategy & Business*, first quarter, 1999.

NPR costs

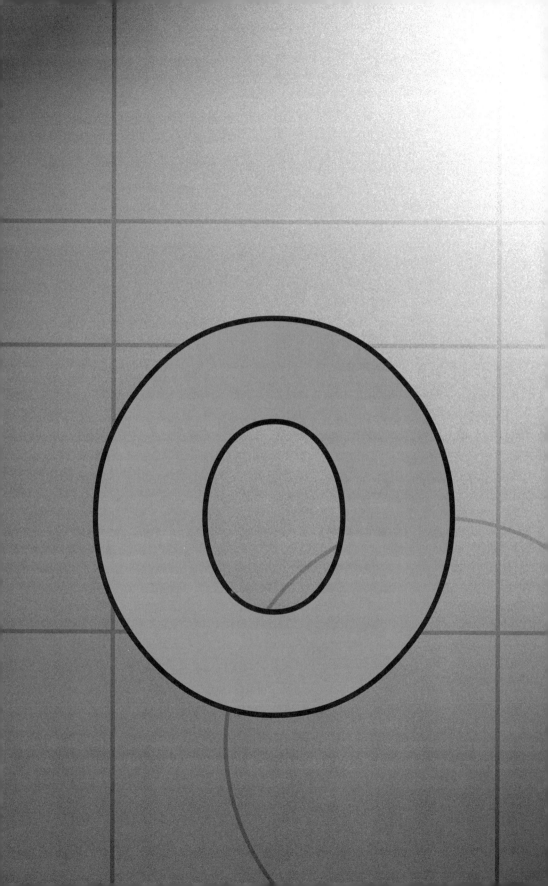

On line analytical processing

You can have all the data in the world, but you still have to do something with it. What you do is what matters. More data means that business analysis is becoming ever more important. Data warehousing enables a larger number of people than ever before to carry out detailed and complex analysis of customers, products and markets. On line analytical processing (OLAP) gives you the opportunity to carry out analysis to discover the reasons behind what is happening. (In the past, databases told you what was happening, but not why.)

The emergence of analysis is mapped out by Sam Hill, of Helios Consulting, who labels this "the age of analysis." "Every time we step up to the counter to buy an airline ticket we step into the age of analysis. The reservation agent quotes a price developed by the airline's yield management system. Every single night this system analyses the capacity available the following day on every plane and every route. It then sets 20,000 fares to optimize the trade-off between discounting prices or losing passengers to other carriers," says Hill. "With every trip to the local supermarket, to the book store, to the doctor's office, we enter the age of analysis. There is as much analysis at work in the supermarket at the corner as in a routine satellite launch. Few of us even give this a passing thought as we wheel our carts down the aisle." Data warehouses enable companies to carry out this analysis to achieve mass customization. OLAP is the most direct route to tomorrow's customer.

SEE: DATA WAREHOUSING; HELIOS CONSULTING

Online Originals

Online Originals is one of those bright ideas which you wish you had thought of first. The British company publishes books by unsung authors, on the Internet. You can browse through sample chapters at the company's site – www.onlineoriginals.com. Then, if you decide to buy, the book is sent to you electronically. The 36 books currently available include everything from Patricia le Roy's novel, *The Angels of Russia*, to the weighty *Evolution in the Systems Age*. All books cost £4, of which the authors receive half. Readers can read the books on their palm pilots.

The people behind Online Originals are David Gettman and his two partners, Doug Alexander and Christopher Macann. They launched Online Originals early in 1997. "The publishing industry is dominated by three huge companies," says Gettman. "So, there is huge commercial pressure on publishers. They can't have loss leaders. They are scared of taking risks." Online Originals is making a mark with its mix of fiction and non-fiction. Books are available in French and English. German is soon to be added. Ideas and manuscripts are pouring in. The 16 original titles have mushroomed. David Gettman and his partners are not quite new Michael Dells. So far, the venture pays expenses and little more. They all have proper jobs – Gettman is a communications consultant – and are willing to watch the business grow. "We have a very valuable brand. Reading books in this way is foreign to many people," says David Gettman. "It is a narrow field, but it will grow."

SEE: ECOMMERCE; BUSINESS BOOKS
MORE INFO: www.onlineoriginals.com

O'Reilly, Tony

O'Reilly is still a big player – though generally quiet with it. While others are rarely out of the media spotlight, O'Reilly slips in and out. Pity. His story is one of the best – from Irish rugby international to head of one of the world's great corporations to an occasionally troublesome reinvention as a newspaper proprietor.

SEE: RUPERT MURDOCH

organizational agility

A neat phrase championed by one of the most thoughtful of American management thinkers, Richard Pascale. Pascale argues that even the most successful organizations eventually find themselves grinding to a halt. Inspiration dries up; enthusiasm dissipates; stagnation results. This can only be avoided if an organization pursues seven disciplines of agility – which range from the self-explanatory "accountability in action" to the more elusive and painful "course of relentless discomfort." The organizational future lies in being flexible while strong; moving nimbly but surely.

Interestingly, Pascale is an admirer of the intensive training methods used by the US army, though he admits that converting their methods into the corporate world is handicapped by the fact that "all it takes is 650,000 acres and a million dollars a day." Even so, organizational agility means that it is preferable to be a ballet dancer than a muscle bound marine. So when the CEO says: "Forget the outdoor training exercise in the mountains, let's go to the ballet," nod knowingly about the lessons in organizational agility which await.

SEE: BUSINESS SCHOOLS
MORE INFO: Richard Pascale, *Managing on the Edge*, 1990

Oticon

The only Danish hearing aid maker to be regularly featured in the business press, Oticon began life in 1904. Based in Copenhagen it is renowned for its innovative approach to management. Its "spaghetti structure" was instigated by president Lars Kolind (born 1948).

Kolind was headhunted to the company in 1988 and introduced some refreshingly different ideas. These included the concept of having multi-jobs, flexible working arrangements, flexible offices and an emphasis on informal communication. To make his point about getting rid of memos, the company's entrance hall was redesigned to feature a huge paper shredder which cheerfully shredded the company's paper production.

In addition to these changes, employees bought 20 percent of the company's shares. The results have been an impressive ad for spaghetti: by 1995 the company was making profits of £42 million on a £78 million turnover.

SEE: KJELL NORDSTRÖM
MORE INFO: www.oticon.com
SOURCES: *Business Life*, February 1998

Owen-Jones, Lindsay

Lindsay Owen-Jones (British, born 1946) began working life selling sachets of shampoo in Normandy, France. He continues to do so as chairman & CEO of L'Oréal. In between he was marketing director for the French consumer products division, president and CEO of the US agent, Cosmair, and vice chairman and general manager of the company.

Since taking over the helm of L'Oréal in 1988, Owen-Jones has transformed its performance. The cosmetics company based in Clichy, a small suburb of Paris, accounts for 12 percent of the world market. It is reported to sell 80 products a second through over 400 subsidiaries and 500 brands. Owen-Jones has helped make it into a truly global company (domestic sales are now 18 percent vs. approaching 40 when he took over; L'Oréal owns Maybelline in the US).

A rugby player and racing driver manqué, Owen-Jones went to Oxford University and has an MBA from INSEAD. He joined L'Oréal in 1969 as a product head. His apprenticeship was a peripatetic one – six countries in 18 years. "I try to be an inspiration, a coach and a critic," he says. He is reported to want managers who are "poètes et paysans," poets and men of the soil.

zeitbite#40
Gary Hamel

"Harder doesn't get you any-where."

SEE: BRANDS
MORE INFO: www.loreal.fr
SOURCES: *Guardian*, July 25, 1998

227

Owen-Jones, Lindsay

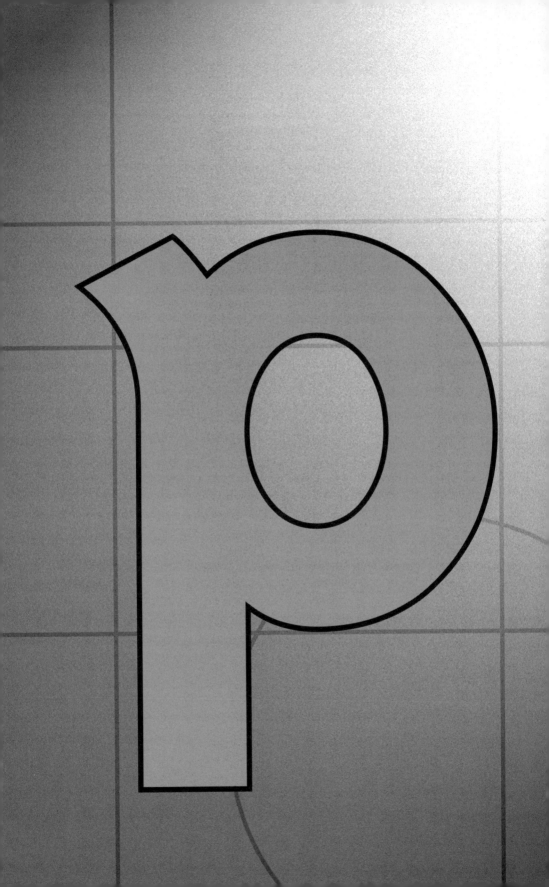

PA Consulting

"Branding is important for consultancies, and it is becoming a lot more important," says Jon Moynihan, executive chairman of PA Consulting Group which has 50 offices worldwide, over 3000 employees and revenues of over $500 million. "The Big Five are spending an absolute fortune on branding. They are determined to turn the consultancy market into a branded market so the client automatically thinks of a shortlist of names. They are all seeking to differentiate themselves from each other. As the consultancy market continues to globalize and a few behemoths get a grip on it, this raises the question of whether branding consultancy is any different from other products and services. We think it is."

Moynihan suggests that in the quest for clients, mass advertising is an expensive sledgehammer to crack an elusive nut. "Buyers are incredibly sophisticated," he says. "It's a mistake to assume that the consumer will be responsive to content-free broadcast branding attempts. The big auditing firms are spending $100 million a year plus. It's money thrown away in an attempt to bludgeon the client. What these firms don't seem to realize is that when you're talking about branding to chief executives, it's not the same as trying to make them buy Coca-Cola instead of Pepsi. Yet all these firms have accepted it. The advertising agencies have boondoggled the consulting firms into thinking this sort of advertising works."

PA, he says, prefers to target key audiences rather than take a blunderbuss and fire it into the crowd. "Thought leadership is the well spring for everything we do," he says. PA is one of the few consulting firms to nail its colors so definitely to the ideas mast.

Des Dearlove

SEE: BRANDING CONSULTING FIRMS
MORE INFO: www.pa-consulting.com

Palm Pilot

Palm Computing brought us the Palm Pilot. It sold over one million units in its first 18 months. The Palm Pilot took off. Dataquest expects 8 million to be sold in 2002. As technology moves on, the

Palm Pilot more closely resembles a PC. It already has a steadfastly devoted fan base – including its own fanzine, the brilliantly entitled, *Brave Palm*.

SEE: MOBILE INFORMATION
MORE INFO: www.palm.com

Pensare

Surfing in on the surge of interest in training is Pensare. Two years old, Pensare is based in Los Altos, California. It is developing software to use corporate networks to help train and appraise employees. Among its projects is a leadership program being developed with Harvard Business School Publishing. The aim is to automate the bureaucracy of training. Its online interactive programs uses emails to contact participants.

SEE: KNOWLEDGE UNIVERSE
MORE INFO: www.pensare.com
SOURCES: *Financial Times*, October 19, 1998

Postel, Jon

Jon Postel, "God of the Internet" according to one obituary, died in 1998 following heart surgery. With his long gray bread and pony tail, Postel was every inch the spokesman of the Internet as world communication tool. His work was deadly serious. Postel was the head of the Internet Assigned Names Association – the only coordinating body for the Internet responsible for issuing the numbers which designate every web address. Postel was closely involved in formulating the future management of the Internet. No one was as qualified. Postel's creation, the Arpanet, was a predecessor of the Internet.

SEE: TIM BERNERS LEE
MORE INFO: www.domainhandbook.com/postel.htm
SOURCES: *Financial Times*, October 19, 1998

power

If Rosabeth Moss Kanter was right when she declared that "power is America's last dirty word," then it is now time for corporates to wear the word on their sleeve with pride.

power

Empowerment was only ever a hollow rhetoric – a feel-good sap to the employee base, to project the image of the "new man"-agement. Like the new man, new management was not afraid to show its vulnerability. It was not reluctant to say that it did not have all the answers – that there could be a different way of approaching the task.

But underneath that vulnerability there still beats a heart of stone - as if we ever believed otherwise. Yes the words have changed – we are "encouraged to consider options" rather than explicitly ordered to do another's bidding. But as Led Zeppelin would remark – "The song remains the same."

It is a song of control and compliance. People want power, not to implement their beliefs but to savor the exercise of power over another. Power is seductive, it is addictive – once tasted it is hard to yield up. Your beliefs and ideals, in fact, are mere rungs on the ladder to success – a means of achieving power – and they mask the selfish drive to savor power once in the "power-club."

Power is essentially an amoral entity – although the blind pursuit of any goal can be damaging. Without power, nothing will happen, but like electricity, power is also capable of great destruction. It is futile to question the "will to power" because we desire what we desire. It is pragmatic to regulate its use, however, for power unchecked will destroy all – including the user.

Gerry Griffin

SEE: REPUTATION MANAGEMENT
MORE INFO: www.powergame.com; Gerry Griffin, *The Power Game*, Capstone, 1999

Powys, John Cowper

Whether it be E.M. Forster, Jane Austen or Henry Fielding, a literary relic is rediscovered to massive acclaim and much talk of movie rights every year. Next up maybe John Cowper Powys author of *A Glastonbury Romance* among others. Powys died in 1963. From a marketing point of view, Powys has the attraction of having connections throughout the UK: Derbyshire; Hardy-country (Dorset);

and Wales, as well as the US – he lived in New York state for a while. He is also largely unknown and unread and thus can be "re-interpreted," modernized and cannibalized at will. Look out for the movie.

pressure groups

Institutions are collapsing all around us. Nation states no longer hold sway. Political parties occupy the ethereal middle ground. Corporations no longer dictate the world of work. The church is on its knees. Among the emerging institutions are pressure groups such as Amnesty International and Greenpeace. They are the respectable institutions of the future.

SEE: POWER; REPUTATION MANAGEMENT
MORE INFO: Gerry Griffin, *The Power Game*, Capstone, 1999

zeitbite#41
Peter Drucker

"99.9 per-cent of your customers couldn't care less about your product or service. You are not that impor-tant in their universe."

Rebuck, Gail

Gail Rebuck (British, born 1952) is one of the most high-profile European executive women. Educated at the Lycais Francais and Sussex University, Rebuck is now chairman and CEO of Random House in the UK. "Books have great influence. They can transform people's lives," she says. Rebuck's personal transformation may lie ahead after Random was taken over by German media company, Bertlesmann.

SEE: COOL BRITANNIA
MORE INFO: www.randomhouse.com

Renaissance Solutions

Consulting firm of David Norton, joint creator of the Balanced Scorecard concept Founded in 1995.

SEE: BALANCED SCORECARD
MORE INFO: Robert S. Kaplan and David P. Norton, *The Balanced Scorecard*, 1996
SOURCES: www.rens.com

Republic Industries

The future of car retailing? Some believe so.

SEE: BALANCED SCORECARD
MORE INFO: www.republicindustries.com

reputation management

In the beginning it was easy if you were a journalist writing about the business world. If you wanted to talk to a CEO, you called them up and spoke. It was a happy and easy relationship – journalists got their quotes and occasional scoops; managers got their free publicity. And then, in a flurry of check writing and press releases, this relationship was re-invented as public relations.

Executives were no longer free to talk at the drop of a hat. Appointments had to be made and their public relations adviser had to be present to ensure not a word out of turn was uttered. "What Jeremy really meant to say ..." they regularly interjected to justify

Company

Republic Industries

Subsidiaries Include

Republic Industries, Inc Alamo Rent A Car/Nat. Car Rental System/AutoNation .

Address

110 SE Sixth St. Fort Lauderdale, Florida 33301 USA

Phone: 954-769-6000 Fax: 954-769-6408

http://www.republicindustries.com

Business

Specialist Retailer – Auto Industry

Statistics Fiscal Year End Dec

Employees	1997	56,000
Annual sales (millions)	1998	$17,487.3
Annual results (millions)	1998	$499.5
Other facts		Largest car dealer in US. Top US car rental company.
Hoover's 500		#164
Fortune 500		#151

their vast retainer. Now, public relations is being reinvented once again as reputation management.

Rep Man, as it is no doubt called by some, is where PR gets all strategic. "Reputation management must be co-ordinated with the traditional corporate functions of marketing, finance, human resources, communications and operations and it must inform relations with all the company's stakeholders," explains one expert in the field, before going on to recommend that companies appoint a chief reputation officer (CRO). Clear?

Reputation management is an attempt to move PR into a bright new world where the charges are higher and PR isn't looked down upon as mere media relations. The beauty of RM (as connoisseurs are already calling it) is that it is all-embracing. It advocates bringing media relations, communication strategies, crisis management and community relations under one comforting umbrella.

238

Cynics – and there are always one or two as soon as PR is mentioned – might suggest that reputation management is simply a means of widening the power of public relations. They, of course, would be right. But this overlooks the sheer genius of reputation management: the name itself. Who, in the corporate world, ever said yes to a bad reputation?

SEE: SPIN DOCTORS; POWER

Robbins, Anthony

The toothsome master of motivation, Anthony Robbins has carved a highly lucrative niche for himself as the Sylvester Stallone of motivational gurus. Robbins is permanently tanned and grins broadly from every publicity shot ever taken. Failure is not on his agenda. Indeed one of his trading names is The Unlimited Success Group Inc. Through his motivational seminars, he promises the world and more. He is, the hype tells us, "one of the greatest influencers of this generation." Robbins' four "infomercials" – thank you so much for sharing them with us Mr Robbins – "have continuously aired on average every 30 minutes, 24 hours a day somewhere in North America since their initial introduction in 1989." Anthony speaks and sells in capital letters. Lower case is for losers. "When you enroll with Anthony Robbins & Associates you will learn how to get all the MONEY, LOVE, LUCK, CONFIDENCE and SUCCESS you would ever want … IMMEDIATELY!"

It may not be subtle, but it works – for Anthony Robbins at least. His daily rate is a healthy $75,000 plus and he is in demand throughout the world. Among his clients are "members of two royal families", Andre Agassi, the Los Angeles Kings, and, somewhat bizarrely, the city of Sheffield.

Robbins is also founder and dean of Mastery University – "a year-long educational experience which he facilitates along with a faculty with unmatched qualifications." Mastery U is not Harvard. Robbins explains: "We are an entertainment culture, living in an entertainment age. Many educational enterprises fail to achieve the results they desire for lack of one simple idea: most people would much rather be entertained than educated. The 21st century educator must be an extraordinary Entertainer who Educates people with the finest tools, and Empowers them to act upon them. I call this philosophy, E3." What would you call it?

SEE: STEPHEN COVEY; MOTIVATIONAL GURUS
MORE INFO: www.tonyrobbins.com
SOURCES: www.tonyrobbins.com

rock star securitized loans

When times were tight, rock stars could usually be persuaded to record an album of cover versions and embark on a world tour. Now, there is no excuse for execrable versions of rock classics or needless tours. Securitized loans mean that aging rock stars can raise money against future royalty earnings in a tax efficient way. It is a win-win deal: jam today and jam tomorrow.

The bandwagon started rocking and rolling in 1997 when David Bowie raised $55 million against future royalties (a deal arranged by Fahnestock, the US investment bank). Bowie owns the master tapes of his recordings, putting him in an exceptionally strong position. (Bowie is also highly imaginative in marketing himself – his initiatives include BowieNet, and downloading singles from his web site).

In April 1998 another rocking relic, Rod Stewart, clinched a $15.4 million securitized loan from Nomura Capital – though, unlike Bowie, he did not own the master tapes. Many more are sure to follow.

MORE INFO: www.davidbowie.com

Rubbermaid Inc.

Rubbermaid Incorporated is a multinational manufacturer with three leading brands and four core businesses. These are Rubbermaid Commercial Products, Rubbermaid Household Products, Little Tikes Juvenile Products and Graco Infant Products. It produces more than 4000 different products in all, sold in 100 countries both at retailers and direct to consumer. The company now employs more than 12,000 staff across the world.

The firm started life in 1920 as the Wooster Rubber Company, a toy balloon manufacturer. At around the same time James R. Caldwell, started to make rubber dustpans after noticing that his own metal dustpan was chipping the paint of the wall from which it was hanging. He soon followed this up with rubber draining board mats, soap dishes and sink plugs. Caldwell called his new venture, Rubbermaid. Before long Wooster Rubber Company and Rubbermaid joined forces, with Caldwell as president, trading under the name of the former but making the products of the latter.

By 1957, the company had changed its name to Rubbermaid Inc., capitalizing on the strength of its brand name. In 1959, it listed for the first time on the New York Stock Exchange and grew rapidly over the following twenty five years. By 1984 it made its first appearance in the Fortune 500 and by the mid-1990s it had exceeded $2bn in annual sales. During this time, it also achieved the distinction of a number one ranking for two years running in the Fortune Survey of "America's Most Admired Companies."

The company has production plants in Australia, Canada, France, Great Britain, Ireland, Japan, Korea, Luxembourg, Mexico, Poland and the United States. The European and Asian Headquarters are located in Belgium and Singapore respectively.

Rubbermaid Inc.

But, aside from the detail, the Rubbermaid story is simply that bright ideas can make the dullest products exciting. If it takes genius to make the mundane exciting, Rubbermaid has it in dustpans full.

Trevor Merriden

SEE: NEW PIG CORPORATION
MORE INFO: www.rubbermaid.com

Rubin, Harriet

Harriet Rubin first came to prominence as the publisher of the original business blockbuster, *In Search of Excellence*. She is founder and publisher of Doubleday/Currency and author of *The Princesca: Machiavelli for Women*.

SEE: BUSINESS BOOKS; FAST COMPANY
MORE INFO: Harriet Rubin, *The Princesca*, 1997

241

St Luke's

In a previous life St Luke's was the London office of the California-based Chiat/Day agency. St Luke's is the rarest of things: an avowedly ethical advertising agency. Barely two-years old, St Luke's is the ad agency behind the British government's £18 million Welfare to Work campaign. With its own distinctive approach to the ad business it is challenging the way companies think not just about advertising but about the fundamentals of running a business.

Based in London, staff at St Luke's hot-desk with a degree of enthusiasm rarely found elsewhere. Telephones are radio-based and small enough to fit into a pocket. Calls follow employees from place to place. Client meetings are held in "brand rooms." Once a client signs up with the agency, they are allocated a conference room which is fitted out in the style and culture of the brand, and which they can use whenever they choose, calling on St Luke's staff as required. (So, the room set aside for Boots No. 17 make-up range is furnished with its target teenage-buyer in mind, complete with bunk beds and posters of pop stars on the walls.)

St Luke's is completely employee owned, with staff – now numbering over 100 – given a further equal equity stake in the business at the end of each year.

Des Dearlove

SEE: ?WHAT IF!; COOL BRITANNIA
MORE INFO: Andy Law, *Creative Company*, 1998

Santa Fe Institute

You may not think that there is much of a connection between ants and share prices. But talk to staff at the Santa Fe Institute (SFI) in Northern Mexico and you will probably come away with a completely different view. The SFI is a private, non-profit research and education center, founded in 1984. It is devoted to the study of what it calls "emerging sciences," in particular the science of complexity, which examines underlying patterns behind a wide assortment of real-world phenomena.

The SFI is unique in that it actively discourages traditional academic barriers that prevent scientists of different backgrounds working together. The reasoning is that while such barriers have been created when dealing with the issues and problems of the past, the issues of the future require fresh approaches across disciplines. At the SFI you will find political scientists and nuclear physicists sitting down with a biologist to discuss, say, the emergence of new life forms.

The 150 scientists working there over the course of a year (there are about 35 in residence at any one time) and visitors range from brilliant but raw undergraduates to Nobel prizewinning veterans. Many of those invited to stay are there for months rather than years but use the contacts they have made to collaborate on long-term projects. And, yes, these include (among many other things) stock market dynamics and the collective behavior of insects.

Trevor Merriden

SEE: BRIAN ARTHUR
MORE INFO: www.santafe.edu

SAS Institute

If a company wishes to attract lots of press coverage as well as the pick of local recruits, it needs to do one thing: look after its employees. This is about as simple as business gets, but it is a point which is proved time and time again. Few companies demonstrate this more vividly than the software company, SAS Institute.

SAS's initiatives are many and varied. Its base in North Carolina includes a large gym (large enough for two basketball courts), a health clinic and day-care facilities. Other benefits include M&Ms distributed every week (employees may not like them, but it is something journalists always write about), massages, family benefits, a 35-hour week, live music in the canteen and so on.

As you would expect if you had read motivational theorists from Douglas McGregor to Rosabeth Moss Kanter, SAS is hugely successful; its 1997 sales were $750 million. More to the point, in an age in which corporate loyalty is rare, SAS has a staff turnover

SAS Institute

rate of 3.7 percent. (The figure is not an aberration – it has never exceeded five percent.) As a result, it makes massive savings in recruitment and training costs – enough to pay for an awful lot of massages.

"SAS places enormous emphasis on three things: employees, customers, and products," says Charles Fishman writing in *Fast Company*. "Employees and customers, for instance, are surveyed every year. The company says, that 80 percent of the suggestions for product improvements that customers make most frequently, eventually find their way into the software. SAS plows 30 percent or more of its revenue (that's revenue, not profit) back into R&D – a higher proportion than any other software company of its size." The message is that good business can be good for you and can be extraordinarily simple.

SEE: LOYALTY; MOTIVATIONAL SPEAKERS
MORE INFO: www.sas.com
SOURCES: Charles Fishman, "Sanity Inc.," *Fast Company*, January 1999

Saturn

Adding value is not about a few added extras at the periphery. The Saturn automobile is a prime example of the shift in emphasis away from tangible product attribute-based value to soft and service-based differentiation.

The Saturn was launched in 1990 and was GM's first new nameplate since Chevrolet. The car itself is fairly spartan. The Saturn has good price points and appeals to the consumers' emotions by being identified with the heritage of hard-working values. Most persuasively, the Saturn is backed by a terrific dealer network which provides truly differentiated sales with no haggling and high quality service. (So low are the standards in the auto business, that loaners and car washes are jewels in Saturn's service crown.)

Saturn has laid out what it calls its "pricing principles": "No hassle means Saturn Retailers are upfront about all elements of a vehicle's price. No last minute add-ons or hidden charges. Nothing up our sleeves. No haggle means the retailer should stick to whatever price it sets. Horse trading and dickering don't fit with Saturn's Philosophy.

Saturn

No Customer should ever wonder whether the Retailer's next Customer will get a better price by 'driving a harder bargain.'"

Saturn demonstrates the use of service as a differentiator of an undistinguished product – once again, it is a differentiator which competitors have so far failed to copy successfully.

None of this is accidental. Saturn's brand development focused on the buying experience, service and support, rather than being narrowly focused on the product. It was concerned with people and processes rather than the product.

According to research by JD Power, the three car brands in the US with the highest customer satisfaction are Lexus, Infiniti and Saturn. The link between them is that all have *de novo* dealer networks designed, developed and managed with an intense pursuit of consistent, exceptional customer service. In 1996, the Saturn was rated best in overall sales satisfaction among all car brands. It was rated seventh in customer satisfaction – the top six were all luxury cars – Lexus, Infiniti, Acura, Mercedes-Benz, Cadillac and Jaguar. Customers even gave Saturn high marks on the service they received when their cars were recalled.

Contrast this with the problems GM has experienced elsewhere with dealerships featuring a variety of its models. In 1995, GM vice president Ronald L Zarrella wrote to 8500 dealers pointing out, rather belatedly, that its autos were not commodities and offering them for sale next to competing brands was not what GM wanted. It was significant that while there are 8500 US GM dealerships, there are 17,000 franchises. Individual dealers can have as many as six franchises operating from the same place. Saturn dealers have no such complications. Their onus on straight talking and value added service remains distinctive.

SEE: BRANDS; LEXUS
MORE INFO: www.saturn.com
SOURCES: Anita M McGahan & Suzanne C. Purdy, "Saturn Corporation in
             1996," Harvard Business School case study 9–797–052
             Copyright © 1996 by the President and Fellows of Harvard
             College.

"My choice in everything is to say nothing and go do it."

247

Saturn

Scardino, Marjorie

After winning a protracted battle to secure Simon & Schuster, Marjorie Scardino – the first female CEO of a FTSE 100 company – is putting her mark on the media giant Pearson. Scardino (born 1947) is a Texan lawyer and journalist who was educated at Baylor University and the University of San Francisco. She and her husband founded *The Georgia Gazette* newspaper.

Before becoming Pearson CEO in October 1996, Scardino ran the *Economist* which she transformed during 12 years from a parochial magazine to an international point of reference. Her introduction to life at the top of Pearson, was an early crisis involving an accounting problem at Penguin in the US, which brought a potential bill of £100 million. Scardino handled the flak with aplomb and moved onto bigger battles. Her major victory has been the $3.6 billion acquisition of Simon & Schuster's education divisions from under the nose of Michael Milken. This created a potent combination of Addison Wesley Longman and Simon & Schuster. Finding a name may be the hardest bit.

SEE: MICHAEL MILKEN; RUPERT MURDOCH
MORE INFO: www.ft.com

Scase, Richard

Richard Scase is one of the select few who spend their entire working day identifying trends and changes in the working world. Scase, currently Professor of Organizational Behavior at the UK's University of Kent at Canterbury is, among other projects, exploring future scenarios for Britain in the year 2010. The future is his domain. And the future, says Professor Scase, will be centered on working flexibly.

"Mobile, flexible organizations require self-confidence," he says. "The capabilities to enable homeworking and the like exist, but in too many cases are not being realized." Scase points out that the barriers to more flexible working practices are mental rather than technical. It can be done. But organizations and, more to the point, managers choose not to. "The culture of management often still equates commitment, enthusiasm and motivation to being physically around. Being there. While people could do a great deal more work away from the workplace, not many organizations possess the self-confidence to allow them to do so. If people work out of the office, you can find that their commitment is questioned. The whole politics of promotion often works against people working away from the workplace."

The end result of this culture of management is that companies are saddled with unnecessarily high overheads – most obviously, expensive and needless office space.

Scase detects that change is in the air. The future will be different. It has to be. "The culture is changing. We are at watershed which will lead to fundamental changes in the relationship between our home and working lives," he predicts, pointing to management consulting firms and high-tech companies where offices have been transformed into attractive meeting places rather than carefully delineated fiefdoms. "With their more relaxed atmosphere, offices of the future will be where you meet up with clients and colleagues," says Scase. "The creative stimulation you get from meeting up with people will still be there, but it will not be static and fixed."

Scase anticipates that beyond the virtual organization lies the intelligent corporation at whose heart lies creativity, the source of innovation. In order to be creative, he first believes you need personal space – "You can't bureaucratize creativity. You can't tell people to be creative. You need to be able to think and play around with ideas in a comfortable environment." The second ingredient is social interaction – "Face-to-face interaction is important. Socializing after work, for example, is extremely powerful and useful. People talk about work in a way they wouldn't do when actually at work."

The future mapped out by Richard Scase is a world of either/and rather than either/or alternatives. Its aim is to get the best of all possible worlds rather than separating activities into physical and mental compartments.

Georgina Peppers

SEE: MOBILE INFORMATION
MORE INFO: Richard Scase, *Managing Creativity*, 1999

Scase, Richard

Schrager, Ian

In the 1970s Ian Schrager opened Studio 54 in New York with the late Steve Rubell. It became the fashionable place to be glimpsed. Then Schrager's gilded existence came to ground with a prison sentence for tax evasion – he served 13 months. Now, he has bounced back with, what he calls, "boutique hotels." He is the owner of the St Moritz, Morgans, the Royalton and the Paramount in New York, the Cliff in San Francisco and the Delano in Miami Beach. Further afield, Schrager is involved in joint ventures at the Sanderson, and St Martin's Lane in London.

zeitbite#45
Peter Senge

"Corporations,
like individuals,
need time out
for reflection."

His hotels are stylish and unique. They are hotel as fashion item. "The design is just one part of the formula, but it's the way the whole things gets put together that touches you in some visceral way. It's like when you go to a great nightclub and you can cut the electricity in the air," Schrager explains.

MORE INFO: www.popart98.com
SOURCES: *Financial Times*, September 9, 1998

Schultz, Howard

Howard Schultz is the chairman and CEO of coffee shop chain, Starbucks. Schultz grew up in Brooklyn and went to college on a football scholarship at North Michigan University. He late became a Xerox salesman. In 1987 he bought out the Starbucks management team for $4 million. (Business trivia: Bill Gates Sr helped Schultz draw up his bid.)

Starbucks now has 1600 coffee shops in the US and turnover of $1.3 billion. It now eyes the world with latte eyes. Starbucks opened in London in 1998 and plans 500 European shops by 2003.

Schultz – the "espresso evangelist" according to one newspaper – has developed a humanitarian management style. "What we've done is we've said the most important component in our brand is the employee," says Schultz. "The people have created the magic. The people have created the experience. The brand is much more than a cup of coffee – it's the experience." His autobiography is suitably entitled *Pour Your Heart Into It*.

SEE: STARBUCKS
MORE INFO: Howard Schultz, *Pour Your Heart Into It*, 1997;
            www.starbucks.com
SOURCES: *Observer*, September 20, 1998

Schwartz, Peter

Peter Schwartz is chairman of the Global Business Network. He trained as an astronautical engineer and spent ten years at the Stanford Research Institute. His books include *The Art of the Long View* and, more intriguingly, Schwartz was also a script consultant on the films *War Games* and *Sneakers*. In his previous corporate life, he succeeded Pierre Wack, the founding father of scenario planning, at Royal Dutch/Shell. From 1982 until 1987, Schwartz ran Shell's scenario planning group. He then returned to the US to set up Global Business Network with a number of former colleagues including Stewart Brand.

Described by one magazine as "an affable, eloquent man with a neat beard and a habit of saying absolutely," Schwartz has created a lucrative niche for himself in the futures markets. His reputation was bolstered in 1982 when Schwartz predicted the collapse of oil prices. Shell piled up cash and then bought oil fields when the price collapsed. All companies could do with scenario planners like that.

Less successfully in Summer 1997 Schwartz published an article entitled "The long boom" with Peter Leyden in *Wired*. It anticipated a "boom on a scale never experienced before." By 1998 Asia was in meltdown and Russia on the verge of collapse. Even so, Schwartz remains the doyen of scenario planning. "Mr Schwartz owes his cachet to his background as a scenario planner, which is about as respectable as futurology gets," observed the *Economist*. If Peter Schwartz has anything to do with it, the future may well be rocket science.

SEE: GLOBAL BUSINESS NEWORK
MORE INFO: www.gbn.org; Peter Schwartz, *The Art of the Long View*, 1991
SOURCES: *The Economist*, August 22, 1998; www.businesstech.com

Sen, Amartya

Amartya Sen (born 1933) is a Nobel prize winning economist with a conscience. His Christian name means "one who deserves immortality." His work on what he calls "the downside of economics" led him to being called "economics' answer to Mother Teresa." This probably says more about the state of economics than Sen's saintliness.

Sen is now Master of Trinity College, Cambridge University, a winding-down (and wine tasting) position after a glittering academic career. Sen studied at the University of Calcutta and Cambridge. He taught throughout the world and spent ten years at Harvard.

Sen argues that economics has overlooked the fact that there is more to wealth than money and material acquisition. People matter and the standards of living of people matter. Economics has to factor in the broader impact of its activities. A market collapse in the West may wreak untold havoc among the poorest countries on earth. Sen is the dismal science's voice of conscience.

SEE: DECREASING RETURNS
MORE INFO: Amartya Sen, *Development as Freedom*, 1999
SOURCES: *Business Week*, October 26, 1998

Shelton, Ken

Ken Shelton, editor of the newsletter, *Executive Excellence*, is the ghost behind one of the biggest business bestsellers of all time, Stephen R. Covey's *The Seven Habits of Highly Effective People*. Shelton has also worked on *Smart Talk* by Lou Tice; *Managing People Is Like Herding Cats* by Warren Bennis; *21st Century Leadership* by Larry Senn and Lynn MacFarland; and is currently working on *21 Keys of Success*. He argues that ghostwriting is simply part of a media process which is radically different from the traditional one. "Publishing today implies multimedia presentation. Often the book is merely part of a package of product that follows a certain line of thought," says Shelton. "The package may include audiotapes, video-based training, CD-Rom games, presentations and speeches. Covey's *Seven Habits* book, for example, was the last item in the *Seven Habits* product-line – the cherry on top." But what a cherry – *Seven Habits* has sold over six million copies.

Shelton believes that ghostwriting is an inevitable and useful editorial service. "Many *authors* can't or won't write. But they may be very gifted as thinkers, presenters, synthesisers, commentators, speakers or entertainers," says Shelton. "I often use a track and field metaphor. If a person is world class at the 400 metre hurdles, does that mean that the same person should also be world class at the 100 metre sprint, the mile run, the high jump or the marathon?" It appears that there aren't many Renaissance men out there.

Little wonder. According to Shelton, "Good ghosts of management books are rather rare because ghosting requires almost as much knowledge of the subject matter as the author has (with one tenth the ego.)" Shelton is choosy. After a big success he can afford to be. "My litmus test to detect the real thing is 1) Has the author ever had a real job? 2) Has the author ever started a business, grown a business, or exercised real leadership in a line position where he or she was responsible for results? 3) Have the concepts of the author ever been applied in a real company with favourable results? And, on a personal level, 4) Does the author's noble mission square with his or her motive, means and message." Then, if the aspiring author passes these tests, there is Shelton's bottom line: "As a ghost, I want to be sure that the *author* has real character, competence and substance. I have found from hard experience that it's hard to create something fresh and meaningful out of nothing."

SEE: GHOSTWRITING; WORDWORKS; ART KLEINER
MORE INFO: www.eep.com

Shih, Stan

Stan Shih (born 1944) is "the high priest of Taiwanese high-tech." More officially, he is chairman of Acer.

Shih was raised by his mother who ran a grocery store. Her business principles and his experience in the store remain fundamental to his business style. He worked in engineering and R&D and developed an electronic watch pen. In 1976, he founded a company which became Acer with $25,000 borrowed from his wife and business partners. The company nearly collapsed in the early 1990s, but has since returned from the brink.

Shih's management style is full of grocery store aphorisms with a smattering of the usual business bullshit. He calls his management

"*The modern Little Red Riding Hood, reared on singing commercials, has no objection to being eaten by the wolf.*"

253

*"Our age cre-
ates a
strange para-
dox. Never
before have
we had so
much infor-
mation, yet
never before
have we so
little inner
certainty
about our
own being."*

philosophy "collective entrepreneurship." Acer's company culture is, he hopes, a "poor young men's culture." An inspiration to Shih is the McDonalds business model. To this, Shih adds idiosyncratic twists – such as "Stan's smiling curve" (speed is more important than the cost to compete) and "Go big or go home." Shih now owns 3.26 percent of the company.

SEE: DAEWOO; LG
MORE INFO: www.acer.com
SOURCES: *Financial Times*, May 18, 1998; Stan Shih, *Me-Too is Not My Style*

SOL

Liisa Joronen is chief executive and owner of the Finnish company SOL. Over the last five years she has transformed SOL from a traditional cleaning business into one of the most progressive companies in the world.

Worker participation is integral to the way the company operates. Staff were asked to help design the first SOL headquarters – SOL Studio – in a converted film studio in Helsinki. More than 1200 concepts for the ideal workplace were generated through a series of workshops. The ideas were then developed in dialog with management and a team of interior designers and were implemented in a record-breaking five weeks. (The process was repeated when the company moved to its current larger premises – SOL City).

The new way of working means that the time staff spend in the office is entirely up to them. They are judged purely on results. The company has also dispensed with the conventional trappings of authority: supervisors are "peer counselors," desks are communal and no one has a secretary.

The bottom line is also crystal clear: SOL has a turnover of $50 million, and is currently growing at around 20 to 25 percent annually.

Des Dearlove

SEE: SAS INSTITUTE
MORE INFO: www.funkybusiness.com

SOL

Shareholder Value

In 1989, the Economist Intelligence Unit found that shareholder value rated a mention in just three corporate annual reports. In 1990, it found 380 mentions for the phrase. Shareholder value arrived with the bang which usually accompanies a big idea. Chief executives brandished their new business technique and consultants were quickly off the mark, selling their particular interpretation of the idea. Shareholder value simply contends that a company should aim to maximize its value to shareholders. Indeed, this should be the *raison d'être* of the company.

To large organizations, this perspective is attractive for a number of reasons. First, it clarifies the reasons for a company's existence with commendable clarity. There is none of the vagueness of making *reasonable* profits and pleasing all the company's stakeholders. It sounds both laudable and achievable – and shareholders are duty bound to like the idea. Second, (if pressed a little) it fits in with the entire idea of the stakeholder corporation. Shareholders are stakeholders and their numbers are increasingly likely to include other stakeholders such as employees. Clearly, adding value to the investments of shareholders can have widespread benefits inside and outside an organization. Of course, cynics are fond of pointing out that the fact that many senior executives hold large swathes of shares as part of their remuneration packages adds a little to the attractiveness of maximizing shareholder value.

255

Another attraction of the concept of shareholder value is that it claims to encourage a longer term view of corporate performance. Instead of desperately seeking to boost quarterly results, executives can channel their energies into creating long-term value growth for shareholders. Institutional shareholders like the long view and this element was vital in the development of the concept. During the 1980s companies lived in fear of the attentions of corporate predators who identified lack of shareholder value as a convincing case for a takeover. As arguments for takeover go this is the one most likely to succeed with shareholders. (The next question must be whether shareholder value is then the best way to run a business. This is a more weighty matter.)

Critics of the concept also voice doubts about whether long-term perspectives are encouraged. After all, they argue, downsizing was

zeitbite#48
Adlai
Stevenson

"With the supermarket as our temple and the singing commercial as our litany, are we likely to fire the world with an irresistible vision of America's exalted purpose and inspiring way of life?"

popular among shareholders who, perversely, often saw the value of their investments go up when a company announced it was downsizing.

While such arguments are difficult to prove either way, what can be said is that value-based management seeks to bridge the gap between the aims of executives and employees and those of shareholders. In the past, companies tended to measure success solely in terms of profits. If profits increased year on year, executives felt they were doing a good job. If, at the same time, the share price underperformed, they offered reassurance to institutional investors, but little else. In contrast, value-based management is as interested in cash and capital invested as in calculations about profitability. "Cash is a fact, profit is an opinion," argues one of the creators of the concept, Alfred Rappaport of Northwestern University's Kellogg School of Management. Indeed, in many ways, shareholder value transports the small business phobia of cash flow to larger corporations.

Indeed, value-based management goes against some of the first principles of corporate life. Most obviously it calls into question the accounting model of measuring corporate performance. Erwin Scholtz of the UK's Ashridge Management College is among those who pour a measure of scorn on the traditional accounting model, whose currency is profits rather than cash. Scholtz suggests that the accounting model is incomplete (as it does not account for the full cost of capital); complex (it uses multiple performance measures); inconsistent (producing conflicting signals); incorrect (as accounting conventions may distort true economic performance); and ineffective (as it is often disconnected from the management systems and operational drivers of the business).

The trouble is that actually calculating shareholder value or, indeed, the value of anything, is a hazardous exercise. Keen to cash in on the fashion for shareholder value, consulting firms have produced a bewildering variety of products which promise to explain – and measure – all. The alternatives include Economic Value Added; Cash Flow Return on Investment; and Value Based Management. These revolve around a variety of measures and approaches.

It is at this point that the going becomes complex. Approaches differ. Alfred Rappaport concentrates on measuring what he labels "value drivers" – these include sales-growth rates, operating profit margins and the cost of capital. Others champion the case for measuring Total Shareholder Return (TSR) which calculates the rate of return from the original purchase; the dividend stream received by the investor; and its sale at the end of the holding period. Still others argue that the three most important things companies need to measure are customer satisfaction, employee satisfaction and cash flow.

Eventually, through one measure or another, a company will be able to assess its value-related performance. Then comes the next step which is equally challenging: what rate of value growth is achievable and desirable? Average performance in the FT-SE 100 over three years requires a TSR of about six to eight percent (plus the inflation rate), while top quartile performance requires an additional five to eight percent.

While skeptics suggest that shareholder value is simply yet another consulting invention, its popularity among companies like Lloyds-TSB Group and top US conglomerates, suggests it is a robust tool to, at least, monitor performance. And, for global businesses, perhaps the greatest advantage of shareholder value is that it provides universally consistent corporate results rather than ones produced to the dictates of local accounting rules.

SEE: BALANCED SCORECARD

SOURCES: Alfred Rappaport, *Creating Shareholder Value: A guide for managers and investors*, 1997; G. Bennett Stewart, *The Quest for Value*, 1991

Smart cards

Only a few years ago, smart cards were the preserve of techno-freaks. Hard-nosed executives looked blank at their very mention. "Come back when it works" was the message. Now they do, and they're back. In fact, hardly a day passes without another announcement of just how clever, sophisticated, useful, and plain smart, cards actually are. There is no question that they work. Indeed, the only question is what can't they be used for?

zeitbite#49
Ralph Waldo
Emerson

"There are always two parties, the party of the past and the party of the future; the establishment and the movement."

Like it or not, we are entering the world of the card. Small, smart and perfectly formed, cards can do anything. Try them. Start with the humble credit card. We can now use our credit cards for virtual shopping on the Internet – safely.

Not that we need credit cards. Smart cards are replacing money and our treasured credit cards are becoming an outdated currency. In Portugal, Multi-banco Electronic Purse (Mep) cards are revolutionizing the way the Portuguese spend their hard earned escudos. The Mep system allows the card to be used to pay for everything from newspapers and cups of coffee to car washes and telephone calls. Over 500,000 Mep cards are now in operation.

Portugal is ahead of the pack when it comes to using smart cards to replace money. In France, the birthplace of the smart card (first developed by Roland Moreno in 1974), smart cards are widely used, but usually for direct debit and credit card payments. Finland and Denmark are also experimenting with the electronic purse concept and, in the UK, the Mondex system has been trialed. It is expected that the European smart card market will be worth $1.3 billion by 2000. No money will undoubtedly lead to big money for companies able to make the best use of smart cards.

Smart card production is estimated to reach 1.32 billion by 2001 according to researchers Dataquest. Fueling growth is the convergence of technologies. A single smart card now has the same power of an early PC.

MORE INFO: www.wlv.ac.uk

Sophia Antipolis
Southern French high-tech and entrepreneurial center. Established in 1988, Sophia Antipolis is only now making significant inroads into business consciousness outside France.

SEE: CLUSTERS; BUSINESS SCHOOLS

Soros, George

George Soros (born 1930) is president of Soros Fund Management. The London School of Economics graduate is one of the most powerful people in the financial world. He has been described as "one-third hard-nosed financier, one-third philosopher-king and one-third latter day Robin Hood." He came to worldwide attention in 1992 when he made £600 million from selling the pound. As a result, Britain withdrew from the European Exchange Rate Mechanism. Power was at work. The event effectively marked the end for the then Conservative government. More recently, Soros called for the devaluation of the Russian rouble in 1998. This promptly led to its collapse. Soros has lamented that "Capitalism was coming apart at the seams." This has not stopped him rethreading his well-armed needle.

George Soros was born in Hungary. He was educated at the London School of Economics, came under the spell of Karl Popper, and moved to the United States in 1956. His career has been built around a variety of investment funds. All have reaped impressive dividends – his Quantum Fund racked up 30 percent returns as a matter of routine and exceeded 100 percent on two occasions. "Sometimes I felt like a gigantic digestive tract, taking in money at one end and pushing it out at the other," Soros has lamented. He has given generously to charitable and other foundations. He has also lectured governments and investors long and hard. The difficulty is reconciling the hugely successful investor, the benefactor and the wisdom-laden sage.

SEE: WARREN BUFFETT
MORE INFO: www.soros.org
SOURCES: *New York Times*, December 6, 1998

spin doctors

In the popular imagination, PR used to be concerned with press releases, column inches and little else. A career in PR got you nowhere particularly fast and the highlights were usually restricted to a few boozy lunches and the distant sighting of someone famous in the foyer of a TV studio. As children contemplated careers as astronauts, footballers or ballet dancers, no one ever proclaimed that they wanted to be big in PR.

Company
Southwest Airlines Co.

Address
2702 Love Field Dr. Dallas,
TX 75235 USA Minneapolis, MN 55402–4302
Phone: 214–792–4000
Fax: 214–792–5015
http://www.southwest.com

Business
Airline

Statistics, Fiscal Year End December

Employees	1997	23,974
Annual sales (million)	1998	$4164.0
Annual results (million)	1998	$433.4
Other facts		SWA has a turned in a 25 year run of profits – without any strikes. It provides 2300 flights to 50 US cities in 25 states daily.
Hoover's 500		# 422
Fortune 500		# 383

Or did they? PR has shifted up a gear. It may not yet possess the excitement of flying through space, or provide the adrenaline rush of scoring the winner in a Super Bowl, but suddenly PR is making waves in the business world and beyond.

In the media age, a new generation of PR champions are emerging. They are not interested in spending years perfecting the press release. Indeed, they are as likely to labor over the details of a press release as their predecessors were likely to order mineral water. They want to wield influence – and, increasingly, they do. Faced with an alarming corporate crisis, the CEO is as likely to call for his PR team as anyone else.

This may appear a superficial response but, in fact, makes sense. The media wields such influence that a badly handled story quickly spirals out of control. A small problem in a distant factory can now have a huge impact on company performance. A few critical lines in a small circulation local newspaper can be picked upon and, before you know it, they are on the front pages of international newspapers and being peddled around the Internet. They may be totally untrue, but once news is out of control, it is all but impossible to rein it back in.

To malign spin doctors – and the growing number of this ilk now emerging – is easy. But, the reality is that spin doctors are simply doing by stealth and contacts what others have been trying to do for decades. They influence the news; they do not control it.

The difference between the spin doctor and the humble PR person of yesteryear is the difference between tactics and strategy. The PR industry was once all about making a short-term splash. Now, it is about influencing the media to achieve long-term goals. It has become altogether more sophisticated and complex.

PR has gone all strategic and the doors of the boardroom have opened. It is only a matter of time before PR executives take another step up and actually become the people running organizations. The stars of the new PR generation may become the real movers and

spin doctors

shakers of the future. Forget manufacturing, balancing budgets and the like: the spin is the thing.

SEE: REPUTATION MANAGEMENT

spread betting

Forget the traditional image of a smoke filled betting shop with abject punters wading ankle deep through discarded betting slips, betting is moving up-market and going high-tech. Witness the betting phenomenon of the nineties: spread betting.

Spread bets are the derivatives of the gambling world. They are the gambling equivalent of trading in the financial markets. Their origins lie in the leisure pursuits of dealers in London's financial markets when many high rolling City traders would gamble on the movements of futures, options, currencies etc. outside of working hours. Traditional fixed-odds betting – a fixed return on your stake – was neither sophisticated nor flexible enough to cope with this new kind of well financed, risk addicted gambler.

A few specialist bookmakers saw an opportunity and applied the mechanics of the financial markets to gambling. Spread betting was born. The bookmaker takes a view on an event and quotes a range within which a given variable will, in their opinion, fall. The gambler bets on either a higher or lower outcome – "buying" at the higher figure (if the bookmaker is too cautious) or "selling" at the lower (the bookmaker is too optimistic). With spread betting, offering a variety of new ways to win or lose money, it wasn't long before it took hold in the sports betting market.

To confuse matters we will use a cricket series as an example. Take the biennial battle for supremacy between the Australia and England cricket teams. First the bookmakers take a view. They might predict England will make between 350 and 400 runs in an innings and quote a spread of 350–400. Then the punter takes a view. If he (sexist, but sadly true) thinks England will score more than 400 runs then he "buys" at 400. If he thinks less than 350, then he "sells" at 350.

So far so good. It's at this point, however, that spread betting differs significantly from fixed-odds betting. If you bet high, then the more runs England make above the bookmaker's prediction the more

spread betting

money you make. So if you bought at £100 a run, every run above 400 is £100 in your pocket. Six hundred runs and you're £20 000 richer. On the other hand, unlike fixed-odds betting your potential losses are not confined to your stake money. If England only score 100 runs (by no means unlikely) you end up £30,000 poorer.

There is some compensation should you find yourself the victim of poor judgment or bad luck. In spread betting you can bet on an event while it is taking place. So if you find yourself on a hiding to nothing you can close out your position before you become destitute (a real possibility as, unlike traditional betting, debts from spread betting are recoverable by law.)

Finally, for those of us unable to pick that elusive winner, spread betting holds another attraction – you don't need to pick the winner.

During the last General Election in the UK one bookmaker, IG Index, predicted the Liberal Democrat party – traditionally third in a three-party race – would win between 23 and 26 seats.

One lucky punter, or shrewd political pundit if you prefer, bet £4000 a seat that the party would do better. The Liberal Democrats duly lost the election, but won 46 seats in the process leaving the delighted punter £80,000 richer.

Stephen Coomber

MORE INFO: www.sporting-life.com
SOURCES: *Independent*, November 1998; www.sporting-life.com

263

Starbucks

In 1971 Gerald Baldwin, Gordon Bowker and Zev Siegl opened a gourmet coffee store in Seattle's Pike Place Market. To launch the business they raised $10,000. The trio called their enterprise Starbucks. (Their belief was that the "St" sound was memorable and alluring.)

The coffee store – pointedly not a "coffee shop" – started as it meant to go by making money. Within a year Starbucks was in profit and, in 1973, began roasting its own coffee. Starbucks evolved and, in 1982, brought in Howard Schultz to help with its marketing. Schultz had grown up in Brooklyn and went to college on a football scholarship at North Michigan University. He later became a Xerox salesman.

In 1983 Starbucks acquired Peet's, and co-founder Gerald Baldwin eventually left to run Peet's. Then the revolution began. In 1987 Howard Schultz bought out the Starbucks management team for $4 million. (Business trivia: Bill Gates Sr helped Schultz draw up his bid.) Schultz remains the company's chairman and CEO.

Schultz broadened the company's horizons. He opened a store in Chicago. It took off. More followed. And then more. The approach was a branding classic. "The goal was to add value to a commodity typically purchased on supermarket aisles," said Schultz. "Our so-called baristas [bartenders] introduce customers to the fine coffees of the world the way wine stewards bring forward fine wines."

Starbucks offered excellent service combined with a rejuvenated product. "Starbucks is not a trend. We're a lifestyle," he proclaimed with all due flakiness. The Starbucks training manual explains how it breathed latte into what was once pond water: "As Americans, we have grown up thinking of coffee primarily as a hot, tan liquid dispensed from fairly automatic appliances, then 'doctored' as needed to make it drinkable ... The opposite of this approach is to treat coffee making as a brand of cooking. You start with the best beans you can buy, making sure they are fresh. You use your favorite recipe. You grind the beans to the right consistency and add delicious, fresh-tasting water."

It did little advertising to build its brand strength. "We concentrated on creating value and customer service," says Schultz. "Our success proves you can build a national brand without 30-second sound bites." Between 1987 and 1998 Starbucks spent less than $10 million on advertising.

Starbucks

Its emphasis instead has been on building a network of alliances which make its products more widely available. It has, for example, established alliances with Barnes & Noble, Costco, Horizon and United Airlines. (The lure can be understood by the fact that the tie up with United exposes 75 million travelers to Starbucks products.) Starbucks has also worked on a wide variety of spin-offs. There is Starbucks ice cream with Dreyer's Grand; bottled Frapuccino developed with Pepsi; and even a (nightmarish) coffee-laced beer with the Redhook Ale Company.

This, of course, runs the risk of getting into bed with the wrong partner. Schultz is confident that this can be avoided: "I don't think we are cannibalizing ourselves as long as we continue to introduce and offer best-of-class products."

Starbucks' approach has been compared to that of Wal-Mart. This is not something the company takes too kindly to. The suggestion is that it has muscled in, using its rapidly increasing size to squeeze smaller competitors. This rests uneasily with the ambience which Starbucks has carefully assembled around its brand. It talks of "elevating the coffee experience" and is keen on new age philosophizing.

In 1992 the company went public. Its stock doubled in value in five months. (Schultz's stake was worth $70 million.) The company's mermaid logo is now omnipresent. Starbucks has 1,600 coffee shops in the US and turnover of $1.3 billion. It aims for 2,000 stores by 2000. It now eyes the world with latte eyes. Starbucks opened in London in 1998 and plans 500 European shops by 2003. When its store opened in Tokyo, hundreds queued.

SEE: BRANDS
MORE INFO: www.starbucks.com
SOURCES: Lori Ioannon, "Making customers come back for more,"
            Fortune, March 16, 1998

Starwave

Five years ago Starwave didn't even exist. Then Microsoft cofounder Paul Allen decided to have another dabble in entrepreneurship. Now Starwave Corporation is a major Internet technology company and creator and producer of the leading on-line sports, news and entertainment services. As with many of these companies, it can be found in Seattle, Washington. The Walt Disney Company acquired Starwave in April 1998 but it didn't have Mickey's ears for long – in June 1998, it reached an agreement to acquire a stake in Infoseek Corporation in exchange for its Starwave holding.

With the backing of Allen, Starwave's chances of success were always going to be good, but its big breakthrough came in April of 1997, when it entered two partnerships with ESPN and ABC News to form ESPN Internet Ventures and ABC News Internet Ventures. These ventures give interactive programming, providing sports, news and entertainment services to millions of consumers on the Web. With the combination of leading-edge technology, editorial production and design skills, and strong media partnerships, plus lots and lots of money, these on-line services seem well positioned to prosper.

Trevor Merriden

SEE: PAUL ALLEN
MORE INFO: www.starwave.com

Steinberg, Leigh

Leigh Steinberg (born 1949) is a sports star agent, and the model for Tom Cruise's character in the film, *Jerry Maguire*. "Show me the money" is Steinberg's unsophisticated but persuasive catchphrase. It obviously works. His law firm, Steinberg & Moorad, represents more than 100 athletes and negotiates multimillion dollar deals for some of America's best known sports stars – including Troy Aikman, Drew Bledsoe, Warren Moon and Ryan Leaf. The news that Steinberg is now exploring ways of expanding his business to include negotiating on behalf of top business talent should be enough to strike terror into the hearts of recruiters everywhere.

For Steinberg, negotiating is a contact sport to be enjoyed by everyone. His approach is that it is a part of everyday life and should be handled in a professional way – with clear focus and a principled philosophy.

"The goal," he insists "is not to destroy the other side, but to find the most profitable way to complete a deal that works for both sides."

This involves the mastery of a number of lessons, including:

- everyone is a negotiator – we all negotiate all the time, but many of us still have a fundamental fear of negotiation;
- negotiate with yourself – a vital step in any deal is introspection; understanding what you want out of the situation; and move from your values to your value – once you understand your own values, you have to understand your value in the world;
- include some kind of ceremonial ritual to complete a deal – whether it's signing football jerseys to cement a multi-million dollar contract or just having a beer together after obtaining a salary increase.

SEE: CEO AGENCY
MORE INFO: www.leighsteinberg.com
SOURCES: *Fast Company*, November 1998

Stevenson, Dennis

Cambridge University educated, Dennis Stevenson (British, born 1945) is remarkably well connected and plays one of those understated but pivotal roles in society. He is chairman of the media group Pearson and of GPA Aviation as well as non-executive director of Lazard Brothers, BskyB and Manpower. It is indicative that he was offered roles by both Conservative and Labour parties.

SEE: COOL BRITANNIA

storytelling

When business leaders were men with a nifty line in regression analysis and the stamina of mules on stimulants, mention of storytelling would have provoked loud laughter. Not so, in the uncertain closing years of the century. Now storytelling is regarded as part and parcel of the leader's art.

Listen to leadership guru Noel Tichy of the University of Michigan Business School. "Leadership is about change. It's about taking people from where they are now to where they need to be. The best way to get people to venture into unknown terrain is to make it desirable by taking them there in their imaginations." Spin that yarn.

Elizabeth Weil, writing in *Fast Company,* has cited examples of companies which have used stories to help build strong cultures. Most famously, there is the example of Hewlett-Packard's Bill Hewlett who found a storeroom door padlocked, and returned to rip the padlock off and post a notice warning against anyone locking the door again. The message? Openness and trust are the way to do business.

This sort of spontaneous behavior is now the stuff of corporate legend. But, it was never planned that way. Bill Hewlett did not think that breaking the padlock would be a great way of building corporate culture. It annoyed him so he just did it. The danger must be that story telling creates mythological leaders or rewrites history. (Even so, storytelling is of emerging interest – look at the work of Art Kleiner on corporate histories and the work of Irish consultant, Sandy Dunlop in linking mythological archetypes with contemporary behavior in his book, *Business Heroes.*)

SEE: **ART KLEINER**

MORE INFO: Sandy Dunlop, *Business Heroes*, Capstone, 1997;
               www.well.com

SOURCES: *Fast Company*, June–July 1998

Strategos

Strategos is a consulting firm founded by strategy guru Gary Hamel. He proclaims that its consultants are "provocateurs, evangelists, architects, teachers, guides." They include Gary Getz, Mike Cornell, Pierre Loewe, Brad Schiarek and Jim Scholes. "We are the enemies of entropy" is one of their off-puttingly propaganda-like slogans.

SEE: **GARY HAMEL**

MORE INFO: www.strategosnet.com

Sull, Don

Don Sull (born 1963) possesses a resumé which has management guru written all over it. Armed with a degree, an MBA and a doctorate from Harvard, he has worked with McKinsey & Company as a consultant and was involved in the $1 billion leveraged buy-out of tire maker, Uniroyal Goodrich. Suggesting that he is as much Renaissance man as new man, Sull's career also boasts a thirst for philosophy, fluent German, a spell as a bouncer in a motorcycle bar, authorship of a musical and membership of the Harvard Boxing Club. He is now an assistant professor at London Business School.

It comes as a surprise, therefore, that Don Sull's research currently centers on something he calls "active inertia." This is a term to describe the corporate tendency to carry on doing what they have always done when they are faced with a crisis. Rather than freezing rabbit-like in the glare of change, managers and organizations carry on in much the same way as before. "Inertia is the enemy of progress. Past insights ossify into clichés, processes lapse into routines and commitments become ties that bind companies to the same course of action. Perhaps the most vital and fulfilling element of a manager's job is to prevent inertia," Sull concludes.

He brings an historical and philosophical slant to business research and education. Sull contends that all the talk of visioning and looking towards the future is all very well, so long as it is does not forget the past: "People tend to think of the past as a hindrance. But you can't have a revolution every day. The past also enables and can be a dynamic force. It confers certain advantages such as trust, brands, reputations and relationships."

His belief that managers, educators and thinkers require a broader view challenges accepted wisdom. He is critical of the view of management as a social science to which a set of formulae and rules can be universally applied. "We are starting to see the limits of the model of management as social science. Management is closest to practical and moral philosophy. How do you get people to act in a proactive way to do the right thing?" he says. "The biggest problem is not that people don't know what to do, just that they don't do it. There is a lack of ambition and imagination."

But, he observes, such limitations are hardly surprising when one considers a business education system which prefers foolproof models to Stoic philosophy: "In the US, business education has been construed more and more narrowly as applied science. Business school professors are engineers and managers are mechanics. Management education is about knowing the right thing to do and getting people to do it. The fundamental assumption is that there are universal laws which can be extracted. I don't believe there are global

Sull, Don

business laws other than in finance. There are useful generalizations, but in management, context, timing, personality and history are everything. The challenge lies in developing judgement, knowing which tool to use rather than reaching for the hammer every time."

SEE: BUSINESS SCHOOLS
MORE INFO: www.lbs.ac.uk
SOURCES: Interviews

Sumitomo Rubber

The 1990s provided a continuing series of challenges for the long-struggling Goodyear brand. Most notable among these was overcapacity in the tire business – estimated at 15 percent or more worldwide. One cost-cutting exercise has followed another. In 1998 Goodyear's sales fell; 2800 lay-offs were announced. Goodyear now has over 95,000 employees; market capitalization of $8 billion; turnover of $13.1 billion; and (1997) profits of $558.7 million.

The most significant response to the problems in the industry which afflict Goodyear came at the beginning of 1999 when the company announced an alliance with its Japanese competitor, Sumitomo Rubber. With total 1997 sales of $4.7 billion, Sumitomo has rights to the Dunlop brand in major world markets. The alliance was aimed at achieving savings of $300 to $360 million. In addition, it combined Sumitomo's strength in Japan with Goodyear's strength in North America and Europe. The new combination boasts 22.6 percent of the $69.5 billion world tire market making it the leading player – Bridgestone manages 18.6 percent narrowly ahead of Michelin on 18.3 percent. Whether the alliance will solve Goodyear's problems is debatable, but it marks yet another Japanese incursion into American dominance.

MORE INFO: www.sumitomorubber.co.jp
SOURCES: "Tread carefully," *The Economist*, February 6, 1999

Sumitomo Rubber

Tapscott, Don

Don Tapscott is a consultant, author and chairman of the Alliance for Converging Technologies. His books provide a commentary on the rise of the net generation. He celebrates the replacement of staid hierarchies with personal chaoses.

"Digital technology is a one-on-one medium, unlike past technological revolutions such as TV and the printing press, which were hierarchical and one-way. The new medium is not controlled by anyone," he says. "When today's youth enter the workforce they will do so, not as ingenues but as authorities. They will find hierarchies in which their boss knows less than they do. They will also find it bizarre how little information sharing goes on, when they are used to exchanging information with strangers online. And they may be puzzled about why it is necessary to go into the office every day."

SEE: ECOMMERCE

MORE INFO: Don Tapscott, *Growing Up Digital*, 1999; *The Digital Economy*, 1997

SOURCES: *The Digital Economy*, *Growing Up Digital*, *Upside* magazine; *Financial Times*

thought leadership

Management consulting is, and has always been, a knowledge-based business. Clients pay for the knowledge and expertise of consultants in a particular area. Yet building, marketing and communicating their knowledge has never been seen as a priority by consultants. Billing clients has ruled the consulting roost.

Now, consulting companies are falling over themselves to prove that they are at the leading edge of management thinking. Thought leadership is all. Suddenly, ideas and information count, knowledge has kudos – because it is the route to more clients and more billable hours.

The irony is that, historically, consultants have held deep suspicions of the world of knowledge. Consultants have, for example, been keen to distance themselves from the ivory towers of academia. While academics dealt in theories, consultants proclaimed themselves to be masters of implementation. Achieving results, solving problems and overcoming obstacles were their measure of success. This was intended to convince skeptical managers that highly paid and youthful consultants really did know what they were talking about.

This overlooked two things. First, big consulting firms recruited their star players directly from the very business schools they sought to distance themselves from. And, second, there is nothing as practical as a good theory. In the immediate and pressured world of business, practice and theory cannot, and never have, existed in isolation from each other.

The first sign that big name consultants were moving into the knowledge business came in the late 1970s. McKinsey & Company, the doyen of consultancy firms, found itself facing intense competition. "Basically, what was going on was that McKinsey was getting beaten up by BCG [Boston Consulting Group] and BCG was beating up McKinsey not because it was better at client relations but because it had bright ideas," says the then McKinsey consultant, Tom Peters.

While McKinsey was selling its own innate brilliance, BCG was selling products and selling lots of them. With its offices filled with some of the world's smartest intellects, McKinsey decided to move into the ideas business. The feeling was that the company had become too process-oriented and its value to clients needed more input from that elusive consultancy ingredient, knowledge. To maintain its exalted position McKinsey needed to know more – and, perhaps more to the point, to demonstrate to the business world that it knew more.

In the years since then, McKinsey has attempted to prove that it has the knowledge businesses need. It now spends between $50 and $100 million a year on knowledge building and claims to spend more on research than Harvard, Wharton and Stanford combined. This positioning is supported by its own heavyweight management journal, the *McKinsey Quarterly*, which makes the *Harvard Business Review* look like *Playboy*, and a steady stream of business blockbusters. Since Tom Peters and Robert Waterman blasted into the bestseller lists with *In Search of Excellence*, McKinsey consultants have been churning out the words: Terence Deal and Allan Kennedy's *Corporate Cultures;* Kenichi Ohmae's *The Mind of the Strategist;* Richard

thought leadership

Cavanagh and Donald Clifford's *The Winning Performance*; *Real Change Leaders* by seven consultants; and Max Landsberg's *The Tao of Coaching* have all hit the bookstalls.

The message is simple: we have the leading ideas and we can make them work in your organization. Indeed, entire consulting businesses can now emerge from a single idea. The passion for re-engineering in the early 1990s fueled the exponential growth of the consulting company CSC Index.

Virtually all the major names in consulting are investing heavily in promoting and developing their knowledge. Most have heavyweight magazines. Arthur D Little publishes *Prism*; Andersen Consulting has *Outlook;* McKinsey has the serious *McKinsey Quarterly* and Booz-Allen & Hamilton weighs in with the impressive *Strategy & Business.*

Consultants and academics are increasingly indistinguishable. This, of course, raises fundamental questions about the role of business schools and their future relationship with consultants.

For all the fashionable talk of knowledge, the job titles and serious discussions, there can only be one leading edge. The competition to occupy it is likely to become ever more intense.

"Consulting firms have just discovered advertising and are very excited. But brands aren't built on advertising alone," warns Sam Hill.

There is another way. The second brand building strategy pursued by consulting firms is what is, sometimes optimistically, labeled thought leadership. This strategy basically positions the brand as being intellectually superior to the competition. In an ideas business, it is a competitive advantage to have more and better ideas.

The battle for thought leadership lacks the glamor of image advertising, but it is incredibly intense. Once again, the traditional leader in this field is McKinsey & Company. McKinsey does not advertise. Its attitude to advertising is best described as aloof. It has long been the intellectual benchmark for consulting firms and, largely, continues to be so. It bolsters its brand through the *McKinsey Quarterly*, a serious, heavyweight publication which has

thought leadership

been around for 35 years and which sometimes makes the *Harvard Business Review* appear frivolous by comparison. Intellectual vigor exudes from each page and this is exactly what McKinsey wants readers to think and experience.

Aside from the heavyweight *McKinsey Quarterly*, McKinsey flexes its intellectual muscles in a number of other ways. In 1990 it set up the McKinsey Global Institute. Its objectives are characteristically bold. It aims, according to the firm, "[to] help business leaders understand the evolution of the global economy, improve the performance and competitiveness of their corporations, and provide a fact base for sound public policy-making at the national and international level." In addition, since the McKinsey-authored *In Search of Excellence* rolled off the presses in 1982, McKinsey consultants have been churning out books with admirable dedication.

Indeed, much of the business book industry is given over to the thought leadership battle between competing consulting brands. Books have become highly expensive calling cards; 400-page ads to be personally inscribed to prospective clients and left in their offices. The books are expensive because often consultants pay ghostwriting firms to do the spade work and, in addition, often buy large numbers of the books to give away. Some have also got into trouble for buying copies in order to ensure that they reach the bestseller lists.

Most of the big strategy-based consulting firms are involved in the thought leadership battle. "Thought leadership is the only place for the top firms. They can't compete on price or on results. But only two firms – McKinsey and the Boston Consulting Group (BCG) – have done it consistently," says Sam Hill. "It is a great strategy. Ideas are the single best source of differentiation. They also mean that you can use PR instead of advertising which is much more credible. The trouble is that it is not easy to do." Hill should know. He was the man who led Booz-Allen & Hamilton's move into the thought leadership melee. In many ways, Booz-Allen's strategy reaped more benefits than most. Prior to taking the thought leadership route, it was largely unheralded, a lesser light next to the intellectual beacons of McKinsey, Bain and BCG. Now, Booz-Allen is actively involved in the intellectual debate. Its consulting stars are quoted and referred to. Column inches are the payback.

thought leadership

Booz-Allen's approach has undoubtedly required a substantial invest-ment. Ideas do not come cheap. Booz-Allen publishes its own heavyweight journal, *Strategy & Business,* initially edited by former *Harvard Business Review* editor, Joel Kurtzman. "When you publish a magazine, you're saying that you recognize and appreciate great ideas – though being associated with great ideas isn't as compelling as being the source of great ideas," Hill explains. Booz-Allen also publishes books in association with San Francisco-based Jossey-Bass and sponsors the Global Business Book Awards alongside the *Financial Times.*

Blur, the book by Stan Davis and Chris Meyer, came out of Ernst & Young's Center for Business Excellence, but Stephanie Shern knows the firm has to pick up its feet in the thought leadership race. Her message is: watch this space. "We've got the knowledge base. The substance is there. Now we have to get the messages out there."

Others are following similar paths with a wide range of publishing and other activities. Arthur D Little publishes the quarterly journal, *Prism.* (Circulation of *Prism* is controlled to maintain the prestige of the publication – according to the firm, "Subscriptions are sponsored by individual staff members as part of their continuing relationships with their clients and other business associates.") Similarly, Mercer pub-lishes its *Management Journal* and made a great deal of the arrival in its ranks of best-selling author Adrian Slywotzky, a real thought leader. "The thought leadership journals are all knock-offs of the *Harvard Business Review.* They have the same quasi-academic style. By and large they are not very effective. None of the firms can say that the dollars spent has led to increased revenues," says Tom Rodenhauser.

Firms also seek to establish their thought leadership credentials through events of various sorts. Ernst & Young runs an annual Knowledge Management conference and the Ernst & Young Entrepreneur of the Year Award – the first winner of the national title was Michael Dell in 1989. AT Kearney runs an annual gathering of 50 CEOs from around the world grandly entitled the Global Business Policy Council.

SEE: BRANDING CONSULTING FIRMS; CHRIS MEYER; HELIOS CONSULTING
MORE INFO: www.ey.com; www.mckinsey.com
SOURCES: *Management Review,* October 1999

thought leadership

Toscani, Oliviero

Photographer Oliviero Toscani has been responsible for some of the most striking images used by Benetton in its controversial ads. "Everything we do is about impulse, about guts," says Toscani. "That's what built Benetton; Luciano didn't test the market for a taste in colored sweaters." The ads are an expression of the brand, of the company and of Luciano Benetton.

This is how the company explains the images it uses to sell more sweaters: "Benetton's communication strategy was born of the company's wish to produce images of global concern for its global customers ... Benetton believes that it is important for companies to take a stance in the real world instead of using their advertising budget to perpetuate the myth that they can make consumers happy through the mere purchase of their product." True enough, but Benetton's "stance" is often difficult to determine.

SEE: BENETTON
MORE INFO: www.benetton.com

Trompenaars, Fons

Fons Trompenaars (born 1952) is a consultant with an impressive pedigree. In the early 1980s, he studied at Wharton where he came across a group of influential thinkers including Russ Ackoff, Eric Trist and Stafford Beer. "I became interested in management and culture," says Trompenaars. "At the time there was nothing in the field. People wondered what it was."

Sponsored by Shell during his PhD research, Trompenaars returned to the Netherlands to work for the oil giant. After setting up his own consultancy, the Centre for International Business Studies, Trompenaars wrote his 1993 book, *Riding the Waves of Culture*. This was one of the first books to focus attention on managing cultural diversity. "When I wrote the book I wrote it for myself. It was not elegant but typically Dutch, forthright," says Trompenaars. "Its sales have increased every quarter. My explanation is that for many managers globalization is just starting and they are only now beginning to realize the implications." The book also involved the British academic, Charles Hampden Turner and the two are now business partners in the Trompenaars Hampden-Turner Group.

zeitbite#51
Warren
Buffett

"I don't try to jump over seven-foot bars. I look around for one-foot bars that I can step over."

277

*"In the past
we said to
employees,
Do as you're
told and you
have a job for
life. Then we
betrayed
them."*

Trompenaars' work is based on exhaustive research. His question-naire on matters cultural has now been answered by 40,000 people. "I love research but wouldn't survive if that was all I did. What I would like to create is a think tank so that we can be at the cutting edge of the development of ideas and of delivery," he says. "The essence of what I do is the transformation of fairly complex models into an appealing, practical setting. There is now a tendency to be too theoretical. It is the transformation into what managers can use that is important. I can look in the eyes of managers and understand them." The hypothesis, says Trompenaars, is straightforward: "Societies which can reconcile better are better at creating wealth."

SEE: DIVERSITY ADVANTAGE

MORE INFO: Fons Trompenaars, *Riding the Waves of Culture*, 1993

Turner, Ted

The CNN chief, husband to Jane Fonda and donor of $1 billion to the United Nations, is a paragon of the modern executive titan. Turner (American, born 1938) is dapper; imaginative and astute; benevolent and ruthless; media shy and media friendly. All the contradictions are there.

SEE: RUPERT MURDOCH

MORE INFO: www.cnn.com

value migration

Defined by Harvard's Benson Shapiro and Richard Tedlow, and consultant Adrian Slywotzky as "the flow of economic and shareholder value away from obsolete business models to new, more effective designs." Strip away the management speak and you have a stark fact of business life. Over any period the needs and expectations of customers change. If a company fails to keep pace, it will find itself left behind.

The trick, therefore, lies in being able to identify the level of value migration and then in doing something about it. And, inevitably, it is here the problems begin. When you are in the throes of actually managing a business, any perception of value migration is likely to be clouded. Paradoxically, the more successful you are, the less likely you are to be able to view value migration with any clarity.

To gain an insight into value migration, Shapiro, Tedlow and Slywotzky suggest that companies ask themselves a number of questions. These begin with "List your most important product and customer service attributes for five years in the future, for today and for five years ago" and also cover market share, percentage of new product failures and ratio of profit from new products. Honest answers to the questions provide a sense of how your company is positioned in terms of value migration. Warning lights flash, for example, if your customers' business is shrinking, if the *quality* of your market share is declining or if your profits from new products are low.

In response to the flashing lights, Shapiro, Tedlow and Slywotzky suggest a number of actions. These include examination of the value migration process within your industry; more intense examination of trends in customer needs; and comparisons with the structure of competitors. Moving early is essential. Instead of being reduced to a panic stricken burst of downsizing, Shapiro, Tedlow and Slywotzky suggest that companies should gradually shift investment away from the old design; invest in new capabilities; and protect the new businesses.

The dividing line between success and failure is narrow. As they point out, IBM – the archetypal "good" company – made $6 billion in 1990 and lost $5 billion two years later. IBM failed to change with the market and only moved when value had well and truly migrated.

value migration

SEE: GARY HAMEL
MORE INFO: Adrian Slywotzky *et al.*, *The Profit Zone*, 1998
SOURCES: *Strategy & Business*, Spring 1997

values

Companies never used to stand for anything in particular. They simply stood, solid and indomitable. The reassurance of bricks and mortar has now given way to the tautology and forked tongues of abstract conceptualizing. What do companies really stand for? In response, many companies have come up with answers. Excessively crafted statements of values are produced, proclaimed and laminated for every desk and every pair of overalls. And that is generally the end of the matter. Statements of corporate values are usually statements of what companies think people want to hear. They are reassuring placebos in a world of hard drugs.

"Less is more."

The reality is that values are abstract. The only values that matter are those which are put into practice. These rarely have any relation to those dreamt up at executive retreats.

SEE: CORPORATE LEGACY

281

Virgin

Richard Branson has distilled Virgin's four core competencies down to the following:

- the ability to identify appropriate growth opportunities;
- the ability to move quickly;
- the willingness to give day-to-day management control to relatively small operating teams: "We try to keep our companies small," he says. (Even though the airline now has 6,000 staff, Branson likes to think it has "retained a small company environment and informality"); and
- the ability to create and manage effective joint ventures.

All this management-speak is a million miles away from 1970 and the start of Virgin's mail-order operation. Branson was fined £7 for using the words "venereal disease" in publicity. A year later, the first Virgin record store opened in London's Oxford Street. (A postal strike made the mail order business difficult.) Virgin was then raided by the UK tax authorities and Branson arrested for purchase tax fraud. The prosecution was dropped after Branson agreed to pay £53,000 in tax and duties over the next three years.

Then Virgin came upon Mike Oldfield and *Tubular Bells* – which launched the company record label. It became one of the biggest selling records of the decade. Later Branson signed up the Sex Pistols.

During the 1980s, Virgin moved into overseas markets, initially through licensing deals but later through its own subsidiaries in France and then elsewhere. It built up the big names – Phil Collins, and Culture Club among them. Diversions included Virgin Vision (forerunner of Virgin Communications) formed to distribute films and videos; a property company is formed; and Virgin Games (computer games software publisher).

Virgin's move into the big league came in 1984 with the launch of Atlantic Airways and Virgin Cargo. Two years later, the Virgin Group, comprising the music, retail and property, and communications divisions, was floated on the London Stock Exchange. (Airline, clubs, holidays and aviation services remained part of privately owned company called Voyager Group).

This proved short-lived and, in 1988, Branson announced a management buyout of Virgin Group – he and other Virgin directors bought the company from other shareholders with loans of £182.5 million. Then he surprised everyone by selling the jewel in the company's crown, the music business, to Thorn EMI. A valuation of $1 billion helped.

The rest is an endless spree of brand extensions – Virgin Cola, bridal wear, Virgin radio, Virgin financial services, Virgin train services. Over extended? Ask Richard Branson.

Des Dearlove

SEE: **RICHARD BRANSON**
MORE INFO: www.virgin.com

Virgin

Wal-Mart

Wal-Mart is bigger than Sears, Kmart and JC Penney combined, with annual sales of $117,958 million. The company serves over 90 million people every week. There are 1879 Wal-Mart stores, 512 Supercenters and 446 Sam's Clubs. Wal-Mart also operates in Canada, Germany, Mexico, Puerto Rico and Brazil, as well as having joint ventures in China and Korea. There are 780,000 Wal-Mart associates in the US alone and a further 115,000 across the world. The Walton family still own around 38 percent of this colossus.

Sam Walton succeeded for a number of reasons. First, he created a brand which had a deliberate, homespun element to it. He was just your old friend running a corner store. Walton helped create the mythology of himself as an all-American success story. It was basically true, but there was more to Sam Walton than apple pie. Positioning the Wal-Mart brand as home grown and loyally American worked despite the reality that Wal-Mart's success drove smaller stores out of business.

The second element in Walton's success was his ability to create a strong corporate culture. Walton gave people responsibility – "A store within a store" gave departmental heads authority. Then there were profit sharing and incentives. Communication directly from Sam was a corny old technique – the multi-millionaire explaining how much he understood and was concerned about the people on the shop floor – but not many other CEOs put themselves on the line directly. Again, it was an old trick but it worked.

Third, Wal-Mart invested heavily in information. It shared information with enthusiasm. Wal-Mart even invested in a satellite communications system so learning and experience were quickly communicated within the organization.

For a homely sort of place, Wal-Mart has embraced new technology with fanatical enthusiasm. It was one of the pioneers of EDI. In the late eighties, Wal-Mart suppliers such as Wrangler and GE were using vendor-managed inventory systems to replenish stocks in Wal-Mart stores and warehouses. Information Technology, such as cash register scanners, means that Wal-Mart is able to obtain a detailed understanding of customers habits and preferences. This information is then fed to

Company
Wal-Mart Stores, Inc.

Subsidiaries include: Sam's Club

Address
702 SW Eighth St. Bentonville, AR 72716-8611 USA
Phone: 501-273-4000
Fax: 501-273-1917
http://www.wal-mart.com

Business
General Merchandisers

Statistics, Fiscal Year End January

Employees	1998	825,000
Annual sales (millions)	1998	$117,958.0
Annual results (millions)	1998	$3526
Other facts		The world's #1 retailer. Founder Sam Walton's heirs own about 38% of the company
Hoover's 500		#4
Fortune 500		#4

zeitbite#54
Charles
Handy

"The market is a mechanism for sorting the efficient from the inefficient, it is not a substitute for responsibility."

suppliers who are told what to produce, in what quantities and where to ship it to. Warehousing and inventory is greatly reduced as a result. This allows the company to use 10 percent of its available space for storage compared to the 25 percent average of its competitors.

Wal-Mart is now using data mining software to detect patterns at its 2400 US stores. The aim, according to Rob Fusillo, director of replenishment systems, is to manage inventories "one store at a time, like [each store] was its own dedicated chain." In fact, Wal-Mart possesses the world's largest data warehouse containing a massive 24 terabytes of data.

The process of information gathering begins at the point of sale. Wal-Mart captures point-of-sale transaction information from each of its outlets and moves it through its network to its data warehouse at HQ in Bentonville, Arkansas. The information is then queried if necessary and sales trends analyzed by item and by store. This enables the company to make decisions about replenishment, customer buying trends, and seasonal buying trends. The aim is to get the right products to the right store at the right time.

The final element in Wal-Mart's success is that it has changed its basic formula but only gradually and with great care. The brand has been extended, but only cautiously. The first Sam's Club opened in Midwest City, Oklahoma in 1983; the first Supercenter in 1988; and the first international store in 1991.

Wal-Mart keeps on growing. Its desire to improve is also one of its unique characteristics. In 1977 Walton declared that he wanted to become a $1 billion company within four years; in 1990 the company declared its aim of doubling the number of stores and increasing sales volume per square foot by 60 percent by 2000. Wal-Mart talks big and then delivers. During 1999 it anticipates 40 new discount stores, 150 new Supercenters, 10–15 Sam's Clubs and 75–80 new operations outside the United States.

SEE: GAP; BENETTON; ECOMMERCE
MORE INFO: www.wal-mart.com
SOURCES: Craig Stedman, "Wal-Mart mines for forecasts," *Computer World*, May 26, 1997

Wal-Mart

Warsi, Perween

In 1986 Perween Warsi began supplying food to her local Indian takeaway. Customers loved her cooking so she set up her own business. The company was called S&A Foods – after Warsi's two sons, Sadiq and Abid. Now, S&A has grown to a firm employing over 600 people with annual turnover approaching £45 million. S&A prepares Indian Balti meals and also produces a meal-for-one range, Ken Hom Cuisine's range of Chinese meals as well as other Thai and Malaysian dishes. Customers include supermarket chains, Safeway, Tesco and Asda, as well as British Airways. The UK conquered, S&A is now looking further afield to export markets. As for the secret ingredient, Perween Warsi says: "I go straight for what I want and I never take no for an answer. I have a clear vision of where I want to go and it never really occurs to me that I might not get there."

SOURCES: *Business Life*, December 1998

Welch, Jack

John Francis Welch Junior was born in 1935 in Peabody, Massachusetts. His father was a conductor on the Boston & Maine Railroad. His mother a housewife. When Welch went to the University of Massachusetts to study chemical engineering, he was the first one from his family to go to college. He went on to study for a PhD in chemical engineering at the University of Illinois.

Welch then joined GE's plastics division at Pittsfield, Massachusetts in 1960 – lured by its proximity to his family home and the $10,500 salary. Welch did not fall in love with GE at first sight. After a year, he tried to leave his job at Pittsfield to join International Minerals & Chemicals in Skokie, Illinois. The youthful, headstrong Welch was frustrated by what he saw as corporate bureaucracy. Welch was talked around. His boss promised to get the bureaucracy off his back.

Welch then began a speedy and spectacular climb up the GE hierarchy. In 1968, at the age of 33 he became GE's youngest general manager. Then, he became senior vice president and sector executive for the consumer products and services sector as well as vice chairman of the GE Credit Corporation. By 1979 he was vice chairman and executive officer. Along the way he built plastics into a formidable $2 billion business, turned around the medical diagnostics business, and began the development of GE Capital. His touch was sure.

The final leap to the uppermost reaches of the GE hierarchy came in 1977 when GE chairman, Reg Jones suggested Welch move to headquarters at Fairfield, Connecticut to join the race to succeed him. Jones knew what he was looking for in his successor. Pretty soon he recognized that Welch fitted the bill.

In December 1980, Welch was announced as the new CEO and chairman of GE. It was a record breaking appointment. At 45, Welch was the youngest chief the company had ever appointed. Indeed, he was only the eighth CEO the company had appointed in 92 years.

During the 1980s, Welch put his dynamic mark on GE and on corporate America. GE's businesses were overhauled. Some were cast out and hundreds of new businesses acquired. In 1984 *Fortune* called Welch the "toughest boss in America." GE's workforce bore the brunt of Welch's quest for competitiveness. GE virtually invented downsizing. Nearly 200,000 GE employees left the company. Over $6 billion was saved.

Perhaps Welch was too brutal. But, there is no denying that by the end of the 1980s GE was leaner and fitter. Complacency was eradicated. In retrospect, Welch's greatest decision may have been to go in with all guns blazing. Dramatic, though relatively short-lived change, was preferable to incremental change.

Having proved that he could tear the company apart, Welch had to move on to Stage Two: rebuilding a company fit for the twenty first century. The hardware had been taken care of. Now came the software.

Central to this was the concept of Work-out which was launched in 1989. Welch has called Work-out, "a relentless, endless company-wide search for a better way to do everything we do."

Work-out was a communication tool which offered GE employees a dramatic opportunity to change their working lives. Work-out was

Welch, Jack

astonishingly successful. It helped begin the process of rebuilding the bonds of trust between GE employees and management. It gave employees a channel through which they could talk about what concerned them at work and then to actually change the way things were done. It broke down barriers. The gales of destruction were past. Creativity was in the air.

The next stage in Welch's revolution was the introduction of a wide ranging quality program. Entitled Six Sigma, it was launched at the end of 1995

Back in 1981 as Jack Welch began life as CEO, GE had total assets of $20 billion and revenues of $27.24 billion. Its earnings were $1.65 billion. With 440,00 employees worldwide, GE had a market value of $12 billion.

By 1997, GE's total assets had mushroomed to $272.4 billion and total revenues to $79.18 billion. Around 260,000 employees – down a staggering 180,000 – produced earnings of $7.3 billion and gave the company a market value of $200 billion.

SEE: GENERAL ELECTRIC
MORE INFO: www.ge.com
SOURCES: Janet Lowe, *Jack Welch Speaks*, 1998; General Electric Annual
            General Meeting, 1990

?What If!

It may be trendy these days to give business a more casual feel, but a London-based company has gone further than most. It has turned the office into a home from home, complete with rugs, armchairs and a table football game, holds client meetings in the kitchen and even runs a company slate at the local pub.

Such eccentric behavior may sound more like student high jinks than a serious business, but at ?What If!, an "invention company" based in London, they are hardened marketing professionals who have grown a £3 million business from harnessing the power of human imagination.

"Seek first to
understand,
then to be
understood."

When Dave Allan and Matt Kingdon left their marketing jobs at Unilever to set up their own business in 1992 they had one simple goal: to create the best innovation company in the world. From experience, they knew they had their best ideas away from the office – hence the home comforts.

They describe the management style as the "serious relaxed business"– something that seems to appeal to big corporates. Their client list includes Heinz, Colgate Palmolive, British Airways, Cadbury Schweppes, ICI, Pepsi Co, Lever Brothers, Thomson Holidays and Royal Mail.

Allan uses the analogy of an oil company: "There are two sides to an oil company. There's the 249,000 people in suits and overalls who exploit the assets of the company today, then there are the people on the exploration side – hairy-kneed, hairy-faced men who search the world for oil – 'gold' – and then as soon as they've found it say, 'OK, where next?'"

It's not just oil companies that need the pioneering spirit, he says. All businesses require people to prospect for the future. Most, however, lose the ability to do so as they get larger. "There's nowhere to play in a big company," he explains, "there's no room for experimentation or invention."

That's where ?What If! comes in. It helps clients explore the frontier between the corporate world – where products are developed – and the real world where consumers actually use them.

For a fee ranging from £10,000 to £250,000, the company works on projects with clients to develop – or invent – new products or services. The approach is summed up by the term "Madness and Measure." Often, this involves challenging the way companies look at problems. For example, the company has a special arrangement with people living in certain streets in London. "We take clients there and say 'knock on any door in this street, and the people who live here will let you into their homes,'" the company explains. "You can see how they use your products and hear what they think of them. It's very powerful because they see with their own eyes."

?What If!

Clients were so impressed that a number asked the company to help them develop their in-house capability. Out of this grew a second string to the business bow. It involves helping companies identify and overcome the internal barriers – including attitudes and behaviors, physical environment, and the way they are structured – which prevent them unleashing the latent inventiveness of their own people.

Between the two activities, the company now has 30 full-time employees. "Have fun to encourage fun," is also part of the management philosophy. As well as a profit-share scheme, the company subscribes to the "James Brown Principle" – a range of initiatives designed make staff "feel good!" These include paid for visits to the office from a yoga teacher; deliveries of fresh fruit; and company accounts at local pubs – where employees go on a Friday night safe in the knowledge that the company appreciates their work and wants to buy them a drink.

Des Dearlove

SEE: COOL BRITANNIA

Wharton Business School

Thomas Gerrity, dean of the University of Pennsylvania's Wharton School, stepped down from the top job in July 1999 to spend more time with his family – and his portfolio of non-executive directorships. After nine years as dean, Gerrity left with Wharton ranked as the best business school in the world. It has topped *Business Week's* influential business school rankings since 1994 and, increasingly, looks impregnable. While Wharton has always been among the business school elite, Gerrity's leadership secured its place as the market leader.

"Gerrity has been more bold than the deans of other business schools," says Wharton MBA Nunzio Quacquarielli, now editor of the *MBA Career Guide*. "Within 18 months of taking over, he had redesigned the Wharton MBA program making it much more international and integrated." This set in train a virtuous circle: Wharton positioned itself as being forward thinking; this attracted funding (Wharton's endowment is now an impressive $292 million

zeitbite#56
Marshall
McLuhan

"There are no passengers on spaceship earth. We are all crew."

compared with $97.4 million when Gerrity took over) and high quality faculty; and also provided a good story for the media and recruiters.

In launching such changes, Gerrity was, in fact, merely practicing what he had successfully preached. Prior to becoming Wharton dean, he was the founder and chief executive of the Index Group for 20 years. Index later became CSC Index and was the driving force behind the fashion for re-engineering at the beginning of the nineties. "He came from a change management background so, in some ways, he just went ahead and did what he had done in his consulting career," says Nunzio Quacquarielli.

If Dr Gerrity's program of change at Wharton can be labeled re-engineering, it was a great deal more effective than the fad as a whole. Crucially, Dr Gerrity got the faculty on his side. This, as countless other deans have found out, is a demanding task akin, it is commonly said, to herding cats. Business school faculty are not renowned for their teamwork or modesty. "I think that Gerrity's fundamental insight about Wharton was that there could be a way to get different academic disciplines to work together so that Wharton graduates would develop well rounded skills and be more effective business leaders," says Wharton MBA Peter Cohan (now a success-ful author and consultant). "Gerrity's academic credibility with the faculty was so strong that he was able to get different departments to work effectively in teams. While Wharton had many strong individual departments, it was the teamwork among them that enabled the school to rise to the top."

While other schools have expanded and, as a result, heaped more work on faculty, Gerrity insisted on the highest academic standards. He increased faculty numbers – now nearing 200 – and sought out innovative ways of enabling Wharton to connect with more students. In most other cases this combination has led to a dilution of academic integrity as faculty are constantly transported around the globe to deliver programs. Wharton's emphasis is on allowing faculty time to travel rather than seeking out a perpetual web of lucrative alliances.

At the same time, Gerrity led Wharton to embrace the latest technology with gusto. Gerrity has a technical background – he has degrees in electrical engineering from MIT and is an authority on the strategic use of information technology. While Wharton has steamed ahead, most other business schools have been circumspect. Harvard, for example, was dragged somewhat reluctantly into the electronic age only recently under its dean Kim Clark. (His predecessor did not have e-mail because he correctly surmised that students would only use it to communicate with him.) Business schools have often invested heavily in technology to little effect. All the PCs in the world do not automatically lead to innovation.

Wharton, however, has developed Wharton Direct, a joint venture with Caliber Learning. In the business school sphere at least, this is probably the distance learning experience which comes closest to matching the power of classroom teaching and interaction. Wharton Direct enables over 250 students spread throughout the United States to take a class simultaneously led by a Wharton academic. From a business point of view, this squares the circle in executive education. Top faculty can educate mass audiences through an interactive medium. This means that the school can charge a premium price for a high quality, mass market product. Previously, such a product was only available on campus.

While Wharton, under Gerrity, has been highly proactive in changing its programs, getting faculty commitment to change and embracing technology, other leading schools have struggled in Wharton's wake. Most famously, Harvard Business School began changing its MBA program long after Wharton had already completed the task and has appeared a reluctant convert to new technology. Then there is its brilliant faculty. "I suspect that Harvard has had more trouble getting its departments to work effectively together and that this has barred it from the number one rank," says Peter Cohan. "While Harvard has a good reputation in the area of strategy with Michael Porter, the school also suffers from more than the usual amount of internal competition. This internal orientation makes it difficult for Harvard to encourage the kind of interdisciplinary work that has made Wharton so effective."

Thomas Gerrity's legacy means that Harvard Business School and the rest have a lot of catching up to do if they are overtake Wharton.

SEE: BUSINESS SCHOOLS
MORE INFO: www.wharton.upenn.edu

Winblad, Ann

Ann Winblad is a partner with the venture capitalists Hummer Winblad Venture Partners. The company (founded in 1989) specializes in investing in software companies. Its investments include Powersoft, Arbor Software, and Wind River Systems. Winblad is a renowned networker who has been known to vacation with a certain Mr Gates.

SEE: BILL GATES
MORE INFO: www.humwin.com

Winfrey, Oprah

The Queen of America was born in Kosciusko, Mississippi. "There is more than sentiment and suffering to Ms Winfrey," no less an authority than the *Economist* has observed, going on to say "She has a good head for business too." Her progression up the ranks of status and wealth has undoubtedly been impressive. In 1985 she opened Harpo Studios; in 1988 came Harpo Productions and now the worthy and hugely successful Oprah's Book Club (which, it is estimated, has sold 12 million books). It takes a keen nose for business to own your own show, the company producing it, the studio and to have two million share options in the distributor. Little wonder that Oprah is worth $500 million.

MORE INFO: www.oprah.com

Wintour, Anna

Sunglass-wearing Anna Wintour (British, born 1949) is the editor of *Vogue*. Educated at North London Collegiate School, she arrived as editor in 1988 and has raised the magazine's circulation to 1.1 million. *Vogue* remains the leader of the feminine magazine pack.

Wordworks

Wordworks is the Boston-based creator of many a business blockbuster. The brainchild of Donna Sammons Carpenter, Wordworks specializes in ghostwriting business books. Its credit in the acknowledgments pages of well-known business books may be familiar.

Take *Reengineering the Corporation* by James Champy and Michael Hammer. This was the business blockbuster of the early nineties. It is not a literary masterpiece, but it is readable and well researched. In the acknowledgments, Champy and Hammer pay tribute to "Donna Sammons Carpenter, Tom Richman, and Abby Solomon, whose extraordinary editorial skills helped turn an inchoate mass into a coherent narrative."

If you open *Jamming*, by Harvard Business School academic John Kao, you also read plaudits to "Donna Sammons Carpenter and her extraordinary team of creative talents." Ms Carpenter is a busy woman. She is also mentioned by Tom Peters in *The Circle of Innovation* and other books of his. Michael Treacy and Fred Wiersma were grateful to her for her work on *The Discipline of Market Leaders*. Michael Milken and Senator John Kerry are also thankful for her editorial support in their literary endeavors.

Carpenter is, according to *BusinessWeek,* "the Queen of ghostwriters." In just over ten years, Wordworks has all but cornered the market in business blockbusters. Its service covers everything. It writes, edits and researches. It will put you in touch with an agent and even send along one of its staff to hold your hand at a key interview. It cannot guarantee a bestseller, but its track record is exceptional.

Almost single-handedly, Wordworks has rewritten the economics of business book publishing. Traditionally, an author receives an advance on royalties from the publisher. If the *author* is using a ghostwriter or a company such as Wordworks, he or she will usually enter into a separate agreement with them. The trouble is that in many cases the publishers' advances fail to cover the ghostwriting charges. The author is effectively using the book as a loss leader, the ultimate calling card to open doors for consulting business or to secure engagements on the lucrative speaking circuit.

One calculation of Wordworks' fees put them at a massive $60,000 for a mere proposal – suggesting that they are going to produce something pretty persuasive. Alternatively, a complete book project could cost $300,000. (Fees for ghosts range from $20,000 to $200,000 depending on the project.) In addition, Wordworks receives royalties. Clearly, in such deals, only massive book sales would allow the authors to recoup their costs.

An added ingredient to the Wordworks offering is that it allows consultants to move fast to meet demand. The average teenage pop sensation has a longer life expectancy than a business fad. Michael Hammer's sequel to *Reengineering the Corporation*, *The Reengineering Revolution* was written, edited and published in six months.

The Wordworks approach is to allow the "authors" to concentrate on what they are good at. "A lot of the authors are very experienced speakers. Typically we outline each chapter and then ask the writer to give a presentation. It maintains the person's voice," says Wordworks' Donna Carpenter. "We are good at identifying whether lack of content is going to be a problem. It is much easier to edit someone who has a lot of material, shaping and pruning it." A typical Wordworks book will go through many drafts before publication – perhaps as many as forty – and the timescale for each differs from 90 days to the more usual one year to 18 months.

SEE: BUSINESS BOOKS; BOOK BUYING; KEN SHELTON; ART KLEINER; GHOSTWRITING

SOURCES: Interviews; *Across the Board*, November/December 1998

World Economic Forum

The junket to end all junkets. Held in Davos, Switzerland, the World Economic Forum involves 1,000 business leaders; 250 political leaders; 250 academics; and 250 media leaders who "come together to shape the global agenda." It is hard work. There is, cynics might suggest, little evidence that they have managed to shape the global agenda to any extent whatsoever.

MORE INFO: www.weforum.org
SOURCES: www.weforum.org

Wyeth

In the beginning there was NC Wyeth. He illustrated *Treasure Island* among many other volumes. Then came Andrew Wyeth. He was made famous by the 1940s painting *Christine's world* of a girl looking towards a house on a hill. His paintings now sell from $95,000 to millions of dollars. And then came Jamie Wyeth whose paintings fetch anything from $18,000 to $350,000. Not forgetting Nicholas Wyeth who handles sales; and wife Betsy who is curator and archivist of the Wyeth oeuvre. The Wyeths have been labeled, by *Fortune* no less, as "America's leading art brand" and the Farnsworth Museum in Rockland, ME has dedicated a center to the Wyeths.

SEE: BRANDS
MORE INFO: David Michaelis, *NC Wyeth: A Biography*, 1998
SOURCES: *Fortune*, September 7, 1998

297

Xybernaut

Kaz Toyosato designed the Sony Walkman. He is now designer at Xybernaut. His new company ("the leader in wearable computing") has brought the world the Mobile Assistant IV. Weighing in at less than 1.75 pounds, it has as much power as a desktop computer. Voice activated, it has 6–8 hours of battery life and 128 Mbytes of RAM. It could also annoy fellow commuters travelling to work.

MORE INFO: www.xybernaut.com
SOURCES: www.xybernaut.com

Xybernaut

Yelland, David

David Yelland (born 1963) was plucked from relative obscurity in 1998 to become editor of the leading British tabloid daily, *The Sun*. The former business reporter had previously worked in New York but quickly found his feet, plunging into controversy by publishing pictures of topless royal brides and the usual tabloid shenanigans.

SEE: RUPERT MURDOCH
MORE INFO: www.thesun.co.uk

Zander, Benjamin

zeitbite#57
Jack Welch

*"Shun the in-
cremental
and go for
the leap."*

Benjamin Zander (born 1939) is the conductor of the Boston Philharmonic Orchestra, a job he has held since the Orchestra's foundation. He has also conducted orchestras throughout the world. Zander has taken advantage of the fashionable link between management and music (see John Kao's book, *Jamming*) and now offers seminars on "orchestrating the executive team," bringing vitality to organizations and "developing a new paradigm for organizations of the 21st century." It is promised that "Benjamin's accomplishments in controlling the orchestral world translate effortlessly into the business world."

Zander's brilliance may well inspire. He trained under such musical personages as Benjamin Britten, Imogen Holst and the cellist Gaspar Cassado. He ran the Boston Civic Symphony until 1978 when he was sacked – Zander's crime was trying out "difficult music." The orchestra walked out with him.

304

Zander is a troublesome challenger of the status quo. (A TV program by Zander was brilliantly entitled "Living on one buttock.") His brilliant seminars – performances in the true sense, with executives trying their vocal chords out on *Ode to Joy* – are backed by the idiosyncratic ideas of his ex-wife Rosamund Stone Zander who is a family therapist.

SEE: MOTIVATIONAL SPEAKERS
MORE INFO: www.speakers.co.uk; www.bostonphil.com; Benjamin Zander,
             Bridges to Possibility, 1998
SOURCES: *Fast Company*, December 1998